THE GIANT BOOK OF
METALWORKING
PROJECTS

TAB TAB BOOKS Inc.
BLUE RIDGE SUMMIT, PA. 17214

FIRST EDITION
FIRST PRINTING

Copyright © 1983 by TAB BOOKS Inc.
Printed in the United States of America

Library of Congress Cataloging In Publication Data

Main entry under title:
The Giant book of metalworking projects.

Includes index.
1. Metal-work.
TT205.G53   1983   671   82-19366
ISBN 0-8306-0357-3
ISBN 0-8306-1357-9 (pbk.)

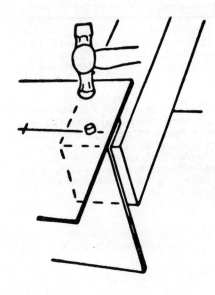

Contents

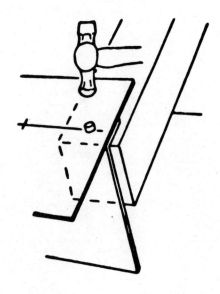

Introduction

THE METALWORKING TECHNIQUES AND PRO-jects described in this book are used in hobbies, business, and industry. Metalworking enthusiasts who are artistically inclined will find metal sculpturing, ornamental iron, and jewelry projects. For the practical metalworker, there are tool-making projects, welding techniques and projects, and sheet-metalwork projects.

There are discussions and projects of interest to beginning metalworkers and some things for more specialized metalworkers. There are sections covering shell molding, die fabrication, metal coating, oxy-acetylene welding, perforated metal, and foundry work.

All of the outstanding projects in this book have been made available by the editors of *School Shop* magazine, the how-to-do-it publication that has printed articles relating to industrial and technical education since 1941. Without their efforts and cooperation, this book would not be possible.

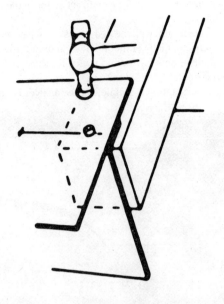

Chapter 1

Metalworking Techniques

T HE TIME HAS COME WHEN IT IS NOT ENOUGH to learn merely the operational skills of the machine-tool trade. As more and more of the functions of the operator are automated, preset, or predetermined, manipulative skill becomes less significant, while the application of knowledge and judgment becomes more essential.

In the machine shop, it is not too difficult to learn how to comprehend operations and the special purposes each fulfills. With a little extra effort, it is even possible to learn how the lathe was evolved by man. But will you acquire the needed understanding of the materials used? What will you learn about metals in particular?

Examine several machine-shop texts. In rare instances they might include some metallurgical data, a brief treatment, and some specifications. Readers are deluded into thinking that such information cannot be very valuable, simply because it isn't stressed in the textbook.

Recognizing the need for understanding metals, some readers try books on metallurgy, only to find themselves mired in terminology, graphs, and diagrams ad infinitum. The problem to teach and how to teach is not satisfactorily solved, but the need grows acute. Progress continues in the development of metals. New alloys must be formed and machined. You must prepare now for work with these metals to become the tradesmen of tomorrow.

In the process of learning the machine-tool trade, you must understand the nature and structure of metal. You must know what its properties are, and why it is alloyed, cold worked, and heat treated to improve these properties. Then you will have the basis on which to more quickly grasp the new, exotic metals, and to more successfully work them.

This premise sounds very interesting in theory and seems to hold real promise. Nevertheless, the question quickly comes to mind, "How can this all be done?" The answer lies in a simplified approach. Recognize the necessity to determine what to study, decide how it can be learned, and obtain the equipment to learn it. To quote a famous physics professor, "Let's consider the possibilities!"

Such consideration entails burning the midnight oil, pouring over eye-reddening texts and references. Obviously, there are many booby traps that will kill your interest. Yet you must investigate, experiment, compare, and evaluate in order to understand. Examining a few of the more important concepts of metallurgy will offer a good start.

By nature, a metal is a crystalline solid. This can be demonstrated by fracturing various kinds of metals and alloys and observing the crystalline structure of the fracture. You can quickly see that some are coarse, some are fine, some are quite distinct, some are rather undefined. Frequently, the individual crystals cannot be seen but rather you can see clusters of crystals that are known as grains. See Figs. 1-1 through 1-4.

This observation introduces the concept of grain structure, the key that unlocks all of the mysteries of metals, and illustrates how structures are identified by characteristic names. The logical conclusion is that the grain size and shape is a significant factor in the nature of metal.

You might well be led to ask: "What makes the difference in kinds of metals? If copper and iron are both crystalline, both have grain structure, then why are they so different?"

The question is simple, but the answer is difficult to

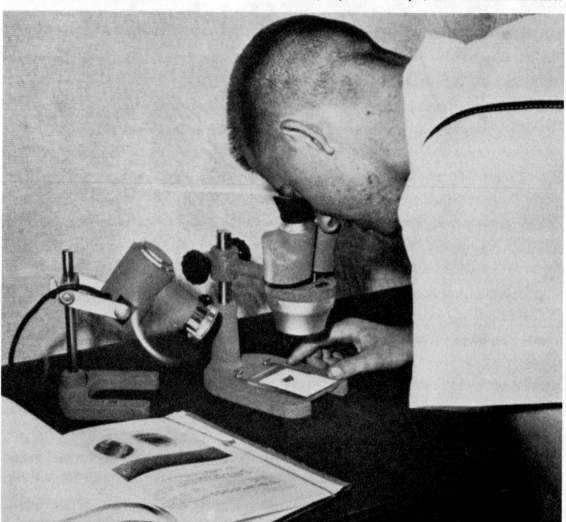

Fig. 1-1. Examining a lathe chip under a stereo microscope. This procedure allows you to investigate metallurgical damage on the chip, revealing what has happened in the cut.

Fig. 1-2. Spark testing a piece of steel, a simple but useful method of training the eye, aids in determining the approximate carbon content of the steel.

have to be centered on specific facts and principles to be satisfactory to the inquiring mind.

The investigation of the essential concepts of metals can be further encouraged by comparing oxide colors, loss of magnetism, change in volume, and other characteristic changes brought about by the application of heat. Observing the effects of heat on metal leads logically into the idea of heat-treatment processes that are used to improve and change the properties and characteristics of both ferrous and nonferrous metals for structural and design purposes.

Grouping Metals. The necessity soon arises for making finer distinctions between the kinds and types of metals, providing the basis for investigation of some of the systems for classifying metals and alloys. Once launched into this maze of crisscrossing terminology, you will have to keep the important systems identified ac-

explain and, unfortunately, there is no simple answer in the references. The answer can only be traced in the crystal itself, its atomic arrangement, and the structure of the atoms that make up the crystals. While this might provide an explanation, it is not a concrete answer because part of it is theory. All that a resourceful reader can do is to get on to other essentials.

This experience bears the germ of an idea. Why not gather samples of the various well-known engineering metals and compare them? You can look for similarities and differences, particularly in such specifics as color, texture, fracture appearance, weight, and hardness.

Even without expensive hardness measuring equipment, some relative differences can be demonstrated with a glass tube and a steel ball. If the samples are the same size and shape, their relative densities can be established with a scale and balance. Once you begin to identify differences and similarities and are able to connect them by association to metals with which you are familiar, your interest will be led into the more specific aspects of the properties and characteristics of metals in relation to their engineering uses and applications.

The need for clear and accurate concepts of the nature and structure of metals cannot be too strongly emphasized. Explanations, even at this elementary stage,

Fig. 1-3. By observing the cooling process of Jominy end quench test, data is obtained for determinng how well a ferrous metal can be hardened, and for plotting a Jominy curve.

3

Fig. 1-4. This machinist, checking the hardness of a case-hardened step block on the Rockwell hardness tester, is performing a basic operation that with minimum instructional effort can be used to advance knowledge of metallurgy.

cording to the underlying purposes of each. For example, general groupings such as stainless steels, tool steels, and cast irons each have composition and structure as their base, but by nature they are application groupings.

In addition, there is the percentage composition systems, such as the SAE and AISI systems, that are used as standards for identification and partial explanation of refining process and chemical content.

4

Strong motivation will be required for learning the systems of distinguishing between various metals, but it will prepare you for the mysteries of trade names. This provides fascinating instructional material, because these names are ordinarily adopted by the manufacturer to give the user a clue to their intended use, their inherent characteristics, or their chemical composition. You can take a collection of trade names and group them according to the key idea in the names and then compare the analyses of well-known types in each group. To go even further, you can find specific examples of the uses of these representative metals in tools, machines, and structural work.

Learning the uses of various metals brings you back to the central theme of metallurgy, which is the idea that need motivates the development of specific kinds of alloys. It is also true that new alloys can be formed by accident as well as design. In these cases, an understanding of the peculiar or unusual properties of an alloy could allow designers to enter new fields of application.

The exotic metals form one group that excites discussion in the present space-age technology. You should take the opportunity to see what these metals are like, to observe the factors they have in common, and to study their location in the periodic chart of elements. Investigations show that there are some logical conclusions to be drawn from the nature of these metals and their location and grouping on the periodic chart.

Experimental Machining. Somewhere in the study of metallurgical ideas, there should be a suitable time to introduce experimental machining operations on some of the less expensive and more available modern metals. They can be purchased from many sources and can be obtained in various forms and sizes. The manufacturers of many of these metals will send samples that can be used to investigate metal-cutting characteristics as well as being used for examination of their properties.

In addition to experimental machining operations, certain tests can also be performed. One of the most widely used scientific methods for determining how well ferrous alloys can be hardened is a test that can be easily duplicated in the shop. A hardness tester should be available along with facilities for running water. These provisions will allow for the performance of the well known Jominy end quench test that reveals on a simple graph not only how well a ferrous metal can be hardened, but also its characteristic curve. This curve will indicate the specific alloy classification of the steel. In short, it is the metallurgist's "fingerprint" system for steel identifica-

tion. Practically all steel companies publish information on the method, the equipment, and examples of Jominy curves. Such information can be used for guidance and comparative reference.

There are other simple tests that can be made in the shop with a minimum of equipment, and they will all add to the fascination of the search. After you have been introduced to some of the concepts of structure, composition, properties, and characteristics of a metal, the study of what happens to the grain structure of metal when it is machined, heat treated, forged, cold worked, and formed by casting, rolling, and drawing processes can be initiated. Once more, it is necessary to resort to collected and identified samples representing as many of these processes as possible. Because metallographic preparation and examination equipment is not found in the average shop, due to high costs and the technical nature of such equipment, actual examination of grain structure will probably be limited to somewhat broader interpretation.

In a simple sense, it can be said that what happens to the metal, happens to the structure. Such things as grain-flow patterns, surface damage, and case-hardening depth can be investigated and observed with a hot acid etch of a sectioned and smoothly finished specimen. This test requires only washing facilities, a small beaker of acid, and a hot plate. Naturally, this type of test must be made under carefully controlled conditions.

Changes in volume brought about by changes in density due to heat-treatment processes can usually be measured accurately by the differences in displacement in liquid. In these measurements, it is wise to use a fairly large piece, because while the proportionate effect is small, the total can be significant.

Machine-shop veterans are aware of the pitfalls in measurement brought on by expansion, and the machinist learns early in life to live with this phenomenon. But how many really understand what happens? By reverting to an elementary version of the atomic theory, the expansion of metals can be explained in a manner that will leave you with a mental picture that will help you understand. In this way, you can learn more about the nature of metal and its behavior.

SHELL-MOLDING TECHNOLOGY

Shell molding is a process that has been growing in importance since its discovery in Germany during the war and its introduction into the United States in 1947. Shell molding has been used by the foundry industry primarily in core-making. However, with some improvements, shell molding is becoming one of the most significant molding processes. These improvements are (1) development of fully-automated shell-molding machines; (2) better methods applied to work with resin-coating sands; (3) development of new methods of making inexpensive metallic patterns; (4) introduction of the wet (hot box) and blowing methods; and (5) increased shell-strength control.

Although shell molding can be included easily in a metal shop, it has not been employed as much as traditional green-sand molding. Shell molding requires a shell-molding machine which is too expensive for most shops. Second, the process requires a metallic pattern that is difficult to make using traditional pattern-making methods.

The purpose of this section is to explain briefly the shell-molding process and to illustrate step-by-step how you can design and build your own shell-molding unit at minimal cost. This unit can be used to make molds to cast metals, plastics, or other materials that can be melted in the shop. The addition of a shell-molding unit would increase the spectrum of educational experiences in the shop.

Materials Required

Many foundrymen have considered shell molding a modification of traditional green-sand molding. Although the primary material in green-sand molding is natural green sand with some binders added, the primary material required to make a shell mold is clear, fine-grain silica sand. For nonferrous metals in the shop, grain fineness number AFS-70 is appropriate.

In the early days of shell molding, the sand was coated in the foundry with phenolic resin, which served as the sand binder. The sand coating required special machines and methods that increased the cost of the process to the point where it became prohitibive. Today, however, readycoated sand can be purchased through any foundry-supplies distributor. Many companies specialize in coating various kinds of silica and sell it either by the bag or the ton. Three or four bags of sand a year would be plenty for a shop.

In addition to the resin-coated sand, a small amount of silicone stripping solution is required. The solution is used on the heated metallic pattern to prevent the cured shell from sticking to the pattern. The silicone solution can also be purchased from most foundry-supplies distributors.

How To Make the Patterns

Traditionally, all shelf-molding patterns were made with metals, aluminum being used most commonly. Pattern parts, sprues, runners, gates, and risers have been cast or machined, split in half, and assembled on one side of a metal plate of appropriate dimensions. The pattern illustrated in Fig. 1-5 was made of aluminum using this method.

This pattern was designed and built by a group of industrial-education students who were assigned the task of making a pattern that would be used to cast nonferrous tensile specimens for tensile-testing purposes. After the students had completed the necessary library research on the subject, they planned and outlined the procedure to be followed in constructing the pattern. This approach could be used to make almost any pattern needed for shell molding in the shop.

The traditional method of making patterns for shell molding is expensive and requires considerable skill. In an effort to find more efficient and economical ways to make patterns, industry has developed several other methods. Two of these methods are the "Fibertool" ("Make Shell Cores without Metal Boxes," *Modern Casting*, Vol. 50, No. 3 (September, 1966), 46.) shell-core box method and the "Wheeldon Process." (A. Woods, "The Wheeldon Process," *Modern Casting*, Vol. 52, No. 2 (August, 1967), 61-63). These methods may be applied for making patterns more efficiently and economically.

Building the Shell-Molding Unit

Many companies specialize in building shell-molding

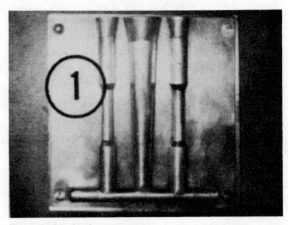

Fig. 1-5. An aluminum pattern.

machines for foundries. Inasmuch as these machines are expensive, consider building your own shell-molding unit.

Shell molding is accomplished by either "blowing" or "dumping" the resin-coated sand against a heated metallic pattern. The sand-blowing machine is difficult to build in a shop. A dumping-box machine, however, can very easily be built in almost any shop. Figures 1-6A and 1-6B illustrate a shell-molding unit based on the dumping-box method. This unit was designed and built as a project by a group of industrial-education students.

The dumping-box shell-molding unit consists of a stand, the dumping-box, and the heating source (kiln). The stand or sand-container was built in a rectangular shape as a working bench 24″ wide, 34″ high, and 50″ long. This part of the unit can be made with angle iron and sheet metal or with wood.

The dumping-box was made in a cubic or rectangular shape with one side open. The box can be made with sheetmetal or with wood. If wood is used, a metallic frame or appropriate-size angle iron should be placed around the edge of the open side of the box to protect the wood from coming in contact with the heated metallic pattern. The box is mounted on trunnions at one end of the stand to permit free rotation.

The heating source (kiln) can either be built or purchased and mounted on the stand at the opposite side

Fig. 1-6B. The finished unit.

of the dumping box. Many different designs of heating sources can be employed, but one that can be heated electrically would be most ideal. The kiln should be capable of heating to at least 1000°F.

In building the unit illustrated in Fig. 1-6B, an electrically heated used kiln was salvaged and repaired to become the heating source. If an old kiln is not available around the shop, a new one can be purchased with a small investment. The unit shown in Fig. 1-6B is only one of many different designs that can be developed.

Once the unit is built, it can be placed on casters to make it mobile. The mobile unit can be stored in the shop at any convenient location.

How To Use the Unit

The primary purpose of the shell-molding unit is to enable you to make both shell molds and cores. Shell molding has numerous advantages over green-sand molding. Shell molding is a precision process that is cleaner and simpler than green-sand molding. In addition, shell molding can be used to make cores and this eliminates the problems that often arise in the shop when making cores by other methods.

Standard foundry safety precautions should be observed at *all* times.

To make a mold with the shell-molding unit, the following steps are necessary:

☐ Clean the metallic pattern with a dry cloth and place it in the heating unit (kiln) *face up* at 450° F., which is the appropriate temperature for most patterns (see Fig. 1-7).

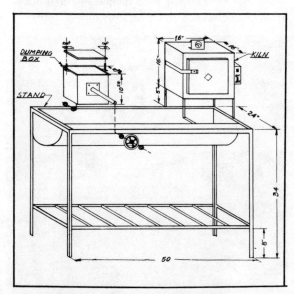

Fig. 1-6A. Diagram of a dumping-box unit.

Fig. 1-7. Place the pattern in the kiln.

☐ While the pattern is being heated, fill the dumping box half full with resin-coated sand from the sand container (see Fig. 1-8).

☐ Remove the heated pattern from the heating unit and apply a film of silicone solution on the face of the pattern and place it *face down* on the open side of the dumping box (see Fig. 1-9).

☐ Fasten the pattern at this position and rotate the dumping-box 180 degrees.

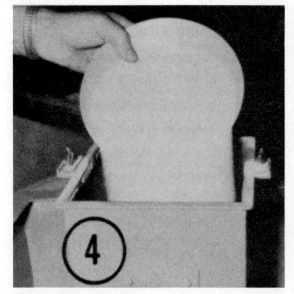

Fig. 1-8. Fill the box half full.

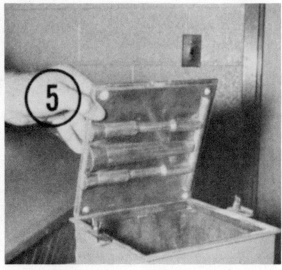

Fig. 1-9. Place the pattern face down.

☐ Keep the entire face of the pattern covered with sand approximately 30 seconds and rotate the dumping-box back to its original position. The step of covering the face of the heated pattern with resin-coated sand is referred to as "investing" (see Fig. 1-10).

☐ Unfasten and carefully remove the pattern from the dumping-box and place it *face up* in the heating source (kiln) until the shell has been completely cured (hardened). This step, referred to as "back curing," takes 2-5

Fig. 1-10. The investing step.

Fig. 1-11. Let the pattern cool.

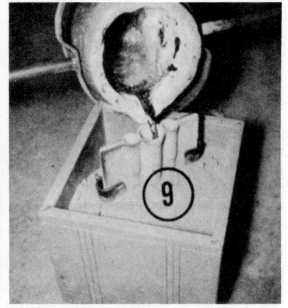

Fig. 1-13. Assemble by clamping.

minutes for nonferrous metals, depending on the thickness of the shell.

☐ Remove the pattern from the heating source and let it cool (see Fig. 1-11).

☐ After the pattern has cooled, strip the shell from it (see Fig. 1-12) by using the injection pins or by tapping the pattern on the opposite side of the plate.

☐ When two half shells have been made as de-

scribed above, assemble them together either by applying adhesive or by clamping (see Fig. 1-13).

☐ Place the completed shell in a box of appropriate size and pack it all around with dry green sand.

☐ Prepare the melt and pour it in the shell through the sprue until the mold is filled (see Fig. 1-13).

☐ After solidification of the mold, break the shell and remove the casting (see Fig. 1-14).

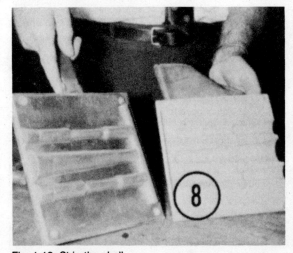

Fig. 1-12. Strip the shell.

Fig. 1-14. Remove the casting.

The procedures described here are intended primarily for nonferrous metals such as aluminum, brass, bronze, zinc, etc. Similar procedure may be used for ferrous metals. The curing temperatures require, however, will be higher. Shell molding is among the most important and fastest-growing processes in foundry technology. A shell-molding unit can be designed and built with a minimal financial investment. Moreover, it is a rewarding educational experience.

METHODS FOR METALS MACHINING

For many years, one of the major profit problems in manufacturing has been the direct and indirect cost of making chips. It has been said that industry spends 10 to 15 billion dollars annually in metal-cutting operations, and industry is continually seeking to achieve improved means of cutting materials.

When new product designs require hard-to-work materials, more pressure is put on the development of cutting-tool materials. Not many years ago carbides came into common use as a material to cut metals that high-speed steels could not handle.

More recently we have seen the introduction of various oxide materials. More commonly referred to as ceramics, they are for machining even harder materials. The search for an improved utilization of cutting tools continues.

A knowledge of cutting-tool applications is extremely important in industry. With the new demands on them, it is extremely vital to understand the capabilities of the various materials and their proper application.

It should be noted that new developments and the utilization of materials in industry doesn't just happen overnight. Although there always appears to be a demand for new cutting tools, engineers also want to see the proof before moving too hastily toward an adoption.

Actually, the applications of cemented carbides became numerous only when high-speed steels became scarce in the early days of World War II. In many cases, carbide was the only tool material available.

In recent years, the ceramics have gained considerable attention. Perhaps, oxide is a better name as a means of distinguishing the material from broken china. A comparison of ceramics to carbides is illustrated in Table 1-1.

The performance of cutting tools depends on the machinist and proper shop care to a great extent. In spite of the progress in machine-tool design, it is interesting to note that the importance of the well-trained craftsman is still very necessary in manufacturing.

Table 1-1. Use of Ceramics and Carbides.

Gear Blank

Material	SAE-5135
Hardness-B_n	170-207
Cutting speed sfm	950
Feed	013
Cut	025
Tool life	1500 pieces

Carbide tools run at 450 sfm under same conditions produced 350 pieces.

Lathe Spindle

Material	SAE 1050
Hardness-B_n	180-220
Cutting speed sfm	700-800
Feed	012
Cut	075
Tool life	9-11 pieces

Output double under same conditions with ceramics.

Shaft

Material	Cast iron
Hardness-B_n	24-280
Cutting speed sfm	600
Feed	010
Cut	015
Tool life	7000 pieces

Carbides produced 1000 pieces at 260 sfm, otherwise same conditions.

Electrical Discharge Machining

The erosion of metals by a spark discharge is known to have been accomplished as early as 1762 by an English scientist named Priestley.

Commercial use of this process, now commonly known as EDM, began about 1941. Unlike conventional machining, there are no mechanical forces involved as are normally found at a drill point or milling cutter.

Figure 1-15 illustrates a circuit diagram in which 110V enters the power supply which then feeds the electrode through its capacitors. The electrode and the workpiece are submerged in a dielectric solution of hydrocarbon oil or, in some situations, carbon tetrachloride. Figure 1-16 illustrates the complete power unit with the front panel of the solution tank removed.

As the electrode is lowered to a predetermined distance (usually .0035" max.) from the workpiece, the solution ionizes and the electrode bombards the workpiece with sparks. Each spark at the area of contact causes heat to the temperature of vaporization. The metal in this vaporized state then ascends through the solution

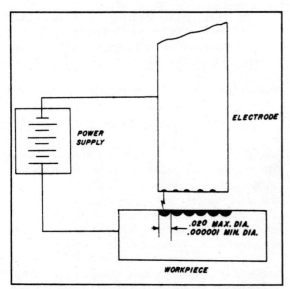

Fig. 1-15. The basic EDM circuit. The size of the craters is determined by the amperage supplied to the electrode.

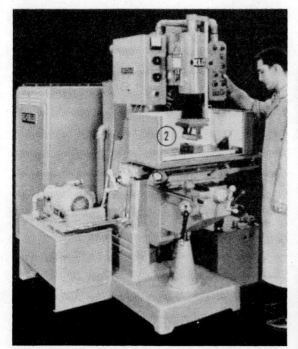

Fig. 1-16. A technician inspecting a wrench forging die on an ExCell-O Model 244. This is the machine that does Electrical Discharge machining (EDM). The front of the dielectric tank is not shown in this photo.

as a metallic cloud leaving a pitmark in the work. The contact of one spark with the workpiece and the resulting cloud constitutes one cycle. The impact of this process is exciting when it is realized that this cycling can take place 10,000 to 100,000 times per second in a machine.

EDM is a very predictable process not only in scientific principle but also in application. It is generally considered that any metal, hard or soft (if it is electrically conductive) can be machined with this process.

The applications of EDM have proven successful in finishing die cavities in the die casting and forging industries. Its value is unique because of its ability to finish complex configurations without the normally required benchwork.

EDM has many other applications which might well lead most of us to believe that the process has really "arrived." Perhaps it has, but like most processes and machine tools it has its drawbacks and its limitations. Figure 1-17 is an example of electrode wear that develops while sinking a blanking die. Electrode wear is a problem in many cases, and excessive wear means more downtime, increased expenditures in supplementary equipment, and specially trained manpower to keep the equipment in top working order. The types of industries using the process are numerous.

Fig. 1-17. The blanking die at the conclusion of machining. Note: electrode wear is noticeable on the punch.

Electrolytic Machining or Grinding

Figures 1-18 and 1-19 illustrate electrolytic action. As current passes from the workpiece to the cathode, the density is greatest at the shortest distances between the anode and cathode surfaces. As erosion takes place in the greatest density areas, the workpiece takes the shape of the cathode profile.

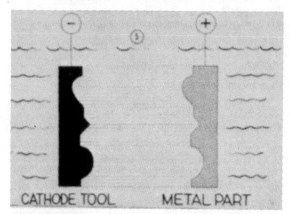

Fig. 1-18. Start of electrolytic grinding. Lines indicate current density where the erosion begins at the points where the density is greatest.

This principle of grinding differs from the machining principle only that a metal-bonded wheel negatively charged is used. The wheel is rotated against the workpiece as in a conventional grinding setup. Nevertheless, the wheel never touches the work, and the pressurized electrolyte between the workpiece and the wheel maintains the circuit and causes the eroded particles to be washed away from the workpiece surface.

The major field of application seems to be in performing work that cannot be accomplished by other processes. It has helped to eliminate the problems of machining the superalloys and tungsten carbides.

Numerical Control

Probably no single manufacturing development has affected industry like the acceptance of numerical control. This is a process of controlling machine tools and manufacturing processes by taped commands. Numerical control of the machine tools employs one of two systems. The point-to-point control system is applicable to drilling and boring where positions with accuracy and precision are important. It is also utilized in other machining operations, although in many cases the second system, continuous path, is becoming more widely accepted. Figure 1-20 shows a comparison of the two systems. It is noticeable that the point-to-point system requires many commands to move along the x-y axes. Figure 1-21 shows the LeBlond Tape-Turn Lathe which utilizes the continuous path method. Please note the absence of gear shift or clutch levers, handwheel, feed clutch, or half-nut levers on the apron.

The more complicated and elaborate contouring systems are usually programmed with a computer. Contouring control systems are designed to generate two-dimensional or three-dimensional profiles on complex parts, thus making the programming function quite difficult. Figure 1-22 provides a good example of a complex programming application. Although the part is somewhat unidentifiable it appears to be the beginning of a stretch form die.

Their differences can be further illustrated by initial costs of approximately 10 times as much for contouring systems as position systems.

Despite high initial costs, the systems offer many advantages over manual operations. It is not uncommon for one numerically controlled machine to outproduce up to six conventional machines.

Now that numerical control has come into its own in industry, it is rapidly compiling some convincing figures to illustrate the feasibility even when production is as small as one piece.

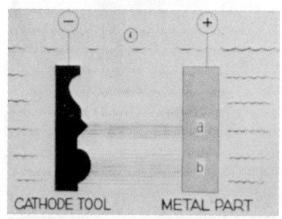

Fig. 1-19. Completion of electrolytic grinding function. Variations in current density result in the configuration of the workpiece at right.

Computers in Manufacturing

The applications of computers in manufacturing are not limited to process programming. Their ability to make

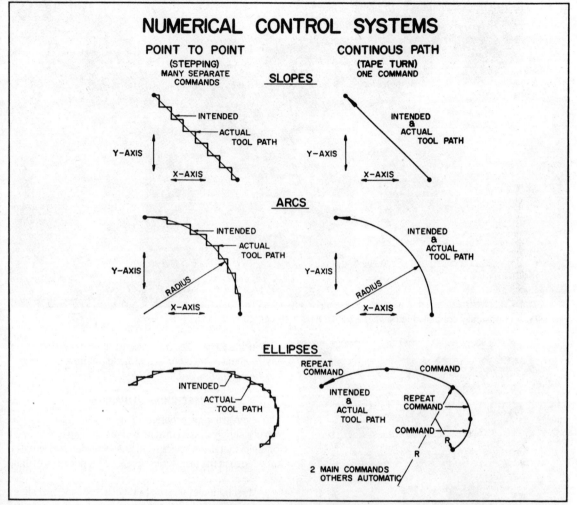

Fig. 1-20. Comparison of "point to point" to continuous path controls and relative numbers of commands.

computations and store information seems to be limit-less. As a result of broad computer uses, entire manufac-turing plants are becoming one big integrated production system.

It's rather difficult to describe computers from the standpoint of design and function. Basically, computers are of two kinds: analog and digital. The analog performs its operation by setting up analogies for the variables, and operating on these variables. The slide rule is a good example; numbers are represented by distances propor-tional to the logarithms of the numbers.

The digital computer is developed from the "count by ten" principle. In many respects, the computer is a sophistication of desk calculators. The significant de-velopment was the change from the decimal system in favor of the binary system.

Computers fall into two class functions: general pur-pose and special purpose. The general areas of use are: routine business calculations, scientific calculations, and systems analysis. Each area has different computer re-quirements.

The special-purpose computers are always designed for particular functions that do not fall in the areas where a general-purpose computer would be feasible. Generally, they have a fixed program, and they cannot handle other problems without some modifications.

These brief descriptions of manufacturing processes cover only a minute segment of the revolutionary tenden-

Fig. 1-21. A numerically controlled lathe with a continuous path computer control.

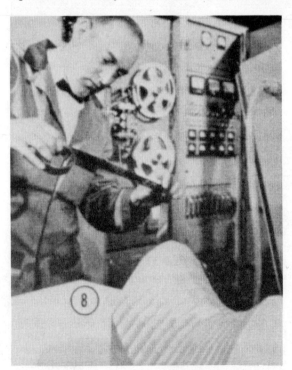

Fig. 1-22. A rough-machined geometric shape with numerical control equipment. The tape for this shape (right) was produced automatically.

cies in industry. We are now firmly entrenched in an environment where our scientific know-how is continually being challenged.

MACHINING ALUMINUM

The ever-growing problem of future shortages in the world's supply of iron ore, as well as the expanding need for light metals in space vehicles, will demand greater knowledge in the properties, uses, and application of light metals.

Most light metals are of a tubular, extruded, or sheet variety, which fall in the general metal-shop coverage. The light metal products produced in industrial machine shops are of a cast or component-parts variety.

The purpose of this section is to show the stability of the most commonly used light metal, aluminum, as a material in the comprehensive machine shop. The model shown in Figs. 1-23 and 1-24 is a half-scale replica of an actual old-fashioned telephone. Care was taken in designing this project to make as many working parts as possible.

The phone could have been made in four parts; but by making it in seven parts, the machining experiences were almost doubled. This complicated project is intended for advanced machine-shop enthusiasts.

The base (detail 1) needs only to be turned, faced, drilled, tapped, and polished. The upright post (detail 2)

Fig. 1-23. Tomorrow's technicians must know the properties, uses, and applications of light metals.

requires turning, threading, male and female radii turning, milling, slotting, and threading. It is recommended that this detail be turned between centers and that everything but the speaker mount be finish turned. The upright is then clamped in a V-block, vertically, and the speaker mount machined to a 9/32″ × 9/16″ block. The block is then slotted to receive the speaker. At this point, the form (as indicated in the side view) is laid out on the side of the block and profiled either on a filing machine or by hand to the layout line and the hole drilled.

Next the cradle housing slot is milled as with any conventional keyway. The speaker (detail 3) is machined by turning, facing, drilling, tapping, and radius turning. It is then mounted in a rotary, three-jaw chuck or V-block and either straddle milled or side milled to a 5/32″ thickness to mate with the speaker mount.

The mouthpiece (detail 4) should be made at assembly. The threads are turned 5/16″ back, and a smaller

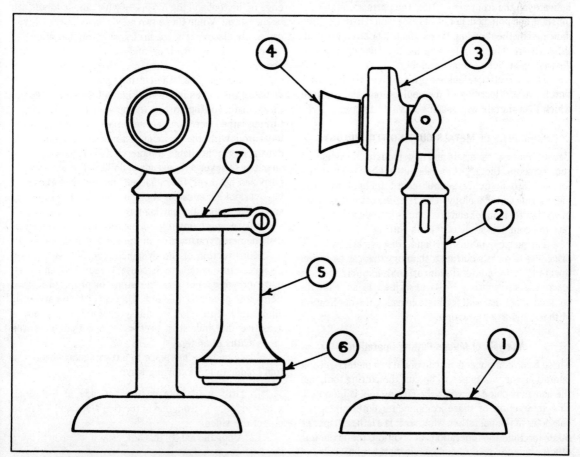

Fig. 1-24. A half-scale replica of an old-fashioned telephone.

15

clearance angle machined as indicated in the drawing. This is then screwed into the speaker and finish machined from that point. This will involve an internal and external tapered radii and an internal facing operation.

The earphone consists of two pieces, details 5 and 6. The earphone housing requires turning, threading, radius turning, drilling, and shoulder boring for its completion. The earphone cap needs turning, radius turning, drilling, internal taper turning, boring, internal facing, and threading.

The cradle, which holds the earphone, is the most difficult part to make. Unless you exercise care, you will repeatedly scrap this part. The first step in this operation should be squaring the block and drawing the layout. First drill the ¼″ hole as indicated by the drawing and then machine the slot that will cradle the earphone. All machining in the top view (detail 7) can then be finished. The next step is the completion of the rest of the part as indicated in the front view. After the parts are all made, finished, and polished, detail 7 is assembled to detail 2, as indicated by the drawing. When this has been completed, the parts are disassembled and anodized and dyed to any desired color before final assembly.

This attractive telephone project gives you a foundation for future learning of the applications and the role which light metals will assume in years to come.

PRINCIPLES OF METALS-CUTTING TECHNOLOGY

Because of new materials and new industrial production requirements, the art of metals cutting has been transformed into a highly sophisticated technology—the metals-cutting technology. This transformation has seen many new techniques and procedures introduced to facilitate the complex study of metals cutting.

The purpose of this section to discuss briefly a few principles of metals-cutting technology that can be incorporated as meaningful educational experiences in machine-shop courses. Also described is an easy-to-construct tool that will facilitate learning the application of these important principles.

Analysis of Metals-Cutting Operation

Three basic components are involved in a metals-cutting operation: the workpiece to be cut, the cutting tool, and the actual machine on which the cutting tool is mounted. The interaction of these components determines the character of the operation, whether it is a lathe, shaper or other machine tool operation. In addition, the economic efficiency of the operation depends on the relationship of these components—with such factors as tool life and types of cutting forces directly affecting the cost of an operation. This means that, for an economic operation, the longest possible tool life and the lowest possible application of cutting force are needed.

The basic elements in a metals-cutting operation that can be varied to increase or decrease its cost are speed, feed, depth of cut, tool geometry, cutting fluid, and to some extent the material of workpiece and tool.

Machine-shop veterans know that (within certain limits) increases in speed, feed, and depth of cut result in a more effcient operation. Also, it is known that when the cutting tool has a certain type of cutting angle (tool geometry), it can cut more efficiently. Usually left unexplored is to what extent these basic elements (variables) really affect the cutting operation.

To understand such matters, you need to be familiar with the kinds of cutting forces that act on the cutting edge of the tool and the means by which these forces can be measured. When these two needs have been met, you can easily discover the means by which an operation can be made more efficient and, consequently, more economical.

An analysis of a lathe-cutting operation may help to visualize the forces involved. Figure 1-25 illustrates the three main cutting forces (components) of a straight turning lathe operation. These forces can be accurately measured with the help of a three-component lathe dynamometer, available commercially at prices entailing an outlay of several thousands of dollars. For all practical purposes, however, the radial and longitudinal forces may be overlooked because their magnitude is relatively small. The tangential cutting force is the principal force, and can be approximately measured with a mechanical dynamometer constructed in the shop at minimal cost.

Construction of the dynamometer can be a useful project. First complete necessary research and then make drawings and plan the steps of procedure. Two items are generally needed: a piece of high-carbon or alloy steel with good elasticity characteristics, and a sensitive dial indicator, preferably one that measures thousandths of an inch.

Machine the steel piece to a rectangular shape as a tool holder in the following way:

☐ Drill a ¾″ hole on the flat side of the stock approximately 1″ from one of the two sides and ½″ from one of the sides.

☐ Along the axis of this hole, saw a ¼″ strip to open the hole at one side.

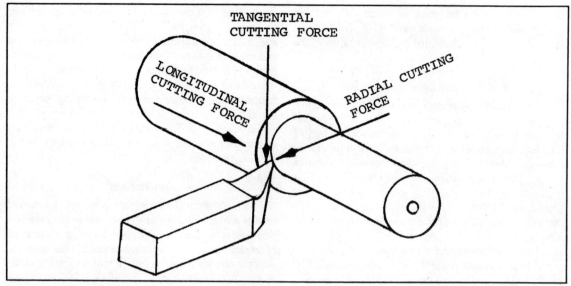

Fig. 1-25. Cutting-force components in a lathe operation.

☐ At the opposite side reduce the stock to form the deflection point (Fig. 1-26). The thickness of this cross section should be about ⅛".

☐ Drill and square the hole necessary to mount the cutting tool bit at the end and drill and tap a perpendicular hole to hold the tool in position as with a regular tool holder.

☐ Weld a small lever at the top (see Fig. 1-26) and mount the dial indicator with its shaft touching the free end of the lever.

☐ Grind and mount a cutting-tool bit at a predetermined distance from the face of the stock. Make sure that this distance is kept constant at all times, as it affects the leverage of the dynamometer and, therefore, its deflection.

Calibration of the dynamometer should be accomplished with dead weights. At the tip of the cutting tool bit, hang a predetermined number of pounds and record the deflection registered by the dial indicator. To verify the calibration, double the weights and observe the

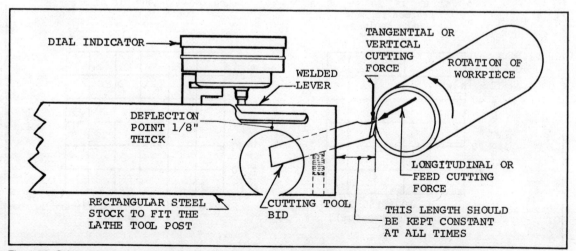

Fig. 1-26. Schematic diagram of one-component lathe dynamometer.

17

deflection that must be twice as much with doubled weight. The number of pounds required to give a deflection of one graduation in the dial indicator constitutes the scale of the dynamometer.

Use of the Mechanical Dynamometer

The mechanical dynamometer can measure the tangential or primary cutting force, which is influenced by the cutting speed, feed, depth of cut, tool geometry, and cutting fluid. The dynamometer can be used to collect data for all these variables, and help derive the optimum condition for an efficient and economical operation for various materials. You can choose to use several cutting tool bits ground with different rake angles to experiment with cutting force and speed. Data can be plotted on a graph as illustrated in Fig. 1-27.

The dynamometer can also determine the machinability of various materials in the shop with a piece of AISI steel, B1112, which has been rated as 100 percent machinable. You can cut on this piece of steel with predetermined speed, feed, depth of cut, and tool geometry, and record the cutting force required. Then, with all factors kept constant, you can vary only the material being cut and record the cutting force required. Using the dynamometer reading for B1112 as 100 percent, the machinability of other materials can be calculated accordingly.

You can explore other uses as you develop skill and competence with the dynamometer as a tool for demonstration purposes.

Implications

As with all other tools in the shop, the mechanical dynamometer will add a new dimension to machine-shop activities and make certain aspects of metals-cutting technology especially more meaningful. Note, however, that the dynamometer is only a tool, and not the final answer to these problems. Therefore, it is dependent on

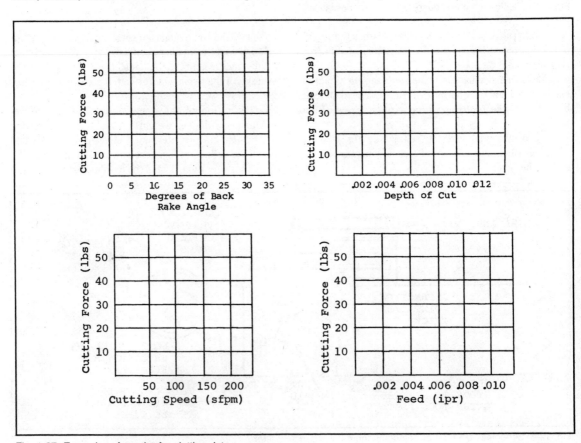

Fig. 1-27. Examples of graphs for plotting data.

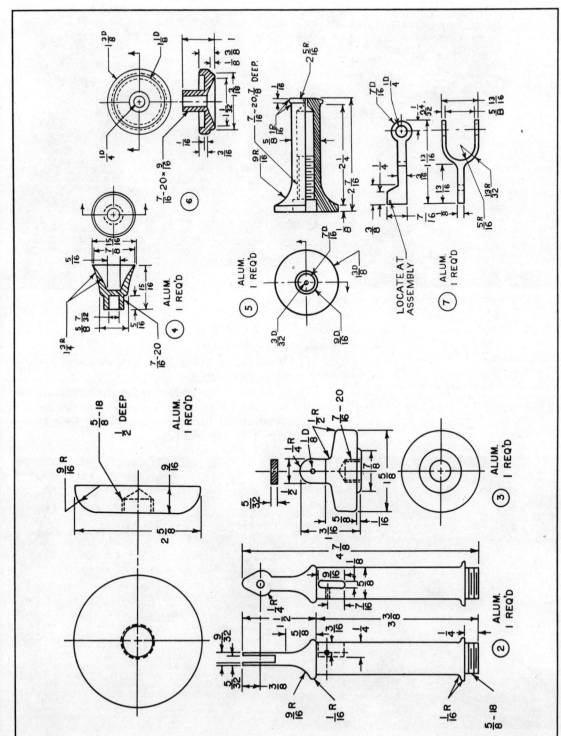

Fig. 1-28. Design details.

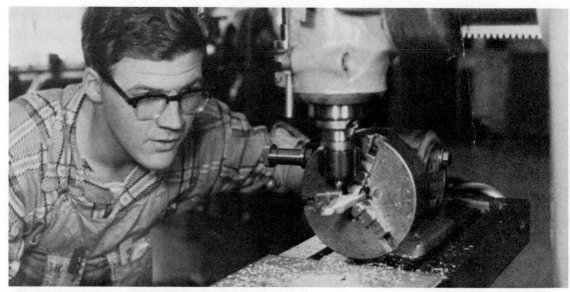

Fig. 1-29. The telephone project offers much machining experience.

your intelligent and creative use of it as a tool to demonstrate the various relationships of the basic variables in cutting operation.

The dynamometer can be effectively used to collect data relative to the cutting-force influence of:

☐ tool geometry.
☐ speeds.
☐ feeds.
☐ depth of cut.
☐ cutting fluids.

It can also be used in determining the machinability of various materials.

However, the greatest benefit of using a dynamometer is in helping you to understand why the variables in a metals-cutting operation behave the way they do. See Figs. 1-28, 1-29, and 1-30.

Fig. 1-30. Here a machinist pauses to examine the upright post .

Fig. 1-31. The dynamometer in action.

POWDER METALLURGY

Powdered metal parts are made by compressing metal particles into a precision die. The compacted metal is then ejected from the die and heated in a controlled atmosphere sintering furnace to bond the metal particles together.

Although Egyptians used powdered metal articles as early as 3,000 B.C., it was not until the 1800s that powdered metals were "rediscovered" in England to produce platinum jewelry. Powder metallurgy became a widely accepted industrial practice during World War II. Today, the process is used to produce gears, self-lubricating bearings, metallic filters, tungsten carbide cutting tools, and many other articles which would be costly to manufacture by traditional machining techniques.

Many types of metal powders have been developed, but copper-base and iron-base materials are the most commonly used. The metals are manufactured into a powder by a variety of processes and once reduced are blended to obtain the properties required by the manufacturer.

Important Terms. Comparing of the powder blend into an article of accurate size and shape is called *briquetting*. Compacting techniques, include mechanical, hydraulic, and isostatic pressing, extruding, rolling, high-energy forming, forging, and slip casting. Pressures range from 15 to 50 tons per square inch.

Sintering is the operation in which the metal particles in the briquette are bonded under heat in a controlled atmosphere. Temperatures are determined by the blend and are usually 60 to 80 percent of the melting temperature of the lowest melting point constituent metal. The atmosphere (hydrogen, nitrogen, carbon dioxide, carbon monoxide, etc.) prevents oxidation of the particles that could weaken or prevent the bond.

Making the Bushing. We used a powdered mixture of 90 parts copper, 10 parts tin, and 2 parts graphite lubricant to produce our blind bushing. The blend is

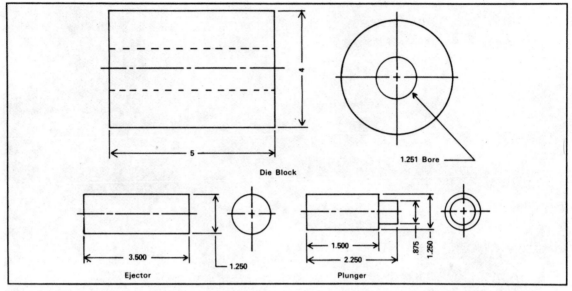

Fig. 1-32. Die components.

readily available, compacts at low pressures, and can be sintered under conditions acceptable in the industrial-arts shop.

The first step is to produce a die, a plunger, and an ejector from hot-rolled steel (see Fig. 1-32). A close tolerance is needed between the bore of the die block and the od of the ejector and plunger to ensure that none of the powder lodges between the mating parts during compression. The steel need not be hardened.

A coating of zinc stearate on the die, plunger, and ejector acts as a lubricant for the parts and as a parting agent for the powdered metal.

Insert the ejector in the die block and pour the copper-tin metal mixture into the chamber. Refer to Fig. 1-33 for the above and following steps. Use a compression ratio of 2:1 to determine the amount of powder. That is, fill the chamber with 2 inches of powder to compact a 1-inch bushing. Place the plunger in the open end of the

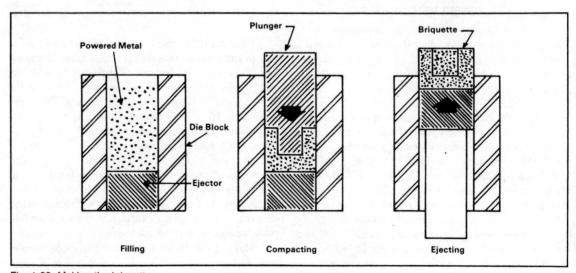

Fig. 1-33. Making the briquette.

chamber and put the entire assembly into a compression molder or a hydraulic press. The plunger must be long enough to extend above the top of the die block.

An 8,000 to 10,000 ppsi compression is sufficient to compact the copper-tin blend. After compression, take out the plunger and then remove the briquette by pushing up on the ejector with a metal rod slightly smaller in diameter than the bore of the die.

Industrial sintering processes require sophisticated, atmospherically controlled chambers and can be dangerous, especially when hydrogen is used as the shielding gas. We sintered the copper-tin bushing in an atmosphere of carbon dioxide. We first placed the briquette into a container of charcoal, then placed the container in a heat treatment furnace for 15 min. at 1600°F. The heat caused the charcoal to emit the CO_2 gas needed for the atmosphere to fuse the powder blend.

HOW TO SELECT HEAT-TREATABLE STEEL

Selection of a tool steel for a particular application is generally not limited to a single grade and may not be limited to a particular family of tool steels. Several different steels could offer a workable solution and the choice might be dictated by material cost, ease of machining, or availability.

Plain carbon tool steels that range from .60 to .95 carbon are most commonly found in the machining lab. These steels are commonly referred to by their Society of Automotive Engineers or American Iron and Steel Institute classification number. For example, SAE 1095 is referred to by the layman as high-carbon tool steel.

Because carbon tool steels are the least expensive of all tool steels and are easily machined, they should be given first consideration when selecting a tool steel for a new application. These steels require no special techniques in hot working or heat treatments. They might, however, lack some of the characteristics required in tooling applications.

The main improvements in tool steel wrought by alloying are greater wear resistance, greater toughness or strength, increased hardenability, and resistance to softening at high temperatures. If a plain-carbon tool steel is not suitable for the intended application, the alloy steels should be examined to find those which have suitable characteristics.

Alloyed tool steels are classified by the system established by the American Iron and Steel Institute. The AISI system of alloy tool steel identification is based on quenching method commonly employed, application, special characteristics, and steels for particular indus-

tries. The commonly used tool steels are grouped, under this system, into six major classifications with subgroups assigned a letter symbol. Classifications are:

1. Water hardening ....W
2. Shock resisting ....S
3. Cold work:
   oil hardening..O
   med. alloy air hardening.......................A
   high-carbon, high-
      chromium ....D
4. Hot work:
   chromium base ....H1 to H19
      incl.
   tungsten base ....H20 to H39
      incl.
   molybdenum base ....H40 to H59
      incl.
5. High speed:
   tungsten base...T
   molybdenum base...................................M
6. Special-purpose:
   low alloy L
   carbon-tungsten....................................F
   mold steels..
      low-carbon ....P1 to P19 incl.
      other types................P20 to P39 incl.

Table 1-2 lists the previously mentioned steel types and compares their properties.

Tools that can be manufactured in the machine shop can be divided into three main classes: cutting tools, shearing tools, and forming tools. Cutting tools include those implements that remove chips from a material, as in machining operations. Steels of this type of service require wear resistance, red hardness, and toughness to prevent tool breakage. Shearing tools are implements used principally to part materials, either hot or cold, using a shearing action. Forming tools transmit their shape to the work. Requirements for any tool of any class are not unique with that class. In general, the following factors must be considered in the selection of a steel for a tool: hardness, wear resistance, toughness, distortion or warping in hardening, depth of hardening, resistance to softening at elevated temperatures, machinability, and cost.

The cost of alloy tool steels is generally one and one-half to two times that of plain carbon steel, figures on a cost-per-pound base for steels in the same condition; comparing cold finished SAE 1095 to cold finished SAE 4340, for example.

The *Machinery's Handbook*, or *Vol. 3—Machining* of

Table 1-2. Comparative Properties of Tool Steels.

TYPE	GROUP	QUENCH MEDIUM*	WEAR RESISTANCE	TOUGHNESS	WARPAGE TO RESISTANCE	HARDENING DEPTH	RESISTANCE TO SOFTENING AT HIGH TEMP.	REL. COST	MACHINING RATING	RESISTANCE TO DECARB-URIZATION
M	HIGH SPEED	O, A, A	VERY HIGH	LOW	A, S: LOW O: MEDIUM	DEEP	HIGHEST	HIGH	45-60	LOW-MEDIUM
T	HIGH SPEED	O, A, S,	VERY HIGH	LOW	A, S: LOW O: MEDIUM	DEEP	HIGHEST	HIGHEST	40-55	LOW-HIGH
H	HOT WORK: CR BASE	A, O	FAIR	GOOD	O: FAIR A: GOOD	DEEP	GOOD	HIGH	75	MEDIUM
	W BASE	A, O	FAIR TO GOOD	GOOD	O: FAIR	DEEP	VERY GOOD	HIGH	50-60	MEDIUM
	Mo BASE	O, A, S	HIGH	MEDIUM	A, S, LOW O: MEDIUM	DEEP		HIGH	50-60	LOW-MEDIUM
D	COLD WORK	A, O	BEST	POOR	A: BEST O: LOWEST	DEEP	GOOD	MED. HIGH	40-50	MEDIUM
A	COLD WORK	A	GOOD	FAIR	BEST	DEEP	FAIR	MEDIUM	85	MEDIUM-HIGH
O	COLD WORK	O	GOOD	FAIR	VERY GOOD	MEDIUM	POOR	LOW	90	HIGH
S	SHOCK RESISTING	O, W	FAIR	BEST	O: FAIR W: POOR	MEDIUM	FAIR	MED. HIGH	85	LOW-MEDIUM
P	MOLD STEEL	A, O, W	LOW TO HIGH	HIGH	VERY LOW	SHALLOW	LOW	MEDIUM	75-100	HIGH
L	SPECIAL PURPOSE LOW ALLOY	O, W	MEDIUM	MED. TO VERY HIGH	LOW	MEDIUM	LOW	LOW	90	HIGH
F	SPECIAL PURPOSE CARBON-TUNGSTEN	W, B	LOW TO VERY HIGH	LOW TO HIGH	HIGH	SHALLOW	LOW	LOW	75	HIGH
W	WATER-HARDENING	W, B	FAIR-GOOD	GOOD	POOR	SHALLOW	POOR	LOWEST	100	HIGHEST

*W-WATER, B-BRINE, O-OIL, A-AIR, S-MOLTEN SALT

the American Society for Metals Handbook Series, are perhaps the machinist's best guides for locating the specifications that the tools or parts must possess prior to their placement in use.

Some Examples. The following examples of material selection procedures are typical of those found in machine shops. One of the first tools a beginning machinist would make would be a chisel, a center punch, or a pin punch. This type of tool, according to *Machinery's Handbook*, would require an as-tempered hardness within the range of 52-57Rc. A tempered martensitic structure in SAE 1095 steel will yield this hardness range. The cost of this steel would be far less than an alloy tool steel (S type) and as long as the dimensional sizes of the heat-treated portion of this tool are small—less than .250" max. thickness—the 50 percent martensitic structure at the center of the part can be obtained. It must be remembered that plain carbon steel has low hardenability and that if larger sections are to be heat treated, an alloy tool steel with higher hardenability should be employed.

The identification of plain carbon steel can be approximated through the use of the spark test performed on an abrasive wheel. A whitish orange, moderately large spar stream with many fine and repeating spurts throughout the stream represents a plain high carbon tool steel approximating SAE 1095 composition. The spark test gives only an approximation of carbon content and the identification of various classes of metals. The selection of steels should be based on the laboratory's identification system—color coded or number-stamped, when received from the supplier. The use of an emissions spectrometer is the most exact method of composition identification of the materials that have lost their identity within the lab. This, however, is an expensive process.

Hot forming (forging) a flat cold chisel or turning a center or pin punch are perhaps the best ways to shape those tools. Final polishing and grinding of the cutting edge should be done after heat treatment, to avoid decarburization and/or scaling.

The heat treating specification for this type of steel is obtainable from many sources. To prevent fracture of the striking end of the chisel or punch, only the working end of the tool should be heat treated, and only that portion that will allow for sufficient reshaping, etc. The specifications call for the heating of this steel to the range of 1450°F to 1500°F. This is above the critical temperature. The rule of thumb for soaking time is one-half hour per inch thickness of the part. This allows sufficient time for austenite transformation to take place.

When holding a part for a prolonged time at an elevated temperature, it is advisable to pack the part in cast-iron chips or to use an atmospheric retort in the furnace to control decarburization of the surface. Flame heating of the chisel or punch is recommended in this case and the temperature can be controlled by noting the bright orange color that accompanies 1450°F to 1500°F, or more accurately by the use of a melting crayon in that range—such as 1500°F temple stick. This tool requires a severe quench in water or brine with agitation. Once the tool has austenitized for the calculated time, it must immediately be quenched in brine or water. When quenched by hand, the tool should be plunged vertically into the liquid to avoid longitudinal distortion. A figure eight agitation motion will increase the rate of heat removal. Once cooled by this method, a martensitic structure will have been created.

This structure must be tempered to relieve the stresses created (i.e. brittleness) in the quenching process. The untempered martensite B.C.C. structure will have an approximate hardness of Rc 67. Tempering specifications for chisels and punches require heating and holding in the range of 525-545°F (purple-violet color) for calculated time. At this temperature, the stresses (brittleness) will be removed and the Rc hardness will drop back to the desired range of approximately Rc 52-57. The tool should now be requenched or cooled in air to room temperature.

Final polishing and the grinding of the cutting edge should now be done to complete production of the tool.

Making a Hob. The selection of a tool steel to produce a hob to cut teeth on a worm gear will now be discussed. The hob is to be 2¼″ in diameter, 3¼″ long, and have an arbor hole 1″ in diameter with a key drive. This hob will be used to finish cut worm wheel teeth on rough cut SAE 1045 cold rolled steel with a hardness of Rc 20.

There are sections on this hob that are .750″ thick and this thickness must be hardened to a minimum of Rc 50. In machining practice, the cutting tool must possess 20 points minimum hardness greater than the material to be cut. Because of the shallow hardening effect of plain carbon steels, an alloy steel with a hardenability band that will encompass the desired hardness at the center of the thickest section of the hob must be selected. The cross-sectional maximum thickness as stated was .750″. One half of this distance in from both sides to the center is equal to 6/16″ in Jominy distance. The two factors—6/16″ distance and minimum Rc 50—should be applied to those sections of tool steels and their respective hardenability bands.

The American Society for Metals *Vol. 1 Handbook* suggests that steels with a Bhn of below 350 are generally cut/hobbed with M1, M2, M10, and T1 high-speed steels. But because, in this instance, only one worm wheel is needed, a steel can be selected that is less expensive, more easily machined, and easier to heat treat but which

possesses the necessary properties for the operation. The hardenability bands in the A.S.M. *Handbook* show several steels with these properties. Three steels—4140H, 4340H, and 9840H—have a guaranteed hardenability within their respective bands. Of these, 4140H is least expensive, but the difference between it and 4340H, the most expensive, is only pennies per pound. Price is a factor, but consideration must also be given to the required heat treatment of the part. The hardening process for all three of these steels is the same. SAE 4340 is most likely to be a stock item in the shop. It might not be 4340H, which is more highly controlled during its manufacture, but 4340 has a higher minimum hardenability at 6/16″ than does 4140 or 9840—hence the selection of a shop grade of 4340 will best meet the requirements.

The hob should be turned, bored, slotted, and milled by conventional machining methods. Grinding again will be a finishing process after heat treatment. The hardening of the hob will be slowly heating up to the austenitizing range of 1500-1550°F and holding for approximately 15 minutes to allow for transformation. This heating should be done in an atmospheric retort furnace. An oil quench is required for 4340 to create a martensitic structure and to cause the least distortion of the three possible quenchants. Tempering this structure is achieved with a temperature of between 400-600°F for two hours to yield an approximate Rc 51. Air cool to room temperature.

WORKING WITH STAINLESS STEEL

The increasing use of stainless steel in both consumer and industrial goods makes it particularly important to know more about the unique properties and applications of this group of alloy steels.

Because of its superior combination of attributes, stainless steel accommodates a wide variety of demands. High resistance to heat and and corrosion—the ability of some stainless steels to work harden or of others to air harden throughout thick sections—are but a few of the characteristics that make these alloys a boon to designers and engineers.

Chromium is the element that gives the stainless steels their corrosion-resistance qualities. Another key alloying element is nickel; it not only increases corrosion resistance, but also improves mechanical and fabricating properties. A third alloying element, manganese, came into use during World War II as a replacement for part of the nickel which was then in short supply.

These three alloying elements—chromium, nickel, and manganese—permit classifying the 38 standard-type compositions into the three basic categories listed in

Table 1-3, i.e., chromium stainless steels, chromium-nickel stainless steel, and chromium-nickel-manganese stainless steels.

If stainless steel did nothing more than resist corrosion, its value would be enormous. Additional factors that further enhance its importance are abrasion resistance, heat resistance, lower maintenance costs, and sales appeal—which may be as important in the manufacture of certain items as resistance to corrosion or high temperatures.

Stainless steel equipment is widely used in the food processing industries and in the manufacture of drugs because it resists corrosion, is easy to clean, and does not contaminate the products involved. Other principal uses are found in transportation, architecture, textile manufacturing, utilities, space experimentation, petroleum, and in the chemical industry by employing the metal's capabilities to withstand exposure to corrosive environments and ordinarily destructive pressure and temperature conditions.

While many metalworkers recognize stainless steel and are aware of some of its characteristics, they seldom have an opportunity to work with it as a project. In many laboratories, stainless steels are either not used at all or are limited to use in projects where fabrication is mainly by machining. Only by working directly with the metal can you gain a better understanding of it.

While it should be remembered that the following procedures are by no means the only ones that can be used, they do represent the operations selected as being best suited for this purpose. In most cases, the hours spent in experimenting far exceeded the hours spent in the actual fabrication of the finished object. For example, bowls were raised from four different gauges of stainless steel to determine how different thicknesses responded to this operation. In constructing a canister, three experimental methods were used to fit the bottom to the sides. In every case, the method adopted was the one which produced the finest finished object.

Materials Used

The austenitic group of stainless steels (AISI 300 Series) was selected because it was felt that the chromium-nickel alloys that make up this group are so widely used that they can provide a standard for comparison. Their many desirable properties make them the first choice for operations that would normally be encountered in an industrial-arts laboratory. The different types chosen were selected on the basis of widespread use and availability.

Because many industrial-arts laboratories do not have the necessary equipment to perform annealing operations, (thermal treatment designed to soften the metal

Table 1-3. Classification Table.

Chromium Stainless Steels		Chromium-Nickel Stainless Steels		Chromium-Nickel-Manganese Stainless Steels
AISI 400 Series		AISI 300 Series		AISI 200 Series
Hardenable by heat treatment	Non-Hardenable by heat treatment	Hardenable by cold working only		Hardenable by cold working only
TYPE NOS.	TYPE NOS.	TYPE NOS.		TYPE NOS.
410	430	302	309 S	201
403	43c	302 B	310	202
414	430 F Se	301	310 S	
431	442	303	314	
416	405	303 Se	316	
416 Se	446	304	316 L	
420		304 L	317	
440 A		305	321	
440 B		308	347	
440 C		309	348	

after working), the examples given are limited to what can be done without annealing the steel.

Also, keep in mind when using stainless steel with highly polished finishes that it is wise to leave the protective covering in place as long as possible to protect the polished surface.

Manual Cutting

Hand Shears. Fully annealed stainless steel in thicknesses of 20 gauge (0.375″) or less can be readily cut with hand shears, providing the shears are sharp and closely adjusted to ensure a clean cut. Cutting austenitic stainless steels requires shears with a 30- to 50-percent greater capacity than is needed for carbon steels. For example, cutting 20-gauge stainless steel requires shears that would cut 16-ga carbon steel without difficulty.

Hack Saw. A wavy-tooth blade of high-speed steel cuts best. For 20-gauge or lighter sheets, the blade should have 32 teeth to the inch.

Care should be taken to keep the teeth of the hacksaw from riding on the steel on the return stroke as this will work harden the metal and make cutting more difficult. When cutting this gauge sheet with a hacksaw, either back the sheet with wood or clamp the sheet between narrow pieces of wood placed near the line to be cut.

Machine Sawing

Band Saw. Use a wavy-tooth blade with 24 sharp teeth to the inch; operate at 115 fpm. Again, be careful to apply light, but constant pressure to the saw; otherwise, the blade may ride the steel without cutting and thus work harden it.

Friction Saw. For 20-ga and lighter stainless steel. Use the same equipment, but increase the speed to 3000 fpm, and use a dull, wavy-tooth blade with 24 teeth to the inch.

Note: Burrs will result from both manual and machine-cutting operations. These should be filed down as soon as possible because they can injure the operator and can mar the surface of the steel in subsequent operations.

Hammer Forming (Raising)

Example: bowl, 5½″ d, 1⅜″ deep (see Fig. 1-34).

Metal: 24 gauge (.025″) annealed, stainless, AISI Type 302 with a No. 4 bright luster finish. (Type 304 may be substituted.)

Bowls can be formed from stainless steel up to a

Fig. 1-34. A hammer-formed stainless steel bowl, 5½″ d, 1⅜″ deep and a stainless steel bowl, 6″ d, 1¼″ deep, formed by spinning (right).

13-gauge thickness (.09375″), although 13 gauge is too heavy to planish satisfactorily. While 20 gauge works quite well, the gauge used in the example produces the best results.

Procedure. Glue together two maple blocks, each 2- × -6½- × -6½ inch (see Fig. 1-35). Be sure the grain of one block is at right angles to the grain of the other to prevent splitting. Attach the resulting 4-inch thick block to the faceplate of a lathe and cut a 1½-inch depression—with the same contour as that desired in the formed bowl—into the block. Drill holes in the corners of

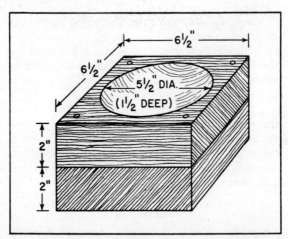

Fig. 1-35. Maple block constructed for hammer-forming operation.

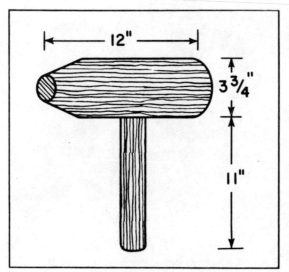

Fig. 1-36. Mallet turned on lathe for hammer-forming operation.

Fig. 1-37. Cylindrical stainless steel canistor (roll formed).

the block for 5/16-inch bolts which will hold the stainless steel sheet in place.

Next, cut a 6½-inch square of stainless steel using the friction sawing method. Remove burrs, drill holes, and bolt the steel to the top of the maple block.

Because conventional forming mallets are too light to be used with 24-gauge (.025-inch) or heavier stainless steel, a heavier mallet is necessary (see Fig. 1-36). With this mallet, which can easily be turned on the lathe, it will be possible to form the bowl with little more difficulty than would be met in a similar operation using softer metals.

Note: Because of the work hardening that occurs, increased springback will prevent the steel from fitting perfectly into the bottom of the form. It will be found that the deeper the cavity, the greater the space between form and block, until at the bottom a space of almost ⅛ of an inch will exist.

When the forming is completed, remove the steel, trim excess from the rim of the bowl with a band saw, and file away burrs. Then planish the bowl. For the final polish, use a loose muslin buff with a 6-inch d, which turns at approximately 3450 rpm, and white rouge as the abrasive agent.

Roll Forming

Example: cylindrical canister, in which both the sidewall and the flange inside the lid are formed on a pinch roll type slip roll (see Fig. 1-37).

Metal: 24-gauge aannealed stainless, AISI Type 302 with a No. 4 finish. (Type 304 may be substituted.)

Procedure: After inspecting the surface and removing all scratches with 320-grit abrasive cloth, protect both surfaces of the stainless steel by covering them with heavy Kraft paper held in place with draftsman's tape. This is necessary because the surface of the slip rolls may be scarred from use. Carefully inspect and clean the slip rolls to remove any foreign particles or burrs which might mar the surface of the stainless steel.

Because the elastic recovery for stainless steel is considerably greater than for carbon steel, the cylinder can be roll formed to the proper size by making a succession of passes through the rolls. Before each pass, adjust the rear roll to produce a cylinder slightly smaller in diameter, until the proper size is reached.

Spinning

Example: bowl, 6″ in diameter, 1¼″ deep (see Fig. 1-34).

Metal: 24-gauge annealed stainless steel, AISI Type 305 (Type 305 has a lower rate of work hardening than either Type 302 or 304, and is recommended grade for spinning) with a No. 4 finish.

Procedure: Cut the disc carefully to produce as perfect a circle as possible. Then place the disc between the follow block and the maple form, centered on the lathe. At a speed of 500 rpm, trim the edge of the disc (as it turns) with a carbide tipped cutting tool. Continue

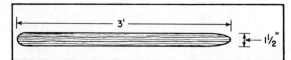

Fig. 1-38. Straight-grained oak.

cutting until the disc is perfectly round and the edge is free from burrs.

Roller-type tools of hardened and polished steel, or smooth, round-nose tools of brass or bronze are recommended for spinning stainless steel. Conventional steel spinning tools are not suitable; the stainless disc erodes the tool, which results in carbon steel pickup on the surface of the disc. A smoothly rounded piece of straight-grained oak, 1½-inch diameter and 3 feet long, can also be used (see Fig. 1-38).

As a lubricant, apply yellow laundry soap liberally and often to both sides of the disc as well as to the spinning tool.

Form a section of the disc ¼ of an inch from the edge into a flange and turn at an angle of approximately 60 degrees to the plane of the rotating disc. This reduces wrinkles caused by forming. Make the flange by inserting the edge of the turning disc about ¼ of an inch deep into a slot cut into the end of a piece of oak (see Fig. 1-39), and then turn the wood to form the flange. The spinning will then proceed as with any other metal.

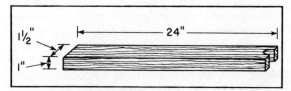

Fig. 1-39. Note the slot cut into the end.

After the bowl is formed and the edge trimmed for the last time, polish the metal on the lathe with successive finer grades of abrasive cloth. For the final finish, polish with grit 320 abrasive cloth, using kerosene as a lubricant.

Drilling

The drilling operations discussed here are limited to drilling holes in sheet stainless steel of 13 gauge (.09375 of an inch) and thinner.

In drilling austenitic stainless steels, best results will be obtained by using high-speed drills with short spirals, with the drill itself being as short as possible for the job in order to provide maximum rigidity and thus reduce breakage. The drill should be ground to a point angle (included angle) of approximately 135° with a clearance angle of about 8°. Web thickness of the drill should be kept at about ⅛ inch of the diameter of the drill in order to reduce the rubbing of the web on the bottom of the hole and thus work hardening the steel.

Because the exceptionally low heat conductivity of stainless results in correspondingly higher temperatures on the cutting edge of the drill, lower spindle speeds should be used in drilling the stainless steels (usually about 60 percent of the speeds used for drilling carbon steels). Because drilling speeds are usually given in surface feet per minute, a conversion table should be used to avoid miscalculations.

Care must be used in center punching stainless steel. Stainless can easily be work hardened by using a round center punch. A triangular center punch struck as lightly as practical will harden the steel less than the round punch.

Turning

Example: small knob for the lid of a canister (see Fig. 1-37).

Metal: AISI Type 304 annealed stainless steel.

Procedure: Use a high-speed steel tool bit ground in approximately the same contour with the same angles as would be used for turning carbon steel. Although special angles have been established for best results in cutting stainless, these angles do not differ greatly from those used in turning carbon steel. When grinding the tool, be sure that the clearance angles are great enough to keep the tool from riding on the surface of the work and causing it to harden.

A speed of 50 surface fpm is recommended for this operation. The rule of "heavy cut with slow speed" works very well; roughing cuts of .015 of an inch and finishing cuts of .003 of an inch can be used.

Finish the knob with successive finer grades of abrasive paper. For the final finish, use 320 grit abrasive cloth and kerosene as a lubricant.

As for joining operations, welding is preferred for joining two pieces of stainless steel.

Silver solder is the only type of hard solder recommended for joining stainless steel. It is also the most satisfactory method of joining stainless steel to nonferrous metals.

Silver Soldering

Example: wire and sheet sculpture. See Fig. 1-40.

Metal: Type 302 stainless steel wire (chiefly

Fig. 1-40. Wire and sheet sculpture fabricated by joining with silver solder.

.051-inch and .035-inch d with spring temper); 24-gauge Type 302 sheet with a No. 8 mirror finish. (Type 304 may be substituted.)

The solder used should contain 50 percent silver, 15½ percent copper, 16½ percent zinc, and 18 percent cadmium. This higher silver content will provide greater strength, and the low copper content will furnish a better color match with the stainless steel. A paste flux can be used.

In the silver soldering of stainless steel, the joint design is of primary importance. A gap of .001 of an inch will provide sufficient clearance to permit the solder to flow by capillary action, but a gap of .003 of an inch or greater will furnish less strength.

Procedure: Thoroughly clean both the wires and the sheet at the point where they will be joined. Abrade the area with 320-grit abrasive cloth, and wipe clean to remove all traces of foreign material.

After aligning and securing the pieces to be soldered, apply the paste flux with a brush, and flux the solder by dipping it into the flux. Flux is easier to remove after soldering if it is permitted to dry before actual soldering begins, or if low heat from the torch is applied to the fluxed area to dry it.

Apply the solder as the flux becomes fluid, and heat the joint until the solder flows in place. After the joint cools, wash it in hot running water to remove the remaining flux. The residual flux is corrosive; all traces must be removed. If hot water does not dissolve the flux, remove it by scrubbing with a commercial laundry detergent and a toothbrush.

Any heat discoloration of the steel can be removed by buffing with white rouge where possible, or by using 600-grit abrasive cloth. Commercial cleaners can be substituted for buffing.

Soft Soldering

Soft soldering can be used successfully where very little strength is necessary to hold the parts together in normal usage. When compared with the tensile strength of stainless steel (ranging from 70,000 to 200,000 psi), soft solders are relatively weak, having tensile strengths of only 2,000 to 7,000 psi, depending on their composition.

Example: small round canister (see Fig. 1-37).

Metal: 24-gauge stainless, Type 302 with a No. 4 finish. (Type 304 may be substituted.)

A 60-percent tin/40-percent lead solder is recommended for this operation. Although the best color match is obtained with an 80-percent tin/20-percent lead composition, strength is considered to be more important in this application than color match (tensile and shear strength are greatest at a 63-percent tin/37-percent lead composition). A liquid flux can be used.

Procedure: Roughen the edges to be joined with a medium-grade abrasive cloth. Then place the pieces in position for soldering and hold rigidly in place.

Because liquid solder flows on any area covered by flux, apply petrolatum near the edges of the joint to keep the flux and solder from being deposited on areas where it is not wanted. Carefully apply the flux with a small brush.

For soldering, use the small flame of an acetylene torch with a very small tip. In experiments with a variety of heat sources including electric soldering irons with heating capacities up to 700 w, the acetylene torch provided the most satisfactory results.

To prevent etching, take care to keep the flux from spattering on parts of the steel not to be soldered. As soon as soldering is completed, rinse the flux away with warm water; then scrub the soldered area with a laundry detergent and again rinse in clear water.

Remove excess solder in the joint with fine abrasive cloth.

Selecting and Purchasing

Major cities throughout the United States have steel service centers where stainless steels of all types and in all forms can be purchased in small quantities. Locations of service centers can be obtained by consulting local telephone directories.

It is necessary to select carefully the type, form, thickness, hardness, and finish in the proper combinations of the stainless steels to be worked. Type 302 (a general purpose type) or Type 304 work quite well for all forming operations except spinning, where Type 305 must be used.

The choice of thickness for raising and spinning is limited to 24 gauge because thicker gauges are too resistant to manual forming operations performed by most secondary-school pupils.

The rapid rate of work hardening of the austenitic stainless steels demands that the material be in fully annealed or "dead soft" condition when it is purchased.

The selection of finish in the material purchased is of great importance. Polishing of stainless steel is time consuming because of its hardness. It is, therefore, practical to select a finish as close as possible to that desired on the finished product. Care must be taken that the surfaces of the steel are protected in handling, working, and storing so that scratches will not appear on the surface which will require much time and effort to remove.

Safety Precautions

The hardness of stainless steel requires that every possible precaution be taken to make the various operations as safe as possible for both the operator and others in the laboratory. Because relatively thin gauges are involved in most cases, special care is necessary in polishing operations; the thin metal can be polished to a very, very sharp edge.

THE CO$_2$ PROCESS: AN APPROACH TO CORE MAKING

Most people will agree that industrial-arts foundry work should include core making. This is not only a valuable experience but the process also permits design of many varied and different foundry projects.

The CO$_2$ core-making process permits core making in the industrial-arts foundry area in a very practical manner. The "mix" is easy to prepare, the core comes out of the core box in a nonfragile condition, the time for fabrication is extremely short, and the cost is low. See Figs. 1-41, 1-42, and 1-43.

The procedure is simple; so simple that a very brief description will permit success at the first attempt. The description of this process follows:

☐ Mix ¼ cup of Stinex (available from Carver Foundry Products, Muscatine, Iowa) with one quart of silica sand. A very thorough mix is important so the ingredients should be "mulled" with an iron bar or some other similar device.

☐ Immediately pack the mixture in the core box.

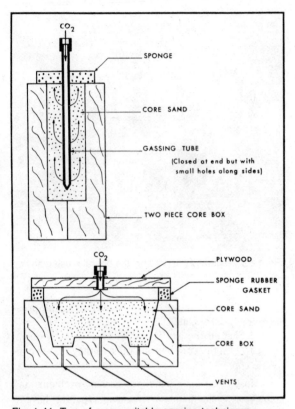

Fig. 1-41. Two of many suitable gassing techniques.

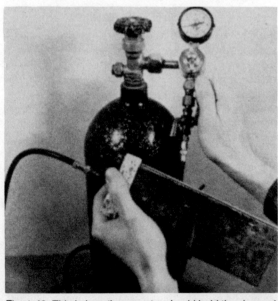

Fig. 1-42. This is how the operator should hold the clamped core box while doing the gassing.

Fig. 1-43. Preparatory to gassing, the operator using an iron bar to mix sand and Stinex.

☐ Gas the mixture, using 10-20 lbs./sq. in. pressure, for 15-20 seconds.

☐ Shut off the gas.

☐ Open the core box and remove the *finished* non-fragile core.

Most cores have individual gassing problems and some design adjustments in the gasing apparatus have to be considered.

EXPLOSIVE METALFORMING

Forming metals to desired shapes by controlling forces generated by explosive charges is not a new discovery. An English patent shows that the technique had been evaluated and judged to be of some merit in 1898. Little was done, however, in the way of developing and applying the technique until the metal requirements for engineering in space research forced a quest for a method of forming the new alloys and metals used in space vehicles.

What does this have to do with metal-working in a shop? Several things. Many large industrial firms are carrying on intensive research and development programs. The major activity is in the area of space research, but several patents have already been granted for tools such as cable cutters and splicers, hole punchers, and similar devices—all employing the principle of explosive force.

The basis of the explosive-forming technique is simple. It is quite the same thing as setting off a firecracker under a tin can. The tin can usually assumes a different shape as a result of this process. If dies are prepared to control the shape of the metal while it is experiencing the force, and the complete operation is contained in a chamber of sufficient strength to allay the fears of even the most timid, then we have a basic description of the process.

After much research concerning pressures exerted by contained explosive charges, to satisfy concern for safety, a "bull nose" (a device used for capping large steel pipe), was selected to serve as container for the charge. Care and precision are imperative in constructing the firing unit as it must be air and pressure tight throughout, and a safety valve must be provided. The leather gasket between the aluminum lid and the flange of the container acts as a seal and also a safety valve for pressure *above* the work piece. The small relief hole at the bottom of the container acts as a safety valve *below* the work. This hole should be ⅛ of an inch or larger.

You can test the unit with a blank 22 cartridge as a charge, using 22-gauge aluminum for a work piece. The charge will not produce sufficient force to shape the metal. You should be able to achieve a perfectly formed shaped with a blank 38 cartridge.

The unit is fired by hand by tapping the firing pin with a mallet. It would be simple to devise a lever-firing system that would permit the operator to stand some distance from the unit. Safety goggles must be worn, of course, and instruction on proper handling of blank cartridges cannot be overemphasized.

Perhaps the best safety precautions are present in the educational benefits. There is ample information about pressures generated by cartridges, and other explosives, and the strength of materials available from manufacturers, and reference books. Professional gunsmiths are another excellent source of technical information regarding pressures and strengths of materials under explosive pressure.

If properly researched, properly constructed, and properly supervised during operation and handling of materials, the danger element is no greater than with many other familiar shop operations. See Figs. 1-44 and 1-45.

A MAGNET WIRE DISPENSING SYSTEM

You can successfully solve the problem of wire handling by the use of inexpensive door stops. These stops are mounted in the center of the wiring table so that their rubber tips can be made to bear against the rims of the magnet wire spools, which revolve on ¼-×-5 inch pipe-nipple shafts attached to the table by means of pipe flanges.

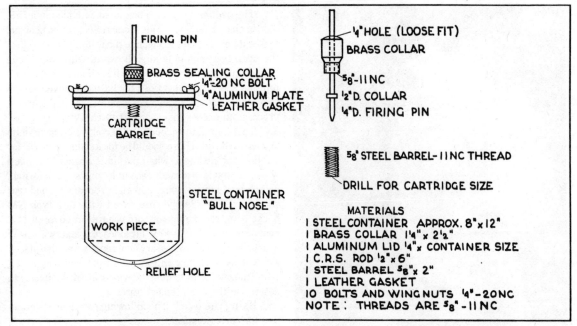

Fig. 1-44. Design details and materials list.

FIRING PIN

BRASS SEALING COLLAR
¼"-20 NC BOLT
¼" ALUMINUM PLATE
LEATHER GASKET

CARTRIDGE
BARREL

STEEL CONTAINER
"BULL NOSE"

WORK PIECE

RELIEF HOLE

¼" HOLE (LOOSE FIT)
BRASS COLLAR

⅝"-11 NC
½" D. COLLAR
¼" D. FIRING PIN

⅝" STEEL BARREL—11 NC THREAD

DRILL FOR CARTRIDGE SIZE

MATERIALS
1 STEEL CONTAINER APPROX. 8"x 12"
1 BRASS COLLAR 1¼" x 2½"
1 ALUMINUM LID ¼"x CONTAINER SIZE
1 C.R.S. ROD ½"x 6"
1 STEEL BARREL ⅝"x 2"
1 LEATHER GASKET
10 BOLTS AND WING NUTS ¼"-20NC
NOTE: THREADS ARE ⅝"-11 NC

This arrangement makes it possible to lock the spools in a stationary position or to permit them to drag, and, thus, put the desired tension on the wire for proper coil winding. This setup accommodates 5-inch and 6-inch diameter spools and even smaller ones, by inserting the proper-sized blocks of wood between the stop and the spool.

This system enables you to wind directly from the spool to the coil and, at the same time, to apply the correct tension to the wire. See Fig. 1-46.

Do not wrap the wire around the stationary coil, but rather rotate the coil instead. Considerable time and wire is saved by this method, and a perfect winding job is possible if reasonable care is used.

All magnet wire spools have the wire size painted on them in white so that there can be no mistake as to gauge. The wire is wound off of 12-inch spools onto 5-inch or 6-inch diameter spools, many of which are in use to avoid delays in winding coils.

A wire gauge should be available for checking wire sizes whenever it is necessary.

OVEN CURES PAINTED ENAMEL SURFACES

Although it is only one aspect of a total project, the finish on articles made of metal should be durable and have a

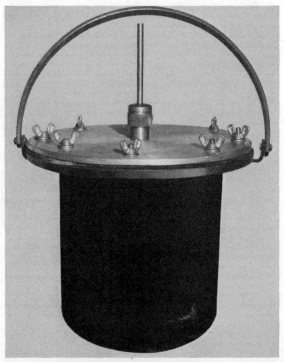

Fig. 1-45. Shop-made unit employs force from a blank 38 cartridge to demonstrate explosive metalforming.

33

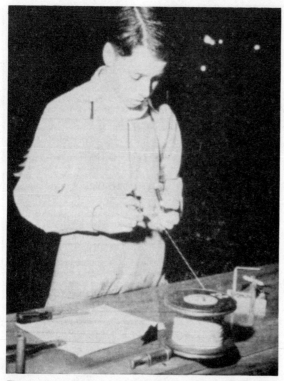

Fig. 1-46. Winding a coil from the dispersing setup. The arrow at bottom points out the door stop, an important part.

The oven is a plywood box lined with aluminum foil held in place by staples. This lining reflects oven heat and makes it unnecessary to insulate the walls. The outside of the oven becomes only slightly warm when the inside temperature is 225 degrees. The lid is hinged to the oven top, and ⅛ of an inch between the lid and the oven serves as a vent. While air movement is necessary in the drying process, an excess may cause draft checking.

There are four independently controlled lamp units housed in the lid. These should be located in the lid center to allow for clearance when the lid is opened. Standard wiring methods are used; each unit consists of a switch, switch box, junction box, porcelain receptacle, and four wire nuts. The switches are wired with 14-2 type NM house wire, and the power cord is a rubber covered 14-2 appliance type. Two 100 W incandescent and two 150 W heat bulbs produce necessary heat ranges. We also placed a 4-×-4 inch window in the oven front and centered a candy thermometer behind the window to make it easy to determine the oven temperature.

Using the oven. The following procedure is effective for curing enamel:

☐ Preheat the oven to 175 degrees, using all four bulbs.

☐ Place the project in the oven. Maintain 175-degree heat for 30 minutes using the incandescent bulbs. If the project is large, it will lower the oven temperature. Apply more heat, using the heat lamps, until 175 degrees is attained.

☐ Next, turn on all bulbs and allow the temperature to reach 225 degrees. Maintain this temperature for 10 minutes. Longer periods at this temperature will scorch and burn the enamel. This phase will speed up the curing process.

☐ Turn off all bulbs and allow the project to cool in the oven. The paint will not attain its toughness until it is completely cooled (about 20 minutes). Total curing time is about 70 minutes. If a large number of projects needs to be cured in a limited period of time, add several ovens, or increase oven size.

The oven has become an indispensable tool because of the variety of other processes we can implement. We have cured epoxy glue joints and dried PEG-treated blocks and small pieces of lumber. When curing epoxy glue joints, the project should be in the oven 24 hours at 150 degrees; temperature can be maintained using two 100 W incandescent bulbs. We found that the temperature varies about 10 degrees in 24 hours. PEG treated blocks and lumber can be dried by leaving them in the oven for

pleasing appearance. Cleaning the metal thoroughly and applying primer prior to painting often doesn't produce desired results.

If you study the factors involved in drying finishes you will find that paint dries three ways: evaporation, oxidation, and polymerization. We decided to try forced drying, which would accelerate polymerizing.

Although industry force-dries objects immediately after finish application, you can get satisfactory results by painting one day and curing the next. This allows the paint to dry to the touch and makes handling easier.

You will need an oven for your laboratory and you can design your own. The oven should be simple, inexpensive, and effective. See Figs. 1-47 and 1-48.

Design. The oven was designed to cure a tool box. The size can, however, be adjusted to meet individual needs. If a larger oven is desired, more lamp units will have to be added. Most of the materials we used were available in our storage room. The remainder were purchased at a hardware store.

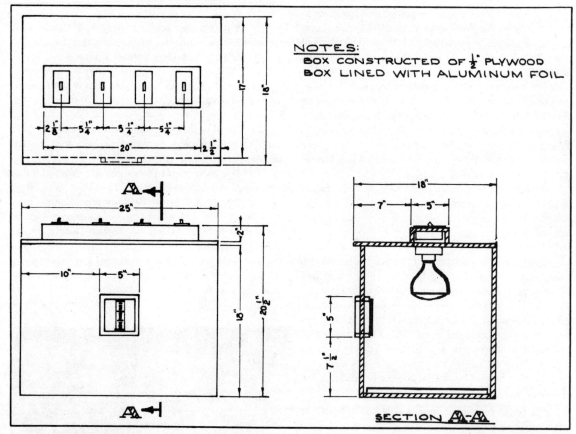

NOTES:
BOX CONSTRUCTED OF ½" PLYWOOD
BOX LINED WITH ALUMINUM FOIL

SECTION A-A

Fig. 1-47. Design details.

three to seven days at 150 degrees (use two 100 W incandescent bulbs).

ETCHING COPPER FOR INTAGLIO PRINTING

The most common method of etching copper for intaglio printing is to cover the copper with an acid resistant coating such as wax or asphaltum. The image to be etched is then scratched to reveal bare copper and the copper plate is etched. There are several variations to this procedure, but they follow approximately the same pattern. See Fig. 1-49.

A method more neatly like that used by many gravure printers utilizes photography and carbon tissue. Mechanical means can be substituted for the photography. This method allows for flexibility in the design to be printed and eliminates scratching the design on copper, which many times makes it difficult to achieve a desirable finished product.

Fig. 1-48. Curing oven, made of plywood, features window-mounted thermometer.

The original design can be prepared for etching in two days. It can be photographed by a copying camera, which will produce a negative of the original. A piece of film exposed to the negative will produce a positive that is like the original design. The positive is then used to complete the process. If no copying camera is available, the positive can be obtained mechanically by drawing on clear acetate with an opaque material such as India ink, or any material that does not allow light to pass through it. Tracing paper may also be drawn on, but the exposure time for the carbon tissue must be increased to allow for the opacity of the tracing paper.

Several office copying machines on the market today, will produce an opaque positive on a clear material that can be used in the etching process. No matter what method is used to obtain the positive, the lines to be etched must be opaque.

Carbon tissue, a gelatin material that is deposited in a thin layer on a paper backing, becomes sensitive to light when immersed in potassium dichromate or bichromate. When light is exposed to the sensitized carbon tissue, the gelatin hardens in the areas exposed to light, and will wash away in unexposed areas. This characteristic of carbon tissue allows it to be used in the gravure printing process.

To etch copper by the carbon-tissue method, the following process should be followed:

1. Sensitive gravure carbon tissue in a 4-percent solution of potassium dichromate at 54 degrees for 3 minutes.

2. Squeeze the carbon tissue onto a sheet of ⅛-inch plastic (gelatin against plastic), forcing all air bubbles from underneath the carbon tissue.

3. Place a sheet of brown Kraft paper, two sheets of blotting paper, and a glass pane over this and allow to dry 1 hour and 45 minutes. When dry, store flat in an air-tight box. Carbon tissue can be used after 2 hours, but is best when it is 7 to 8 hours old. It should not be kept longer than 2 days after being sensitized, unless it is stored in an air-tight container in a freezer.

4. Clean copper with a solution of 18-degree Baume muriatic acid (4-ounce muriatic acid, 1 cup salt, 1 gallon water). Use a fine pumice for final cleaning. The copper must be water-receptive in all areas.

5. Expose carbon tissue 4 minutes to carbon arc light. (The correct exposure must be determined according to the light source used.)

6. Flood the copper with distilled water, place exposed carbon tissue against copper, and quickly squeeze to copper with a hard rubber roller.

7. Allow to fan dry 10 minutes.

8. Flood paper backing of carbon tissue with methanol alcohol until the backing becomes pimply.

9. Soak in 120-degree water 2 minutes.

10. Pull carbon tissue backing away from copper.

11. Swab excess carbon tissue lightly with cotton until image is visible and soak again in 120-degree water 5 minutes.

12. Flood with 50-percent methanol alcohol. Flood again with 90-percent methanol alcohol, and fan dry quickly. Do not allow spots to accumulate.

13. Use asphaltum to block out any exposed areas that should not be etched.

14. Obtain a solution of 40-degree Baume perchloride of iron and a solution of 43-degree Baume perchloride of iron. Watch the copper closely during etching procedure.

15. Swab the copper with cotton approximately 2 minutes with the 40-degree solution of perchloride of iron. Lines to be etched should darken.

16. Swab the 43-degree solution approximately 4

Fig. 1-49. A positive (left) was made by drawing with India ink on frosted acetate. On the right is the etched copper, now ready for printing.

minutes. Do not mix the two solutions as they can be reused.

17. Flood with water to stop etching action.

18. Remove asphaltum with naphtha, remove all carbon tissue with muriatic acid solution.

19. Clean copper with a fine copper cleaner and print.

This process, while appearing to be very complicated, is quite simple once the materials are collected. A little sophistication in the photographic operation, addition of a step between 4 and 5 for a 5-minute burn of a straight-line screen before exposing the design, and slightly different etching procedures can yield results similar to those obtained in the gravure printing industry.

COPPERPLATE NONMETALLIC ITEMS

Electroplating is a fascinating activity for the shop. There is something magic-like in this process that always intrigues young and old alike. You can gain first-hand experiences with theories of electrolysis and electroplating. You can also learn how to set up and operate simple plating equipment.

An electroplating area is useful not only in electric, sheet-metal, and art-metal shops of both unit and general type, but also in the general shop itself. It is with copperplating of nonmetallic objects made in the crafts shop that this discussion is concerned.

Nonmetallic copperplating is a special kind of electroplating in which nonconductors, such as wood, Keene cement, leather, plastics, etc., are covered with a thin coating of copper by electrochemical means. The process is especially useful in the crafts area where objects cast in Keene cement can be made even more beautiful if copperplated and given an antique finish.

Equipment Needed

Only a surprisingly small amount of equipment is needed to do nonmetallic copperplating. Anyone can devise a satisfactory setup using shop-made equipment. The major kinds of equipment and materials needed include:

☐ a tank.
☐ an electrolytic solution.
☐ a source of direct current.
☐ a rheostat, and

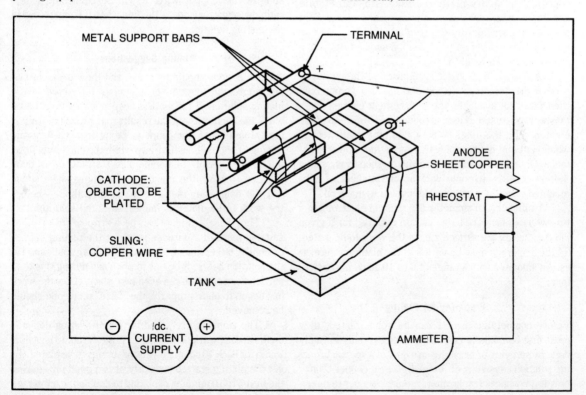

Fig. 1-50. Design details.

☐ an ammeter.

A typical hookup is shown in Fig. 1-50. Descriptions of each of the aforementioned items follow:

Tanks. The tank can be a glass jar, a crock of glazed earthenware, an old aquarium, or a storage-battery case. Good tanks can be made of wood. Wooden tanks, though, should be lined with tar or pitch. The following inside dimensions are satisfactory for tank size: length 14 inches, width 8 inches, height 10 inches. This tank will hold approximately 3 gallons of solution and it is large enough to meet most plating needs in the shop.

Solution. The following solution will produce good copperplanting results on nonmetallic objects: 5 pounds copper sulfate (blue vitriol); 12 ounces sulfuric acid; 1½ teaspoons corn syrup; and water to make 3 gallons.

Crush the copper sulphate crystals. Then dissolve them in about a gallon of hot water. Add the remainder of the water to make 3 gallons. Slowly add sulfuric *acid to water*. Stir in the corn syrup.

Current Source. Only direct current can be used for electroplating. Some good sources of direct current are a storage battery, a battery charger, a tungar-bulb rectifier, or a dry-plate rectifier. An automobile generator, driven by a small motor, makes an excellent source of current for electroplating. Also, certain transformer-rectifier units of the kind used on HO-gauge model trains can be used.

Rheostat. A rheostat is required in the circuit to control the amperage during plating. If a commercial rheostat is not available, the replacement element for a toaster can be used. A lead is connected to one end of the element with the other lead clipped on the element at whatever point is necessary to provide the proper resistance. Or, a rheostat can be made in the shop by wrapping 30 feet of #22 nichrome wire around a sheet of mica mounted on a sheet of suitable insulating material.

Ammeter. An ammeter is a must in electroplating for two reasons: (*a*) The amperage required for a given job depends on the surface area of the work to be plated; (b) the amperage must be varied as the plating progresses. An ammeter with a range of 8 to 10 amps is satisfactory.

Preparing for Plating

Before nonmetallic objects can be copperplated, they must first be made to conduct electricity. This is easily done by spraying or brushing on a coat of a special bronzing solution consisting of: 1 ounce *cleaned* copper bronze powder, ½ ounce clear lacquer, ½ ounce lacquer thinner.

The copper-bronze powder must be cleaned chemi-

cally before it can be used. If this is not done, satisfactory plating cannot be expected. To do this cleaning, place the powder in a small bottle of acetone. Shake the bottle vigorously. Allow the bottle's contents to settle in a flat pan or dish, and then pour off the acetone. The powder that remains should be clean and free of the grease that previously coated each particle.

The ingredients in the bronzing solution must be measured carefully. If too much lacquer is used, the conducting quality of the bronze powder will be impaired. If too much thinner is used, the bronze powder might tend to flake off during plating.

After the work has been coated with copper-bronze paint, it must not be allowed to become dirty or oily before plating. Even handling the work with bare hands should be avoided. The work should be inspected, however, after the copper bronzing has been applied. When the work is dry, a finger touched to the surface should show some copper-bronze powder. If none shows, then either too much lacquer or not enough lacquer thinner was used.

The work to be plated should now be suspended in a sling of fine copper wire. It will be connected to the cathode (negative) side of the line when it is immersed in the plating solution.

Plating Suggestions

All connections should be made, and the current turned on, before the work to be plated is immersed in the plating solution. If the work is suspended in the solution while the current is off, the results may prove unsatisfactory. Even when the work is being inspected during plating, it should be withdrawn while the current is flowing in the circuit. In nonmetallic painting, it is good practice to have the electroplating going on—that is, actually depositing metal on a "false" cathode—before the work to be plated is immersed in the solution.

The "false" cathode can be a strip of tin or other suitable metal. Its purpose is to get the plating started promptly. Otherwise, the work might hang suspended in the solution before it begins to plate and during this time partial disintegration can even take place. After the work has begun to plate properly, the "false" electrode should be removed.

The amperage required for electroplating depends on the area of work to be plated. A rule of thumb is: Allow 1 amp for each 10 square inches of surface to be plated. To get the plating started promptly, it is a good idea during the first 5 to 10 minutes of plating to double the amperage that normally would be required. Following this beginning period, the amperage should be cut back to normal. In other words, if the area of the work requires 2 amperes for proper plating, 4 amperes should be used during the first 5 to 10 minutes of plating, or until the work begins to take on a pinkish glow, indicating that plating has begun. Then the current should be reduced to 2 amperes for the remainder of plating time.

Color Guide

If plating proceeds properly, the work soon takes on a light reddish color. After 15 to 20 minutes of plating, the work should be withdrawn from the solution (current left on) and inspected. The proper color should be, of course, a bright tinge of new copper. If the color is a dark pink, the work should be washed with water, buffed lightly with fine steel wool, or emery cloth, and immersed again in the solution, this time with reduced amperage. If rough spots, sometimes called "orange peel," develop, these should be smoothed. This condition can be corrected by:

—the plating should be continued at a reduced amperage.

—the work should be moved farther away from the copper anode.

—both should be done.

It is desirable from time to time to agitate the solution and to move the work so that it faces another direction in the solution. This will ensure smooth and even plating. Occasionally, the work should be withdrawn and moved to a new position in its sling to prevent the formation of marks where the sling touches the work.

In nonmetallic plating, the copper will not cover the work immediately. The plating will seem to be "taking" in spots that spread until the entire surface is covered. Sometimes it might be necessary to retouch, with the copper-bronze solution, a particular spot that seems unwilling to be plated. One purpose of inspection is, of course, to ensure that plating is occurring evenly all over the surface.

Depending on the amperage and area of work, a satisfactory thickness of copper should be deposited in 2 to 4 hours. Smoother plating results can usually be obtained by using a low amperage for a long time than a high amperage for a short time.

Antique Finishing

After a copper coating of sufficient thickness has been deposited, the work should be removed from the tank, washed thoroughly in water, and buffed lightly with a soft, wire, scratch wheel (brass preferred). Although copper-plated objects can be preserved in their natural color by light buffing with rouge or a cloth buff, antique finishing tends to make them look richer and less gaudy.

Antique finishing is easily done by buffing the work with a soft, wire brush, and then immersing it into a solution of 3 ounces of liver of sulphur in 1 gallon of water. The work should then be washed and rubbed lightly with fine steel wool to bring out the highlights. A coat of clear lacquer will preserve both the color and the finish. See Figs. 1-51 and 1-52.

Safety Suggestions

Electroplating is not a dangerous activity. Nevertheless, care should be exercised in handling chemicals and in dealing with electricity. This is just good common sense. Some specific safety suggestions to follow when electroplating are:

☐ Avoid getting chemicals or chemical solutions on the hands, face, or in skin breaks. Wear rubber gloves, if necessary. Keep hands clean by thoroughly washing them with soap and water.

☐ Avoid inhaling fumes which may be given off during plating. Special ventilation is unnecessary in ordinary use of the equipment described herein.

Fig. 1-51. An incense burner made from plaster of Paris that has been copperplated by the technique described here. Copperplating makes this figure even more exotic.

Fig. 1-52. Each of these figures is made from a material not generally associated with copperplating. The fish (from top to bottom) is ceramic; the pitcher is glass; the baby shoe is leather; and the cat is Keene cement.

☐ Protect your clothing and yourself by wearing aprons (rubber preferred).
☐ Avoid spilling and splashing chemical solutions.

ABRASIVE BLASTING

Here is an abrasive process that can be used to etch glass, formica, and metal, remove paint and rust from various materials, and clean castings. Abrasive blasting, commonly called sandblasting, has been used in industry for nearly a hundred years. Before seriously considering this process, the following questions should first be answered:

☐ What equipment is needed?
☐ Are there safety hazards involved and special safety precautions to be taken?
☐ Is the operation of the abrasive blaster feasible?
☐ Will this be of value?

The answers to these queries form the basis for the following discussion. The equipment needed for abrasive blasting consists of abrasive blasting gun, cabinet, air compressor, storage tank, and motor, and abrasive material. The blasting gun can be purchased or an efficient gun, such as the one shown in Fig. 1-53, can be easily constructed.

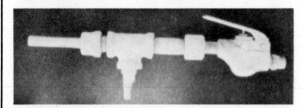

Fig. 1-53. Abrasive blasting gun.

Booths or cabinets designed to reclaim abrasive material and prevent dust problems can be purchased. They can also be built in the shop. The materials used for the construction of the abrasive blasting cabinet shown in Fig. 1-54 were ½-inch fir plywood for the upper portion of the cabinet and 26-gauge galvanized steel for the hopper, which is needed to reclaim the abrasive material and return it to the abrasive reservoir. Four pieces of fir stock were used for the legs. Inside the cabinet a light was installed to adequately observe the work. Double-strength glass was used for the window in the upper part of the cabinet and sleeves from an old shirt with tight fitting cuffs were fastened to arm holes with embroidery hoops. The abrasive reservoir, connected to the hopper, was made from an empty 1-gallon turpentine can.

Although it is true that in abrasive blasting the higher the air pressure the faster the cutting, an air compressor capable of producing 100 psi and a 7-8 gallon storage tank capable of maintaining 70 psi were found satisfactory for decorating and cleaning articles. An efficient and inexpensive compressor unit can be assembled by using an old refrigerator compressor, surplus storage tank, and a ⅓-hp motor.

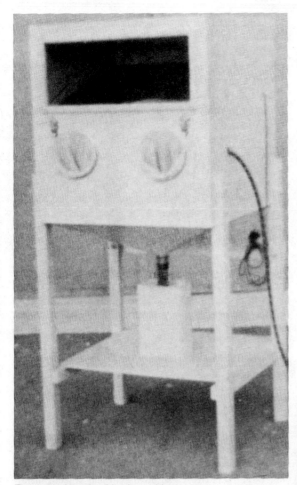

Fig. 1-54. Abrasive blasting cabinet.

Sand is the most easily acquired abrasive for blasting purposes. Other abrasives, including aluminum oxide, silicon carbide, and steel grit, can be purchased from some supply houses for abrasive blasting. In industry, sand is used to a limited extent because it breaks down quickly and creates dust problems. In the shop, these undesirable aspects of sand are almost negligible because of the required low pressure and short blasting time. Thus, sand is one of the most economical abrasives available for shop use.

As long as the abrasive blasting is done within the cabinet, you can safely operate the blasting gun. When blasting, canvas or rubber gloves should be worn as a precautionary measure to protect the operator's hands and any jewelry worn near or on the fingers. Common sense will dictate the use of safety glasses and filter masks wherever these precautions are necessary.

The operation of the device is relatively simple. By keeping the air pressure regulator set at about 60 to 70 psi, all you have to do is squeeze the lever on the blow gun and direct the abrasive blast perpendicular to the surface to be cleaned or decorated.

Rubber matting with an adhesive backing, drawing paper, and masking tape all work well as stencil materials. The key to making a good stencil for use in an abrasive blasting operation is to hold the stencil knife perpendicular to the stencil to avoid undercutting.

A variety of materials can be decorated by abrasive blasting, such as aluminum and copper. Metal material should be buffed before it is etched to avoid "loading" the etched area with buffing compound.

The etching of glass is easily done using sand at 30 psi—as illustrated by the drinking glass shown in Fig. 1-55. Also, glass used with lamp bases, signs, and other objects can be similarly decorated. Wood and stone can be successfully carved, while ceramic materials can be etched in the same manner as glass and metal.

Formica can be etched at a pressure near 80 psi using steel grit as the abrasive. If a sharp contrast is desired between the etched and unetched surface, paint can be wiped on and then off the formica. This procedure

Fig. 1-55. Glass etched at 30 psi with sand.

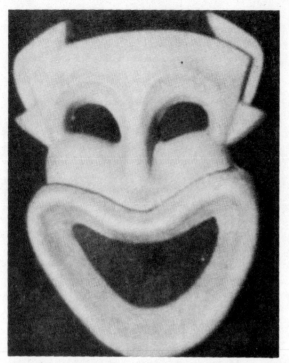

Fig. 1-56. Aluminum cleaned at 70 psi with steel grit.

will leave a sharp contrast between the design and the formica.

Abrasive blasting is an invaluable tool for cleaning rusty tools, castings, and removing paint and other finishes from wood and metal.

As shown in Fig. 1-56 the upper portion of the aluminum casting was cleaned using steel grit as the abrasive at 70 psi. Sand and silicon carbide worked well for this particular cleaning operation, but did not cut as rapidly as the steel grit.

When rust develops on tools it is usually difficult to remove, especially on such areas as the twist of an auger bit. Abrasive blasting with sand readily removed rust in these hard-to-get-at places. The upper portion of the piece of band iron shown in Fig. 1-57 illustrates the efficient removal of rust using sand at 40 psi.

Abrasive blasting, a relatively old industrial process, can be a safe and inexpensive aid. The simple operation of the blasting gun can prove beneficial for purposes of cleaning various materials and obtaining special decorative effects on projects made from a variety of materials.

VISUALIZING FLOW CHARACTERISTICS

The following experiment, done in a foundry, has proved very useful in demonstrating flow characteristics and it is also fun.

Take the electric coil unit from any electric stove and break off the ends to make it flat. Using it as a pattern, make three rammed up molds ready to pour. The sprue should be at one end of the coil and the riser at the other end. Using standard clean aluminum and silicon, make three equal batches of metal ready for pouring. If facilities are available, all three molds can be poured at once for quick comparison; if not, one at a time will do.

The first batch should be only pure, clean aluminum. The second batch should be 25 percent silicon and aluminum. The third, 40 percent silicon and aluminum. Measurements are by volume. Now make the pours and the results are clear and concise.

The pure aluminum batch, when poured, will flow approximately one-third of the distance along the coil.

The second batch (25 percent silicon) will flow approximately two-thirds of the distance along the coil. The third batch (40 percent silicon) will flow to the riser or just short of it. See Fig. 1-58.

Increasing the size of the sprue, riser, and gates or pouring temperatures will give a greater flow, with the converse also holding true. Therefore, the sprue, riser,

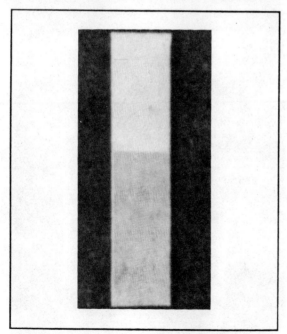

Fig. 1-57. Rust removed from band iron at 40 psi with sand.

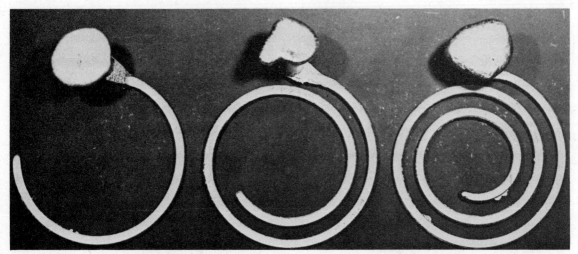

Fig. 1-58. From left to right, pure aluminum, aluminum and 25 percent silicon, and aluminum and 40 percent silicon.

and pouring temperatures must be held constant for true results.

With this simple experiment, you will open a whole gamut of projects involving alloys, flow characteristics, density, melting point (higher in silicon alloy than in pure aluminum), etc.

MINI METAL FORMER

Controlled hydraulic metal forming is not really a new process, but new and bigger applications are making it an important factor in the metalworking industry.

Industrial hydroforming employs a punch and a rubber diaphragm die backed up by oil or water pressure. The fluid chamber is lowered until the diaphragm covers the blank and initial pressure is applied. Then the punch is raised and the pressure is increased to draw and form the shape. Many metals and their alloys can be hydroformed; the easiest is aluminum. Other metals include beryllium, brass, copper, platinum, molybdenum, mu metal, nickel, nimonec, and waspalloy.

Pressure capacities in industrial units range from 5,000 to 15,000 psi. Some machines can take a blank 25 inches in diameter and a depth of draw of 13 inches. The machine is entirely self-contained except for the electrical control panel.

XDA Hydroform. We have designed and built a small working model of the hydroform. Its forming pressure is supplied by a 3-ton hydraulic jack with a punch pressure of about 2,200 psi. Maximum draw is just under an inch.

The XDA is simple to operate. Place an aluminum blank on the blankholder ring and close the release valve on the jack. Pump up the jack until the springs reach their full compression. Release the pressure and the blackholder drops for removal of the formed part.

Punches can be interchanged in minutes. They are polished to keep the part surface smooth. Best drawing results are produced by a dome-shaped punch, because the XDA has a relatively low forming pressure. Punches with vertical walls are less efficient because more pressure is needed to draw the metal into sharp corners.

Construction Notes. The fluid forming chamber is a three-piece assembly. It is machined 1¾ inches deep and will hold a 5-inch d rubber diaphragm. The chamber may be filled with either oil or water at a ½-inch plugged opening.

The bottom flange is bored out to an id of 3½ inches. The hole is an alignment guide for the blankholder ring. The bottom of the reservoir and the flange have offsetting grooves which tightly pinch and hold the diaphragm without cutting it.

The blankholder ring is a four-piece assembly with six springs. The base is screwed into the center shaft. The base and top of the blankholder are counterbored ⅛ of an inch to hold the springs. The top sits on the springs and surrounds the centershaft. The punch is a steel cap that screws into the top of the center shaft and holds the top down.

This design allows the springs to apply pressure around the entire edge of the blank. As the springs com-

Table 1-4. XDA Parts List.

NO.	NAME	SIZE	MATERIAL	AMOUNT
1	Base Plate	3/4 x 8 x 10	HRS	1
2	Hydraulic Jack	3 ton		1
3	Support Rod	3/4 x 21	HRS Threaded Rod	4
4	Spacer	1 x 18	Steel Pipe	4
5	Flathead Screw	1/4-20 x 1-1/2	Steel	1
6	Blankholder (Bottom)	3-1/2 x 1/2	CRS	1
7	Blankholder Spacer	1-1/2 x 3	CRS	1
8	Spring	3/4 x 3	Spring Steel	6
9	Blankholder (Top)	1-1/2 x 3-1/2	CRS	1
10	Punch Form	1 x 1-1/2	CRS	1
11	Punch Screw	1/4-20 x 1-1/2	Steel	1
12	Cap Screw	1/4-20 x 1	Steel	6
13	Collar	1 x 4-1/2	CRS	1
14	Diaphragm	1/8 x 4	Neoprene	1
15	Diaphragm	1/16 x 4	Neoprene	1
16	Reservoir	3 x 4-1/2	CRS	1
17	Plug Screw	1/2-13 x 1-1/2	Steel	1
18	Top Plate	3/4 x 8 x 10	HRS	1
19	Cap Screw	1/4-20 x 1	Steel	1
20	Plug Cap	3/4 x 3/4	CRS	1
21	Cap Screw	1/4-20 x 1	Steel	1
22	Hex Nut	3/4-10	Steel	8

□ Select a round-nose turning tool.

□ Position the straight toolholder and cutting tool parallel with the side of the compound rest and in the center of the tool-post T-slot (Fig. 1-60(A)).

□ Locate and secure the carriage so that when the compound rest is swung the machining will begin at the desired place on the stock, and so the carriage will not move.

□ Slightly loosen the compound-rest bolts so the rest can swivel.

□ Back the compound-rest screw—counter-clockwise—until the tool bit is on the opposite side of the pivot-bolt center. The size of the ball produced is contingent on this adjustment; the further back the cutting tool is positioned from the pivot center, the larger the ball can be.

□ Adjust the cross-feed screw to take a cut of a few thousandths, then swivel the compound rest (see Fig. 1-60 (A, B, and C)). Continue this procedure until the ball

press, the punch is exposed, uniformly drawing and forming the part. See Table 1-4 and Fig. 1-59.

BALL AND ARC TURNING SIMPLIFIED

Convex and concave shapes are commonly produced on the conventional engine lathe by designing sophisticated devices that attach to the compound rest, using specially-formed tool bits, or using the cross-feed and carriage hand wheel to turn the curves. These techniques can be time-consuming and, at best, produce mediocre results. But ball and arc turning on the conventional engine lathe can be simply and accurately done *without* special tools or accessories and with only a few minor adjustments.

Ball Turning

Ball turning can be accomplished on some lathes without trial-and-error, and without the aid of special attachments. The following procedure will yield excellent results on these lathes:

□ Select the diameter of stock desired and chuck it in the lathe, allowing sufficient length for chucking and turning (see Fig. 1-60(A)).

□ Machine off enough material to permit the compound rest to swing as shown in Fig. 1-60 (A, B, and C). A sufficient amount of stock must be left to give support for the spherical turning.

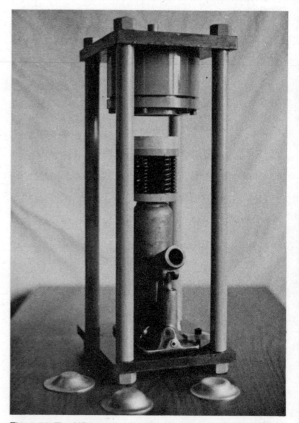

Fig. 1-59. The XDA uses a 3-ton hydraulic jack for pressure. It can draw aluminum blanks into a variety of shapes.

44

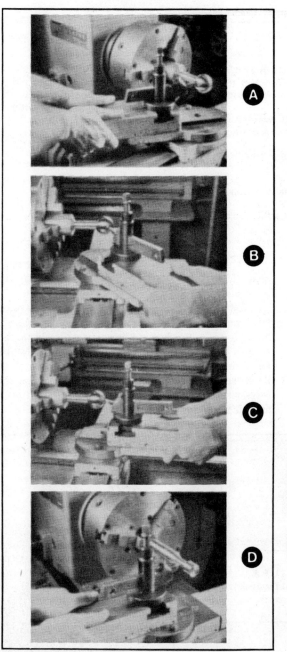

Fig. 1-60. Ball and arc turning techniques.

is complete. *Note:* A firm hold on the compound rest helps in assuring a smooth cut.

    ☐ After machining is accomplished, the ball can be polished to the desired finish.

    ☐ The ball can be separated from the stock by using the cut-off tool or the hacksaw.

    An infinite number of ball sizes can be machined by this procedure. The ultimate diameter will be dependent on the type of lathe used.

Arc Turning

The procedure for ball turning can be easily modified to produce convex arcs (see Fig. 1-60D). For arc turning, step 2 can be completely eliminated. In step 7, the cutting edge of the tool bit will not be brought to the opposite side of the pivot-bolt center, but will remain in the usual position. Other changes from the ball-turning to the arc-turning sequence can be easily deduced.

    The size of the arc produced is increased by turning the cross-feed screw in a clockwise direction.

    The next time a project requires ball and arc shapes, try producing them this easy way. The savings in time and effort alone will be amply rewarding.

METAL COATING

Coating protects metal from rust. This is important because most metals projects are made of mild steel, which machines easily and is relatively inexpensive, but oxidizes rapidly. Coating improves the appearance of the metal and this gives added incentive to produce quality work. Projects that quickly discolor, tarnish, or rust tend to decrease motivation.

    You can usually coat a project in less than 30 minutes. Therefore, 45 to 55 minutes, including clean-up, is ample for the entire process. The method is self-instructional through the use of a step-by-step chart (see Table 1-5).

    Storage and maintenance of chemicals are no problem. Cover the containers to avoid spills and contamination by foreign particles, and leave on a shelf or counter top. The chemicals have a shelf life of a year. Follow the manufacturer's instructions on mixing of chemical baths for the best results.

    A coating unit can easily be made using the flowchart shown in Fig. 1-61. A number of industrial chemical suppliers offer coating sealers under various trade names. Quality does not vary much from manufacturer to manufacturer. Most coating solutions and sealers contain a detailed set of instructions on setup and maintenance of chemical baths. See Table 1-6 and Fig. 1-62.

FINISHING METAL PROJECTS

The finish on a product could make or break it as far as

Table 1-5. Self-Instruction Procedure for Coating of Mild Steel Projects.

Coating Instructions for Mild Steel	Time
Step 1. Clean large metal pieces from project.	N/A
Step 2. Place part into plastic parts basket.	N/A
Step 3. Place part (in basket) into Tub #1 to clean and degrease.	30 sec.
Step 4. Place part (in basket) into Tub #3; cold water rinse.	30 sec.
Step 5. Place part (in basket) into Tub #2 (muriatic acid) to etch metal.	30 sec. agitate lightly
Step 6. Place part (in basket) into Tub #3; cold water rinse.	30 sec.
Step 7. Place part (in basket) into Tub #4; black coating.	10-90 sec. agitate lightly
Step 8. Place part (in basket) into Tub #3; cold water rinse (stops chemical blackening).	30 sec.
Step 9. Allow part (in basket) to dry.	5-15 min.
Step 10. Place part (in basket) into Tub #5; sealant (emulsion of acrylic polymer and dry film lubricant).	60 sec.
Step 11. Let part air dry, aging 24 hours increases adhesion and abrasion resistance.	10-15 min. (24 hrs.)

pleasing appearance is concerned. Modern industry has devoted a great deal of time and money in the study and research of developing more appealing, durable, easily applied finishes and processes and adapting them to production methods.

Phosphatizing and *anodizing* are two good examples of such progress in metal finishing. In phosphatizing, the surface of the metal is treated with a chemical such as Bonderite, a product of Parker Rustproof Company, Detroit, Michigan. This process not only creates a corrosion-resistant surface but also etches a strong primer surface into the metal for successive coats of enamel. Phosphatizing is especially applicable to wrought-iron products.

Anodizing, such as the Alumilite process, patented by Aluminum Company of America, Pittsburgh, Pennsylvania, is an electrochemical process that is almost the reverse of electroplating. The resulting surface can be left plain or dyed beautiful pastel colors that give a metallic sheen. Anodized surfaces can now be seen on ash trays, drinking tumblers, fishing equipment, and even athletic trophies.

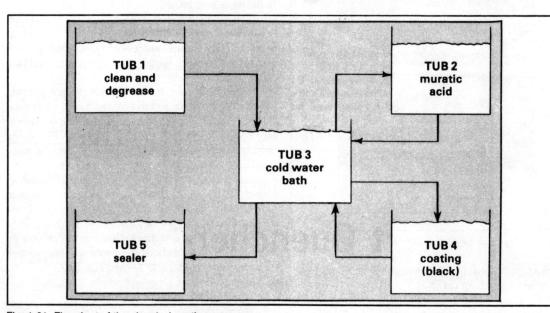

Fig. 1-61. Flowchart of the chemical coating process.

---

5 plastic or stainless steel tubs with lids
  (various sizes)
supply of cold water including a drain
2 lengths (as needed) of rubber tubing
chemicals: degreaser and cleaner (per-
  chloroethylene or ultrasonic cleaning),
  muratic acid, coating, sealer.

Here are a variety of simple and practical finishes for general metal-shop projects that will take them just a little out of the ordinary, as far as appearance is concerned, and make them a great deal more attractive. Some are new, some quite old, but all have been tried and are easily applied in a shop situation.

Highly Polished Art-Metal Projects. You want a finish that is clear, will not run or streak, is easily applied, will preserve the polish, and will not chip. Wipe on a thin coat of a "wipe-on" wood finish such as Royal Finish, and the project will dry dust-free in the ordinarily dusty shop atmosphere. Cost and cleaning trouble for brushes involved in using clear lacquer is also eliminated.

Protecting Wood Furniture. Apply a good coat of flock such as Suede Tex, available at craft-supply houses, to an adhesive undercoat on the bottom surface of the project. This will give a soft felt-like coating that is easily applied. Flock can also be put to good use as a padding under glass on such projects as wrought-iron window shelves and coffee tables.

Preserving Steel Projects. Use an improved and simplified version of the old gun-bluing process. Gun blues available today, such as Minute Man, are easily applied cold and are effective when the simple directions are followed. Emery cloth, running water, and a cotton swab are the only additional materials needed.

Finish it with a shiny coat of wax and you will have a well-protected, blued steel with plenty of appeal. Another good preservative finish for such projects is achieved by applying a thin coat of boiled linseed oil and burning it dry. This will give a shiny black coating that is easily applied if you can stand the odor during the process.

A Charcoal Finish for Wrought-Iron Projects. Go over the entire project with No. 40-grit emery cloth for final smoothing. This removes loose scale and leaves a good surface for the primer to grip. Then apply a coat or two of automotive-type grey metal primer-surfacer. When the primer-surfacer is thoroughly dry, rub it down

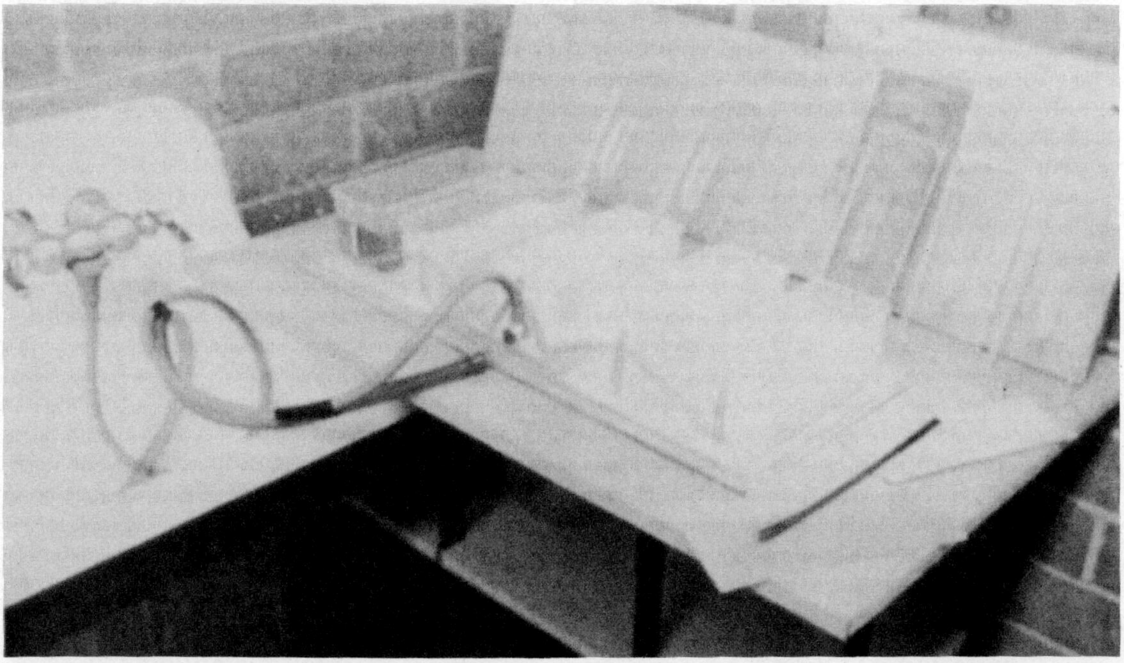

Fig. 1-62. The coating apparatus is in operation, with the cold water bath, center, surrounded by the various chemicals. Avoid spills and prevent contamination by covering the chemicals when not in use.

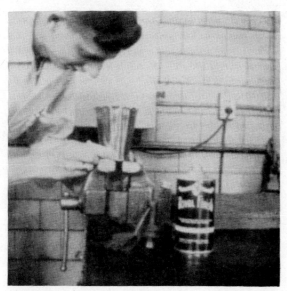

Fig. 1-63. Commercial products give a clear, attractive finish to highly polished, art-metal projects.

heat-resistant aluminum paint such as Thermalite. This aluminum paint is available at hardware stores and will stand 500 degrees or more. It is also useful around the shop on furnaces and pipes. Ordinary aluminum paint is good on most other exterior projects while projects subject to extreme weather conditions should be coated with such "rust" paints as Rust-Oleum or Nev-A-Rust, available at paint and hardware stores.

Variations in Finishing Methods: If the project is made of aluminum, there is practically no limit to the variety of finishing effects easily applied in any shop. Frosted finishes can be achieved through the application of caustic soda. Satin finishes can be produced with wire brush or wire brush wheel; changing the brushing angle gives a variety of effects.

Swirl finishes can be applied simply by twisting steel wool or emery cloth under your thumb; nevertheless, some lubricant such as soap suds or coal oil should be used. A very fancy spot finish can be achieved by inserting a piece of emery cloth in the split end of a dowel rod and mounting the work in the drill press.

For an antique finish, hand hammer after heating over a coal fire. A highlighted or two-tone effect is possible by masking off buffed or painted areas and applying one of the above finishes.

There are as many finishes available as there are types of projects and processes. And in most cases, it is just as easy to apply a finish appropriate to the project. See Fig. 1-63.

lightly with about No. 300-grit emery cloth, and finish with a medium coat of flat-black enamel. The grey primer is a good base color for the charcoal finish, yet is enough difference to tell where you have painted. The flat-black will dry quickly to a beautiful soft charcoal.

Preserve Exterior Projects. The barbecue grill would get too hot for ordinary paint. Use several coats of

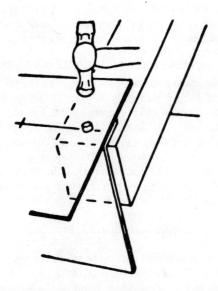

Chapter 2
Tools

PROPERLY FINISHING A SHOP PROJECT INVOLVES more than a "lick" or two with a file and a "swipe" or two with a polishing cloth. This can be exasperating however, when the task itself is so tedious. To help solve this problem, you can use a polishing disc as an attachment for your metals lathe. This method gets a better and faster finish on projects.

The disc itself is cast aluminum and can be foundry cast from a wood pattern with the face turned smooth. See Figs. 2-1, 2-2 and 2-3. The steady rest is built from a piece of channel iron with a handle welded into place. This piece must be hardened after forming to prevent chatter. The polishing disc is attached to the headstock in a three-jaw chuck. The steady rest handle is secured to the tailstock with an adjustable drill chuck. Rubber cement will hold the polishing cloth (emery cloth) to the polishing disc.

A GAUGE FOR HIGHER MACHINING STANDARDS

Machine metalworking laboratories are often hampered by the cost of gauging equipment. But a simplified version of a go/no-go, or snap limit, gauge can be made in the shop.

Commercial od gauges have cast-iron C frames with standard hardened anvils and buttons with contact surfaces that are ground and lapped. Properly adjusted, they offer greater precision and accuracy than micrometers or vernier calipers. In the simplified version discussed here, a modified C frame is constructed from mild crs and fastened together with socket head cap screws. The anvil is made from tool steel that can be machined from 1-inch drill rod. The buttons are made from 5/16-inch drill rod. The contact surfaces of both are wear surfaces, so, if the drill rod is not hardened, the gauge will have to be calibrated fairly often. Commercial anvils and buttons are hardened to around a Rockwell 60 on the "C" scale (file hard). Hardening is advisable if facilities are available. The contact surfaces should be ground to as high a microinch finish as possible.

Once the anvil is fastened in place, the buttons can be "set" at the desired limits. Commercial gauges have an adjusting and locking system that includes an adjustment screw in the frame above each button. This allows adjustments to .0001 of an inch. The simplified version has only two set screws to lock the buttons in place. Nevertheless, with a little practice, there should be no problem adjusting the buttons to within .001 of an inch.

If gauge blocks are not available, it might be neces-

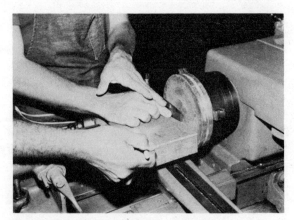

Fig. 2-1. Polishing with the lathe adapter.

sary to grind a set. A few common sizes, along with the .001 of an inch and .002 of an inch leaves from a feeler gauge will allow a fair job of gauge setting to be done. Don't forget the possibility of using the ring or "O" gauge standards that often come with micrometers. Drill shanks can also be used—but mike them first.

The example of the gauge shown in Figs. 2-4 and 2-5 has a spacer for setting the buttons in the .750-inch range. The spacer can be lengthened or shortened according to the setting desired. It is a good idea not to extend the buttons more than about ⅜ of an inch. Frequent handling will cause the frame to accumulate oxidation or rust. A coat of gray or black paint, expecially a crackle finish, will give a professional touch. Commercial gauges usually have an aluminum disc screwed on the side with the go

and no-go limits stamped on it. Plastic adhesive labeling tape can be used and will hold up for some time.

A set of gauges can also be made as a production job and will give some additional experience in designing and building simple jigs and fixtures. If more information on gauges is desired or students wish to follow more sophisticated gauge design, *Machinery's Handbook* gives the standards used in commercial gauges and gauge making.

AN EDGE LOCATOR CUTS TIME AND EFFORT

When you are boring holes in anything but the ends of round stock, it is usually necessary to locate the holes from a side and end of the work piece. It is often convenient to use tool-makers' buttons for locating these holes when you are doing the work on certain types of machines. Tool-makers' buttons require a considerable amount of time for accurate work. If the design and accuracy of the machine will permit, it is much faster and more accurate to use the machine itself to make the set over from the specified side and end. All jig borers and many milling machines and boring mills have the required accuracy.

Once you have decided to use the machine to measure the distance from the edge of the piece to the center of the hole, you must next establish the location of the edge of the piece. One method of doing this is to set the side of the tool or the side of the spindle up against the side of the work, and then move the work one-half of the width or diameter of the tool (or spindle) so that the side of the work is directly in line with the center of the spindle. Unfortunately, it is difficult to judge the pressure

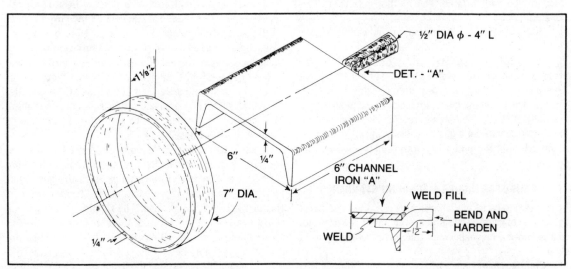

Fig. 2-2. Lathe polishing disc and steady rest.

50

Fig. 2-3. The polishing disc is simply attached to the lathe headstock in a three-jaw chuck.

half way between sides A and B, and because side B is on the edge of the work, it is only necessary to move the table one-half of the distance between sides A and B to place the center of the spindle directly over the edge of the work.

Actual construction of the edge locator (Fig. 2-6) is simple. Machine each of the two pieces all over, leaving approximately .010 of an inch for grinding. Because the two pieces should be hardened and drawn to about 55 on the Rockwell C scale, they must be made of tool steel. After heat treatment, grind sides B and D, working for a very flat, smooth surface.

Lap these two sides if extra precision is desired. Set up side D perpendicular to the surface of the grinder chuck, and grind sides A and C without changing the setup, again striving for a very flat, smooth surface.

Assemble side C against side B, using two 5-40 socket-head cap screws. Grind all remaining surfaces except the relief slot. Measure the distance between sides A and B, using gauge blocks. Record one-half of this distance for future use.

Because this is a precision gauge, it should be handled with care. A simple felt-lined box will help to protect it from rust and nicks.

of contact when the tool (or spindle) is up against the edge of the piece, and eccentricities in the tool (or spindle) are not taken into account.

The edge locator described here eliminates these difficulties, for when it is set up as in Figs. 2-5A and 2-5B, the table is adjusted until the dial indicator gives equal readings on sides A and B of the locator when the spindle is rotated 180 degrees. The center of the spindle is now

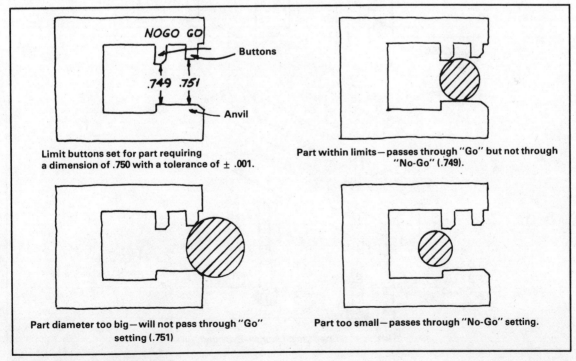

Limit buttons set for part requiring a dimension of .750 with a tolerance of ± .001.

Part within limits—passes through "Go" but not through "No-Go" (.749).

Part diameter too big—will not pass through "Go" setting (.751)

Part too small—passes through "No-Go" setting.

Fig. 2-4. Edge locator design details.

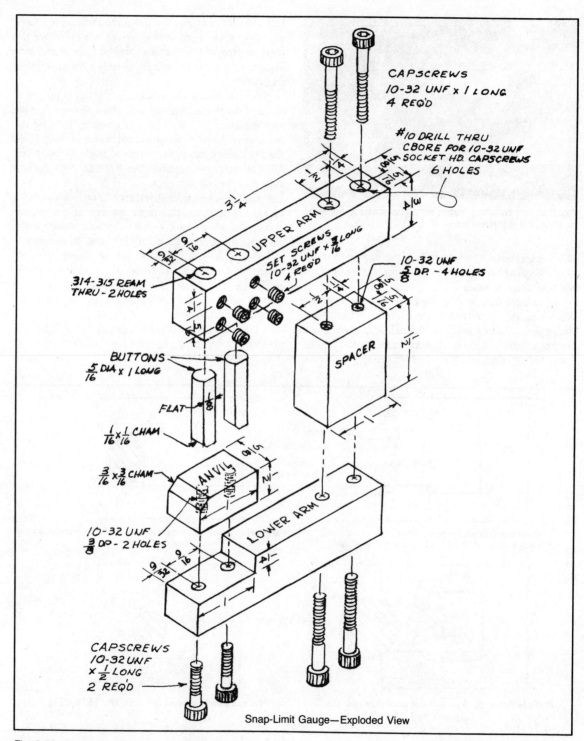

CAPSCREWS
10-32 UNF x 1 LONG
4 REQ'D

#10 DRILL THRU
CBORE FOR 10-32 UNF
SOCKET HD. CAPSCREWS
6 HOLES

UPPER ARM

$3\frac{1}{4}$

$\frac{1}{2}$

SET SCREWS
10-32 UNF x $\frac{3}{16}$ LONG
4 REQ'D

10-32 UNF
$\frac{5}{8}$ DP. – 4 HOLES

.314-.315 REAM
THRU – 2 HOLES

SPACER

BUTTONS
$\frac{5}{16}$ DIA x 1 LONG

FLAT $\frac{1}{8}$

$\frac{1}{16}$ x $\frac{1}{16}$ CHAM

$\frac{3}{16}$ x $\frac{3}{16}$ CHAM

ANVIL

LOWER ARM

10-32 UNF
$\frac{3}{8}$ DP – 2 HOLES

$\frac{9}{32}$ $\frac{9}{16}$

CAPSCREWS
10-32 UNF
x $\frac{1}{2}$ LONG
2 REQ'D

Snap-Limit Gauge—Exploded View

Fig. 2-5A. An exploded view of a snap-limit gauge.

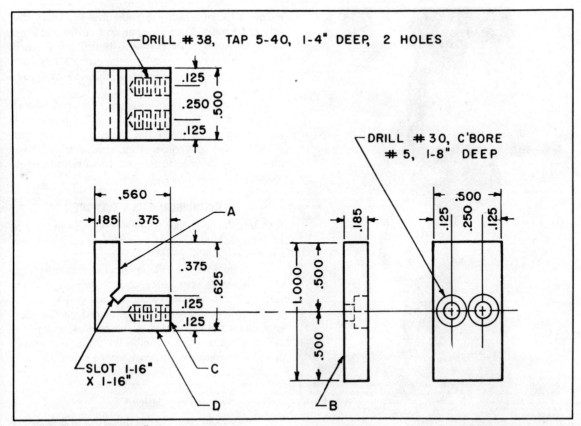

Fig. 2-5B. Edge locator details.

A TAILSTOCK TURRET

To develop and mass produce a paper punch with foundry, sheet metal, and machine metal hardware, you will need mass-production-type tools. You can construct two turret attachments for a basic engine lathe.

Both attachments—the fairly simple tool post turret, not pictured here, and the tailstock turret will prove their value for increased lathe production.

The tool post turret holds tools for external lathe operations such as turning, facing, and cutting off. These turret blocks, as they are often termed, are merely blocks of steel slotted on all sides to hold and clamp four lathe tools. When in use, they are clamped to the compound rest T-slot in place of the regular tool post assembly.

The tailstock turret (Fig. 2-7) is capable of holding and positioning six different tools for internal lathe machining.

No feed stops are provided for the tailstock turret, but the depth of cut can be controlled by reading the tailstock spindle graduations. A dial travel indicator can

be mounted to the tailstock turret if greater accuracy is necessary.

The turret tool base is constructed of mild steel and turned to the given dimensions. The center hole is drilled 7/16-inch diameter through each piece to receive the threaded stud. The turret top is then bored to 31/64 inch and finally reamed to ½ inch. Extreme care must be given to accurate placement of the index holes in the underside of the turret top. The index pin should slide easily in the turret assembly without binding. The pin bushing is reamed to fit the pin and silver brazed into the underside of the turret base.

A No. 2 Morse taper shank can be purchased or machined from cold, rolled steel. A drill chuck arbor can be used with the short taper turned straight. The straight end should be turned .002-inch larger than the diameter of the hole in the turret base. A shrink fit is made by heating the turret base and driving the shank into place.

Tool holes on the turret top are ⅜-inch diameter to allow the use of ⅜-24NF threaded-back drill chucks.

mounting the lathe tailstock, with turret in place, on the drill press table. Place a center drill in the drill press chuck. Clamp the tailstock base to the drill press table in the proper position for drilling the clamp screw hole. Center, drill, and tap the first hole, then index and complete holes.

To install the turret attachment, clean the tailstock taper sleeve and insert the taper shank. The proper tooling may be placed in the tool holes and secured with ¼-20NC Allen set screws. When a run of work is completed it is advisable to remove the turret so that its tooling cannot be damaged.

CYLINDRICAL-STOCK SUPPORT

A project should include not only new skills and related information, but it should also reinforce skills and knowledge previously acquired.

Designed for the milling machine, this cylindrical stock support is a device for supporting long, cylindrical material rigidly in place during machining. The support fulfills the above requisites for advanced machine-shop enthusiasts admirably, and in the process, makes the milling machine more versatile. In effect, the support provides an adjustable tailstock for the miller.

Design

The stock support described in this article was designed

Fig. 2-6. Demonstrating an edge locator being used with a dial indicator. The table is adjusted until the dial gives equal readings for sides "A" and "B" of the locator when spindle is rotated 180 degrees.

These chucks provide a versatile method of holding and changing small round shank tools. Special tooling can be constructed. Tool holes must be drilled and reamed on the lathe on which the attachment will be used. Mount the assembled turret in the lathe tailstock spindle. Clamp a center drill in the lathe spindle chuck and accurately start each tool hole by indexing and clamping the turret top to each tool position and feeding the work to the drill with the tailstock hand wheel. Drill each hole to 7/32-inch diameter to the proper depth. Finish by reaming to ⅜-inch diameter. See Fig. 2-8.

Tool clamping screws may be accurately located by

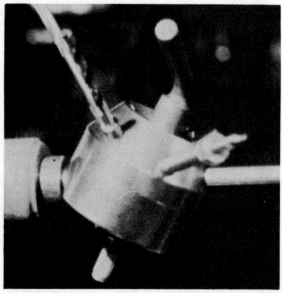

Fig. 2-7. The tailstock turret.

54

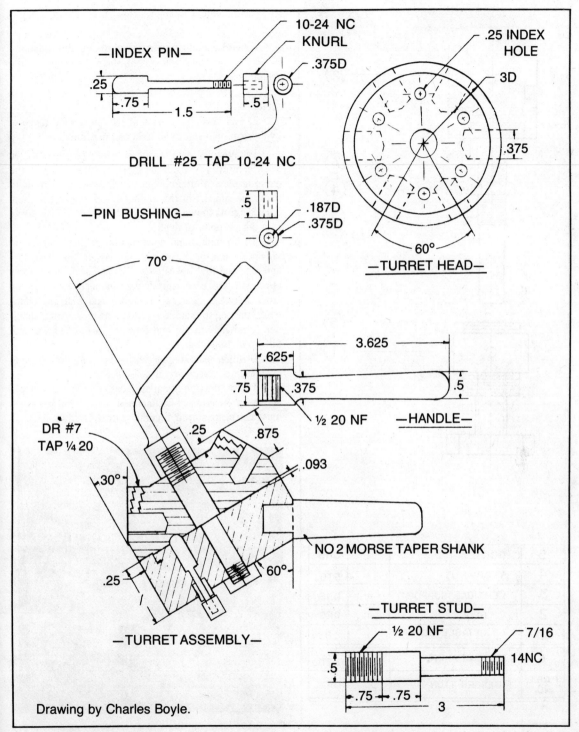

—INDEX PIN—

10-24 NC
KNURL
.375D

.25
.75
1.5
.5

DRILL #25 TAP 10-24 NC

.25 INDEX
HOLE
3D
.375
60°
—TURRET HEAD—

—PIN BUSHING—

.5
.187D
.375D

70°

3.625
.625
.75   .375   .5
½ 20 NF   —HANDLE—

DR #7
TAP ¼ 20

.25   .875
.093

30°

60°

NO 2 MORSE TAPER SHANK

.25

—TURRET STUD—
½ 20 NF   7/16
14NC
.5
.75   .75
3

—TURRET ASSEMBLY—

Drawing by Charles Boyle.

Fig. 2-8. Turret design details.

55

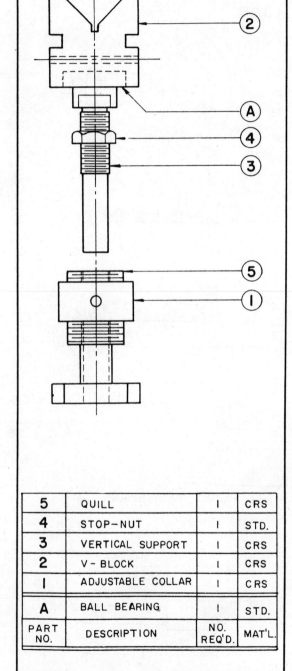

5	QUILL	I	CRS
4	STOP–NUT	I	STD.
3	VERTICAL SUPPORT	I	CRS
2	V–BLOCK	I	CRS
I	ADJUSTABLE COLLAR	I	CRS
A	BALL BEARING	I	STD.
PART NO.	DESCRIPTION	NO. REQ'D.	MAT'L.

Fig. 2-9. Cylindrical stock support and parts list.

by M. T. Lewellen. Special design features of the support are:

☐ vertical adjustment above the mounting table.

☐ longitudinal adjustment along the length of the mounting table.

☐ the support clamps directly to the mounting table.

☐ the clamping device allows for a wide range of cylindrical material to be held and machined.

Dimensional data are intentionally not included on the assembly drawing of the support. You can modify the existing plan to either improve the basic design, or to make the support fit the milling machines in your shop. The design as shown in Figs. 2-9, 2-10, and 2-11 can serve as a design point-of-departure.

The planning and construction of this support involves design, blueprint reading, layout, and hand-tool and machine-tool operations. Examples of these latter operations are: centering stock, grinding tools, mounting stock between centers, three-jaw and four-jaw chuck work, turning to diameters, precision measuring, shoulder turning, external and internal thread cutting, and filing and polishing.

Drilling, reaming, and boring holes on both flat and cylindrical surfaces are also required.

The production of flat surfaces on cylindrical stock, and the production of flat inclined surfaces on bar stock must also be mastered, together with the milling of slots.

Fig. 2-10. Attaching the cylindrical-stock support to the mounting table.

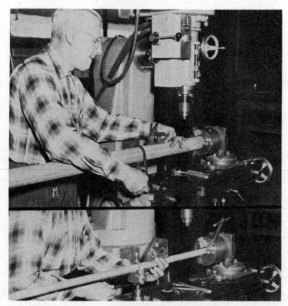

Fig. 2-11. Two kinds of devices for holding stock in place in the support.

Most metals are manufactured in standard shapes and sizes. The value of manufacturers' catalogs can be demonstrated when specifying and ordering the ball-bearing assembly and the roller chain.

Cutting speeds and feeds, tolerancing, coolants, and a great many "how" units—such as "how high-speed drills are manufactured, specified and sold"—are all examples of related, useful information.

The device is slipped into place in the center slot of the mounting table of the milling machine and tightened rigidly in place by running the adjustable collar ("1" in the drawing) down to the table top with a spanner wrench.

The "V"-block assembly (2), which is free to rotate 360 degrees about the vertical support's (3) horizontal axis to allow for possible nonalignment of the workpiece, is then adjusted up or down to receive the cylindrical workpiece at the proper elevation.

The stop-nut (4) is then tightened against the quill (5) to prevent unwanted vertical movement due to vibration, etc.

Depending on the diameter of the workpiece, a roller chain and locking pins (or a brass shackle and locking pins for small diameter work) is then adjusted to the diameter of the stock to hold the material securely against the "V" block. Final adjustment in elevation of the vertical support ("3") might then be necessary.

The workpiece can then be machined along the en-tire length of the mounting table with no loss of rigidity or accuracy.

The cylindrical-stock support for the milling machine is an excellent project for introducing new concepts and for reinforcing others in the machine shop. The milling machine will be more useful and versatile with the support at hand ready to use.

One of the chief values you will derive from planning and constructing the support will be that of redesigning the existing plan to either improve the basic plan or to make the new unit fit existing facilities.

SAND BLASTING EQUIPMENT

The acquisition of sand-blasting equipment is often prohibited by the cost of commercially-available equipment. It is possible, however, to build a useful unit from angle stock and sheet metal and to improvise a suction-type, sand-blast gun for a very reasonable amount.

Having such equipment not only adds to the industrial processes, but it also facilitates some chores around the lab that ordinarily prove both time-consuming and tedious. Paint and rust can be removed, castings can be cleaned, and other jobs of this type can be handled with minimum expenditure of time and temper.

Wood can be textured, glass etched, frosted, and even drilled. Matte finishes can be applied to many surfaces. The decorative possibilities of a sand-blasted finish in contrast with a polished surface preserved by masking are limitless.

How It Was Made

The cabinet shown in Fig. 2-12 was fabricated from 20-gauge sheet metal and mounted on an angle-iron frame. The size and method of construction were dictated to some extent by the capacities of metalworking machines available, something to keep in mind when improvising. Most folds, bends, and cuts were made by machine. A few had to be made by hand. The window consists of a piece of double-strength window glass topped by a sheet of plexiglass to prevent injury in the event of breakage.

The plexiglass proved too prone to sand pitting to be used alone. Sealing around the lid was accomplished by applying self-adhesive automobile weather stripping. Builders caulking was used to eliminate other small leaks. The arm holes are guarded by pieces of old air hose slit and applied over the raw edges of the metal. The hose serves to retain one end of the canvas sleeves through which the operator's arms enter the cabinet. Elastic sewn into the wrists prevent loss of sand through the arm holes.

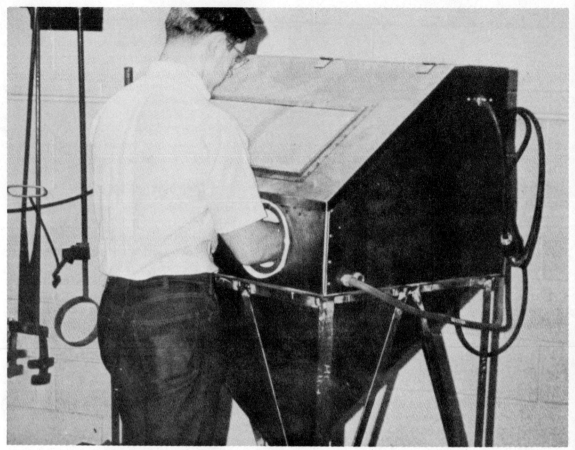

Fig. 2-12. The completed sand-blasting apparatus.

Light in the cabinet is a necessity and can be added easily by an inexpensive porch-light assembly fed by a three-wire line and grounded to the cabinet.

The sand-blast nozzle is made of mild steel rod, hydraulic brake-line tubing, and ⅛-inch black iron pipe. Hoses used are standard ⅜-inch-id air hose and ¼-inch-id oxygen hose.

An electric conduit coupling provides a sand-proof hose entrance to the cabinet. The nozzle shown is adapted to fit a DeVilbiss Type P-DGB, Series 502 dusting gun, but can easily be fitted to most guns of similar type by changing the thread. Because no sand actually passes through the gun, there is no wear and it can easily be converted back to its original use.

Sand Returns To Nozzle

The nozzle shown blasts sand adequately at an air pressure of 40 psi, and a consumption of 3.3 cfm is within the capacity of most air compressors found in labs.

Sand returns to the bottom of the hopper where it is again picked up by the sand hose and returned to the nozzle.

The abrasive used in the unit shown in Fig. 2-13 is silica sand of the type known as sawing sand and is reasonable in price. An 80-pound bag lasts indefinitely because only about 20 pounds are charged into the machine at a time. When too dirty for further use, it is discarded and replaced.

Other abrasives are available and can be used as long as they are not so heavy as to resist the siphoning action of the nozzle and provided that the particles are small enough not to cause clogging.

Available are glass beads, aluminum oxide, steel grit, and nut shells. Silica sand is usually available locally at ready-mix plants or lumber yards.

The novelty and many uses of this equipment more

than justifies the effort and minor expense of its construction. Try it. You'll find it well worthwhile.

KEEP YOUR WHETSTONES WET!

Have you ever noticed how thirsty a whetstone gets when it is stored in a dry condition? The solvent is absorbed almost as fast as it is applied to the stone. This often results in the stone being used too dry and becoming clogged with metal particles. This, of course, greatly reduces the honing effect of the whetstone.

To provide a workable tool-sharpening center—inexpensively and efficiently—follow this procedure. Cut the top from a rectangular 1-gallon can and suspend it, as shown in Figs. 2-14 and 2-15, in the center of a shelf. The stones can then be stored in solvent to keep them saturated. If this is done, they can be used without additional solvent being applied. If they are being used for a long period of time, about 15 minutes or more, they might require an occasional squirt of solvent. This is stored in an oil can kept readily accessible.

The evaporation factor is negligible if there is a lid on the can. The lid shown is hinged to the shelf. The solvent needs replenishing only once every two to three months.

The arrangement described here not only saves time, but keeps the whetstones constantly "seasoned" and ready for immediate use.

A PORTABLE OILSTONE HOLDER

A portable oilstone holder, such as the one shown in Figs. 2-16 and 2-17, serves as a safe way to maintain oilstones. The unit can be moved about the shop or it can be stationed near the grindstone. The oilstones can be individually removed from the holder. An attractive oilstone

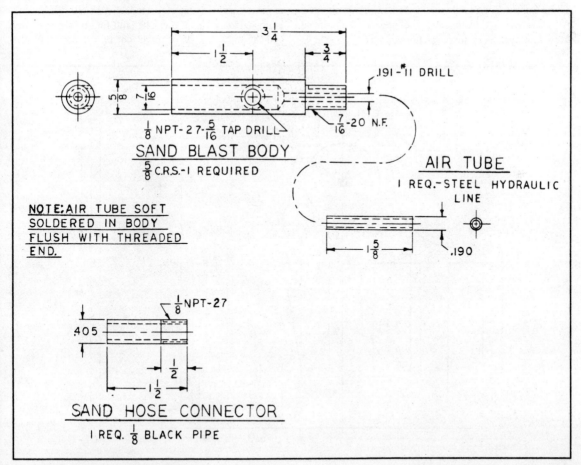

Fig. 2-13. Details of the nozzle assembly.

Fig. 2-14. "Honing shelf," with lid cut out and hinged, holds salvaged 1-gallon can. Wooden dividers can be constructed and lowered into can to hold stones in upright position.

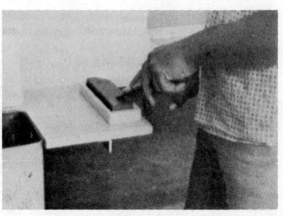

Fig. 2-15. Brackets built into the shelf make convenient holders for stones while they are in use, as demonstrated here.

holder encourages metalworkers to keep tools sharp.

This portable oilstone unit is of special convenience because it conserves space, an item of major importance in most general industrial-arts laboratories. It is easy to build and keep clean. It can be built for any set of stones and the oilcan might or might not be included with the

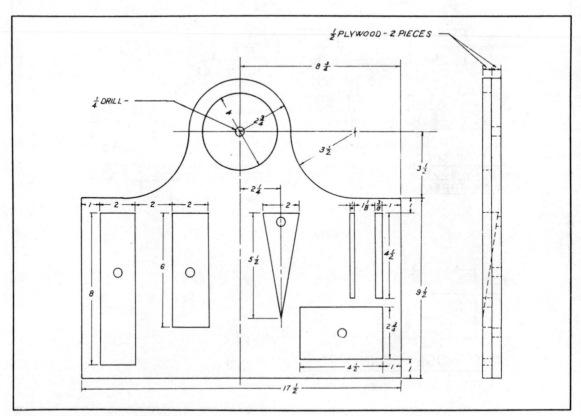

Fig. 2-16. Oilstone holder design details.

Fig. 2-17. Oilcan and stones are instantly available with this setup.

on the bandsaw. All edges are sanded for final finishing. A ¼-inch hole or larger is drilled through the bottom piece for the oilcan and the four larger cavities. Several smaller holes can be drilled for the slip-stone cavities if desired. These holes permit waste particles to fall through and help to keep the unit clean. A block of wood to which a

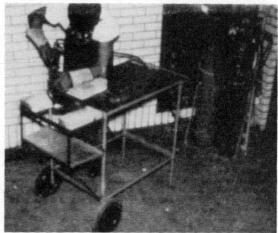

unit. The holder presented here requires two pieces of ½-inch plywood, 17½- ×15¾ inches as described in the detailed plan (See Fig. 2-16).

Layouts of the various shapes of stones and oilcan are drawn on the top piece of plywood. Holes are drilled through these spaces and then cut out with the jigsaw. All edges are filed and sanded. The place for the gouge slip is carved out with carving tools so that it will remain in a horizontal position for outside bevel whetting of the hand gouge.

When the various shapes have been cut out, the top piece of plywood is fastened to the bottom piece with flat-head screws, making one solid piece of wood 1 inch thick. The curves at the top of the unit are then sawed out

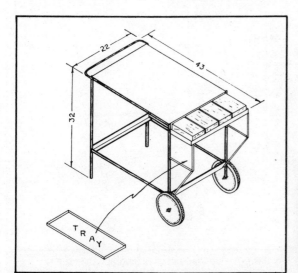

Fig. 2-18. Dimensions for the portable welding bench.

Fig. 2-19. The portable bench is used for cutting (top) and for electric welding.

piece of leather strop has been glued is shown in the lower right-hand corner of the detailed sketch and photograph. The unit can be finished with several coats of shellac.

PORTABLE WELDING BENCH

If you need an extra pair of hands to help hold a large or long object while welding or cutting and adding a cutting bench or another welding table is simply out of the question, a portable welding bench for gas and electric welding as well as for cutting might be the answer.

Materials include ½-inch pipe, old wagon wheels, ⅛-×-1 inch flat stock, and ⅛-inch sheet steel. Dimensions can be changed to fit individual needs and uses for your area and storage for rod, flux, or C-clamps can be added if desired. See Figs. 2-18 and 2-19.

A NEW APPROACH TO THE NOMOGRAPH

Speed and ease of computation are the great advantages of a nomograph (see Fig. 2-20). A straightedge laid across the three axes will give the torque in pound-feet for the corresponding load in grams and pulley radius in inches, with *no* unit versions or calculations required, even where slide rules or calculators are available, this facility of computation can represent a considerable savings of time and energy, and of course nomographs can be obtained for a fraction of the expense of slide rules and calculators.

Principle. Briefly, the principle of the nomograph is that of the slide rule, without the "slide." While simple to operate once completed, the necessary steps for its construction, as described in technical literature, call for some extensive mathematical manipulation to obtain "scale moduli" and to calculate the ratios between the input and output axes. A simpler approach is clearly needed.

Criteria. The primary requirements for a nomograph is a calculation involving multiplication, division, powers, or roots. Even comparatively simple calculations might benefit from a nomograph in the absence of a slide rule or calculator. The two nomographs described here both represent three or more such operations. Some possible applications of nomographs might be in computations involving: power loss ($E = I^2R$), wire resistance ($R = 10.371 \times$ length/area), piston velocity-area-gallons/min., areas of shapes ($\pi d1$), volumes of solids ($\pi r^2 1$), power-circuit-voltage, cutting speeds—tool diameters—rpm.

Equipment. A slide rule (10 inches) is the only required equipment in the construction of this type of nomograph. Other lengths of slide rule might be useful if a log cycle is required that is not one of the three on the standard slide rule, but there are other ways of meeting this requirement. The use of a drawing paper such as Albanene facilitates the tracing of scales from the slide rule or sliding log scale.

Accuracy. Because slide rule scales are used in the nomograph, one cannot expect accuracy greater than that of the slide rule, although with certain combinations of scales, slide rule accuracy could be exceeded. The trial nomographs constructed while preparing this section were made quickly, with little regard for drafting niceties or accuracy in scale marking and interpolation. Even then the nomograph results were within 2 percent of those computed by slide rule. More carefully drawn nomographs were found to be within one percent of results computed by standard methods, an accuracy which was

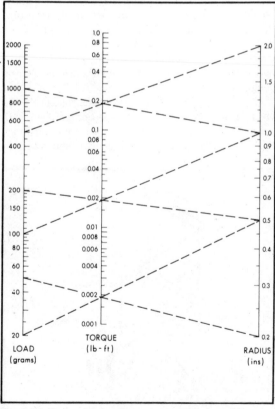

Fig. 2-20. Torque-load-radius nomograph (nomo #1).

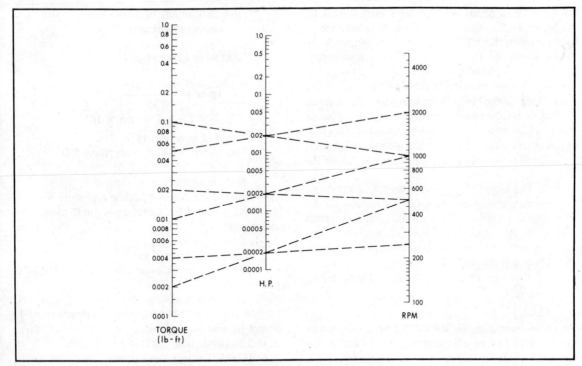

Fig. 2-21. Horsepower-torque-rpm nomograph (nomo #2).

considered satisfactory for normal shop applications. It is also evident that the finer the subdivisions on the log cycles, the greater the resulting accuracy.

Procedure. The construction of the two nomographs illustrated in Fig. 2-20 and 2-21 is described below. The first is a nomograph deriving torque in lb-ft from load in grams and pulley radius in inches (Nomo #1). The construction steps of this nomograph are given in detail as an explanation of the technique used. The second nomograph is one deriving horsepower from torque in lb-ft and revs/min. This construction is given in abbreviated form and serves as a summary of the construction procedure, while illustrating the problem of the output scale which does *not* correspond to one of the three scales on the standard slide rule.

Nomo #1 (torque-load-radius)

1. Reduce relationship between variables to a simple expression. To find torque (ft-lbs) given load (g) and radius (in.):

$$T = L \times R \text{ (g-in.)}$$

Divide by 454 to convert L to lbs. and by 12 to convert R to ft.

$$\text{Therefore } T = \frac{L \times R}{454 \times 12}$$
$$= 1.8 \times L \times R \times 10^{-4} \text{ lb-ft}$$

2. Determine range of input variables. Based on lab equipment capacities, the ranges for the present nomograph are: load: 20-2000 g and radius: 0.2-2.0 in.

3. Select scales for input variables. Normally one or more of the three scales on a 10-inch slide rule are suitable, but longer or shorter slide rules might also be applicable. Load range is 20-2000 g, a factor of 100-fold, therefore a scale of *two* full log cycles is required, i.e., the A (or B) scale on the slide rule. Radius range is 0.2-2.0 in., a factor of 10-fold, therefore a scale of *one* full log cycle is required, i.e., the C (or D) scale on the slide rule.

4. Draw and divide the input axes. Leaving sufficient margins for scale values, lightly draw two vertical axes.

   a. Load axis; Using the A scale, mark on the axis the exact limits of the A scale. Label the lower limit 20 and the upper limit 2000. Line up the 2 on the A scale with the lower limit and mark the major division opposite 3, 4, . . ., 10, 20, 30, . . . , 100. Move the A scale up until the 10 coincides with the 100 mark on the axis and mark the divisions opposite 11, 12, . . . , 20. Insert approximate scale values as illustrated between 20 and 2000 g.

b. Radius axis: Using the C scale, mark exact limits. Label lower limit 0.2 and upper limit 2.0. Line up the 2 on the D scale and mark the major divisions opposite 3, 4, . . ., 1. Move the D scale up until the 1 coincides with the last marking and complete marking opposite 1.1, 1.2, . . ., 2. Insert remaining scale values between 0.2 and 2.0 inches.

5. Plot and locate the output axis. (As noted earlier, there *are* mathematical procedures available for determining the scale of the output axis and its location relative to the input axes. The following technique achieves both concurrently, and incorporates useful self-checking features.)

a. Consider our previously obtained expression:

$$T = 1.8 \times L \times R \times 10^{-4}$$

For the moment *disregard* the 10^{-4} factor. If the product of the L and R factors in the expression were 10 then the value of T would be 18. Find two values each of L and R which make a product of 10. For example: L = 20, R = 0.5 and L = 50, R = 0.2

b. Draw lines connecting these two pairs of values. They intersect at point 1 on Fig. 1.

c. Repeat the process for L × R = 100 and L × R = 1000, resulting in intersections at points 2 and 3 on Fig. 2-20.

d. Draw a line through the three intersections. Check that (1) the line is *parallel* to the other two axes and (2) the distances between the intersections are *equal*. The axis location and magnitude of the log cycle are now determined.

6. Insert scale values on output axes. The values of T at the three intersections are 18, 180, 1800. The 10^{-4} factor must now be replaced, making the intersection points 0.0018, 0.018, and 0.18. Find a log scale that fits the distance between the intersections. In this case it is the K scale on the slide rule. Line up 1.8 on the K scale with the lowest intersection and mark off the major divisions from 1.0, 1.5, . . ., 9, 1, for the three cycles on the K scale. Insert the scale values from 0.001 to 1.0 lb-ft.

The nomograph is now complete. As a check on its accuracy, it is advisable to select some values of load and radius within the range of the nomograph, compute the torque values and compare to the torque values obtained by the nomograph.

Summary of Nomo #2
(horsepower-torque-rpm)

1. Obtain the expression:

$$hp = \frac{torque \times rpm}{5250}$$
$$= 1.9 \times T \times rpm \times 10^{-4}$$

2. Range of input variables:
torque: 0.001-1.0 lb-ft (from Nomo #1)
rpm: 100-5000
3. Scale input variables:
torque: as in Nomo #1 (slide rule scale K)
rpm: factor of 50, therefore A (or B) slide rule scale suitable
4. Draw input axes:
T-axes: copy from Nomo #1
rpm-axes: 1-½ cycles of scale A, lower limit 100, upper limit 5000
5. Draw output axis:
Disregard 10^{-4} factor. Select combinations of T and rpm to give products of 1, 10, 100. Obtain three intersection points (Fig. 2-21) of 1.9, 19, 190.
Draw axis through three points. Check for parallelism and equality.
6. Scale output axis:
No slide rule (10 inches) scale fits the log cycle of output axis. There are three alternatives: (a) Try to find a log scale that fits the cycle (simplest solution). Perhaps a 6-inch slide rule has a suitable scale. (b) Use a sliding log scale such as that in Fig. 2-22.
Locate required log cycle width and mark off divisions on output-axis, bearing in mind that intersection points are 0.00019, 0.0019, 0.019 (after 10^{-4} factor is replaced). (c) Use the closest log scale available, eg., K

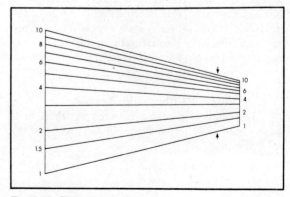

Fig. 2-22. Sliding log scale.

scale on slide rule. Mark off K scale divisions on laid-off line, and project over to the output axis, again with intersection points at 0.00019, 0.0019, and 0.019. Insert values from 0.0001 to 1.0 hp.

Flexibility. The scales of the two nomographs shown here were selected to enable you to enter the nomograph with empirical data such as load and rpm readings and come up with findings in the proper units. Once constructed, however, a valuable feature of the nomograph is that it can be used for any multiple of the input variables, with appropriate scale adjustment. Thus, we also have a V8 + dynamometer rig that supplies data such as torque of 150 lb-ft at 4000 rpm. The intersection of a line joining 4000 rpm and 0.15 (150×10^{-3}) lb-ft is at 0.12 hp, and replacement of the 10^{-3} factor gives the output as 120 hp.

ADD ECM TO YOUR METALS LAB

If you're looking for a way to start electrochemical machining (ECM), but cannot begin because of budget problems, don't give up hope. The machine shown in Fig. 2-23 can help you solve the problem. It was developed for a graduate level project to design, construct, and test an experimental ECM system that could function for demonstrations and light production in a metals lab.

ECM is used by the aerospace and automotive industries for many machining operations that include high-temperature turbine and forging dies. Although it can compete with some conventional machine tools, ECM is usually used in high volume, difficult jobs that cannot be completed by conventional methods.

How Does it Work? ECM emerged from the laboratory in the early 1950s when new grinding methods for carbides were being researched. Its first application was in the electrolytic grinding process (ECG), in which grinding efficiency was increased by initiating a flow of direct current between the wheel and the work. The electrically charged wheel and workpiece contacted each other while they were flooded with a salt water electrolyte solution. The result was an increased cutting rate with little or no wheel wear. In 1962, the process was carried one step further; the wheel was replaced with a shaped cathode tool. That tool could be fed toward the anode workpiece so that the workpiece material was deplated. The process can be conceptualized as electroplating in reverse; an ECM system is merely a sophisticated version of Michael Faraday's original electrolytic cell. The metal-removing capabilities of this process are still governed by the same laws discovered by that nineteenth century physicist.

An electrolytic cell is composed of an anode (workpiece), cathode (tool), electrolyte solution, and direct current power supply. The cathode is formed into a shaped tool that directs the current and indirectly generates the desired configuration in the workpiece. That tool is often a mirror image of the shape to be produced, and is positioned adjacent the workpiece in an insulated, water-tight enclosure. The tool and workpiece should never touch; therefore, a gap of .005 to .015 of an inch is maintained between them. The electrolyte solution normally flows through the tool to supply the machining gap with a constant flow of conductive liquid.

When the tool and workpiece are connected to a dc power source, electron displacement or electrolysis will occur. This phenomenon is so consistent that one of the most common scientific units, the coulomb (C), can be defined as the quantity of electricity required to deposit electrolytically .00111800 grams of silver.

Fig. 2-23. Tool is mounted on ram inside work enclosure on experimental ECM unit. Standard dc welding power supply is connected to lugs at rear of machine.

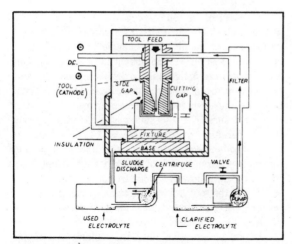

Fig. 2-24. The relationship of the individual ECM components.

The schematic shown in Fig 2-24 shows the arrangement of the basic ECM components. When the tool is fed downward toward the work, electrolysis in the machining gap causes dissolution of the workpiece, and the displaced metal is rapidly flushed away by the electrolyte solution.

Applications. ECM applications parallel those of conventional machining methods, and can be used to produce most standard configurations. Operations such as hole machining, shaping, turning, die sinking, deburring, honing, and planing may be performed on various types of ECM equipment. ECM is most suitable for long runs that require complex cavities in hard materials. The cathode tool never touches the workpiece; there is no tool wear or machining stress. Most of the newer ECM systems are capable of removing over one cubic inch of workpiece material per minute.

An Instructional System. Although it is simple by industrial standards, the ECM system pictured includes all of the basic components in commercial units. For demonstrations and basic experimentation, this unit could be simplified even further. The basic system must include:

☐ a cathode tool prepared with an approximate mirror image of the configuration to be machined in the workpiece.

☐ a workpiece and workpiece holding device.

☐ a means of supplying electrolyte solution to the gap between the tool and workpiece.

☐ a source of dc electrical power sufficient to maintain a current density of 100 amps for a 1-square-inch tool.

The cathode tool should be supported in some type of machine frame that incorporates a tool feeding device. The feed system can be either very elaborate or simple, depending on the overall machine design. For a laboratory ECM system, a simple feed could be devised by placing the cathode tool on a slide which moves up or down. Dead weights could be placed on the tool to adjust the gap as the pressure of the pumped electrolyte tends to force the tool away from the work. A more elaborate geared drive mechanism was used in the machine shown in Fig. 2-23.

The Cathode Tool. The tool can be constructed of any metallic material, but sintered copper-tungsten is preferred by industry because of its resistance to arc damage. The simplest tool consists of a section of tubing joined to an electrolyte manifold, and is used for round hole machining. The manifold is bolted to the tool feed mechanism and connected to the electrolyte supply pump. Electrolyte flows from the supply reservoir to the manifold through the tool and out between the machining gap. A tool for producing hexagonal holes and an accompanying test workpiece is shown in Fig. 2-25. This tool is constructed of brass fittings and tube sections brazed together and coated with an insulating layer of epoxy paint.

The Power Supply. It is not necessary to construct a high-priced power supply. Industrial units incorporate many spark detection circuits that reveal conditions leading to short circuits and arcing in the machining gap. An experimental system will function without the detection circuits, but there will be some tool damage.

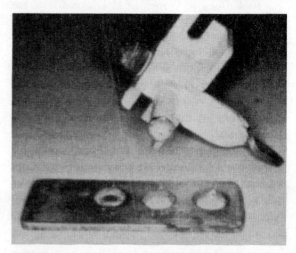

Fig. 2-25. The center hole in this workpiece was made by the cathode tool behind it.

In the unit pictured, a 250-amp-dc-arc welding machine was used for the power supply. The sample workpiece in Fig. 2-25 shows three hex-shaped holes that were cut using the welding power supply. Large industrial units are normally rated at over 10,000 amps, but those current values are certainly not necessary for demonstrating the process.

For the most accurate results, the voltage of the power supply should be less than 15V. Surplus dealers or the electronics lab might be able to furnish a dc power supply if a welder is not available.

The Electrolyte. The most common electrolyte consists of a sodium chloride and water solution, with approximately 1 pound of NaCl per gallon of water. As was previously mentioned, this solution must be circulated through the tool and between the machining gap. This phase of the system presents the most design difficulties because of the problems in storing and piping corrosive salt solutions. Electrolyte reservoirs and piping must be constructed of either AISI 316 stainless steel or plastic components to prevent rapid deterioration. The pump should be capable of delivering 5 gpm at approximately 20 ppsi. The pump should be made of either plastic or stainless steel, and these materials are expensive.

Because the machining waste is deposited in the electrolyte solution, industrial machines use various kinds of filtration systems. The run-and-dump method is most practical. When the electrolyte is completely contaminated, short circuits and arcing are likely to occur, so that replacement at frequent intervals is necessary.

Safety. ECM systems employ a high amperage/low voltage power supply. Typical units with 10,000 amp capacities will seldom exceed 15V, so that the danger of electrical shock is not great. Obviously, common precautions for handling liquids around electricity, and approved wiring practices must be observed. All metallic parts that are part of the electrolytic cell must be well-insulated in a leak-proof enclosure.

Avoid electrolyte solutions that are powerful oxidizers and might constitute a fire hazard. Salt water solutions are both safe and inexpensive. Sodium nitrate and sodium chlorate are highly flammable.

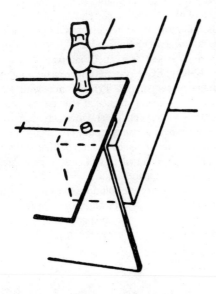

Chapter 3
Sheet Metalwork

A PERPETUAL PROBLEM FOR METALWORKERS is finding interesting sheet-metal projects that combine utility and good looks with vital problem-solving experiences. All projects should challenge you with new problems and ideas, calling on you to use your acquired knowledge and past experiences as mental "tools." This project fits such a description. The assignment: to design a mail holder that combines structural and functional qualities with esthetic value.

BUILD A MAIL HOLDER

The long, open-drawer style is ideal for holding mail of all shapes and sizes easily, while providing easy access to the mail. A cover is necessary to shield the open drawer from the elements. A slightly tapered cover is considered more pleasing than the conventional rectangular shape. Additionally, the roof of the cover is slanted to drain off any water. For better protection from the weather, the drawer is also indented under the cover. After determining the basic shape of the mailbox, consider ways of opening the drawer. The basic sliding drawer concept can be eliminated due to lack of depth. Hinges require a catch or clasp that could fail in use.

Because something simple and reliable is desirable,

the laws of gravity were utilized. Putting trunnion pins in the lower front corners made the center of gravity exert a leverage to keep the drawer closed.

Nevertheless, the possibility that mail could collect near the front of the mailbox and shift the center of gravity did exist. The bottom, therefore, was slanted toward the rear to prevent the center of gravity from shifting. In fact, the heavier the load, the tighter the drawer would close. The final shape (Fig. 3-1) is shown in profile in Fig. 3-2. The sides of the drawer were trimmed as shown so that the drawer would rotate freely about the pins.

Shaping Up and Around

The layout procedure is based on simple rectangular principles. Nevertheless, a few unusual problems did arise because of the shape. The sloping top is obtained by tapering both front and back sides of the cover flaps. The drawer ends were offset proportionately. The complete layouts are shown in Figs. 3-3 and 3-4.

In making the mailbox, layout dye was used to make the scribed lines contrast. The pieces were carefully cut out and smoothed. The hems were folded on a bar folder adjusted to round the hems slightly, to add both safety and rigidity to the pieces.

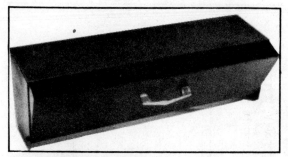

Fig. 3-1. The completed mailbox.

The seams were tinned (see Fig. 3-5) before the pieces were folded to shape so that an orderly assembly would be easier. After the seams were tinned, the pieces were folded to shape on the box and pan brake (see Fig. 3-6). To fold pieces, that cannot be readily bent in the brake, the method depicted in Fig. 3-7 was employed.

The Proof Is in Assembly

After the pieces (see Table 3-1) were bent to shape and soldered, the unit was given a trial assembly. The fit was very tight! The top arcs of the drawer were filed to permit smooth action; the unit was then disassembled and painted. After drying, a pull was attached to the drawer and the unit was reassembled. The finished product is shown partially open in the lead illustration.

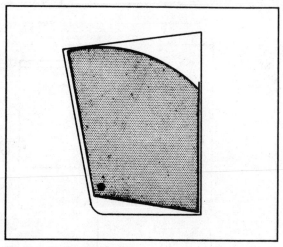

Fig. 3-2. Profile of the mailbox.

SHEET-METAL SHELL TOTE

This shell tote incorporates good sheet-metal operations in its construction. Besides learning basic operations in its fabrication, you will have a serviceable item when the project is completed.

Start by developing a template for the body of the tote, the ends, the top, and the handle. Once this is done, work on the necessary folds will progress rapidly.

A box or pan brake is desirable to make the

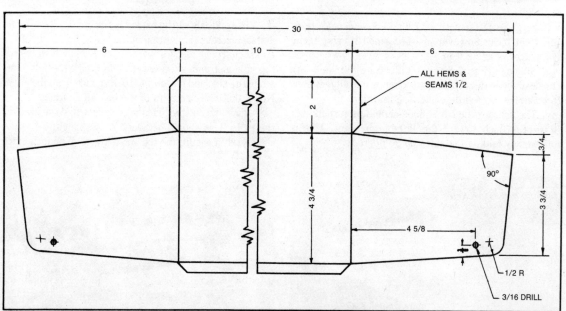

Fig. 3-3. The cover layout.

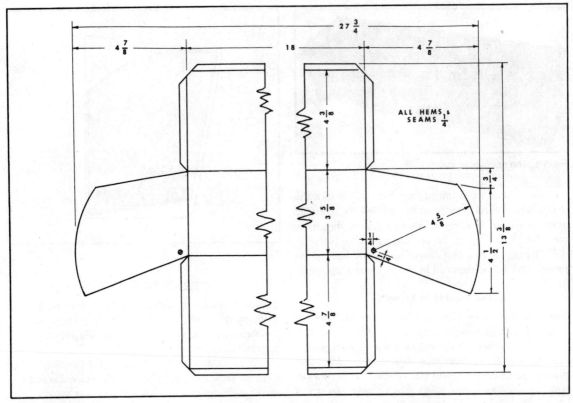

Fig. 3-4. Drawer layout.

Pittsburgh seam (sometimes called a *hammered lock* or *hobo lock*). It can, however, also be formed in a vise, using two pieces of angle iron.

Although Figs. 3-8 and 3-9 illustrate the shell tote and describe in detail its construction, some suggestions to make the job a little easier are in order.

The hem for the cover slide should be turned over 3/16 of an inch toward the Pittsburgh seam. This is followed by folding the sides up 90 degrees.

The ends should be made ¾ of an inch wider than the distance across the bottom of the box. The length of the end should be made ⅜ of an inch longer than the height of the side just under the cover slide. Mark the fold lines along the side and bottom, 5/16 of an inch from the edge. Notch the lower corners of the box 45 degrees.

Place the end piece in the brake and fold the lap over the ends. This should be about ¼ of an inch.

Next, measure the top and allow ⅜ of an inch more

Fig. 3-5. Tinning the seams before bending.

Fig. 3-6. Bending on the box and pan brake.

70

Fig. 3-7. Bending with clamps.

Table 3-1. Materials List.

1 pc. 13⅜″ x 27¾″ 24-ga galvanized
  sheet steel
1 pc. 7¼″ x 30″ 24-ga galvanized sheet
  steel
2 10-24 rh machine screws
2 spacing washers
1 chromed drawer pull
flat black enamel

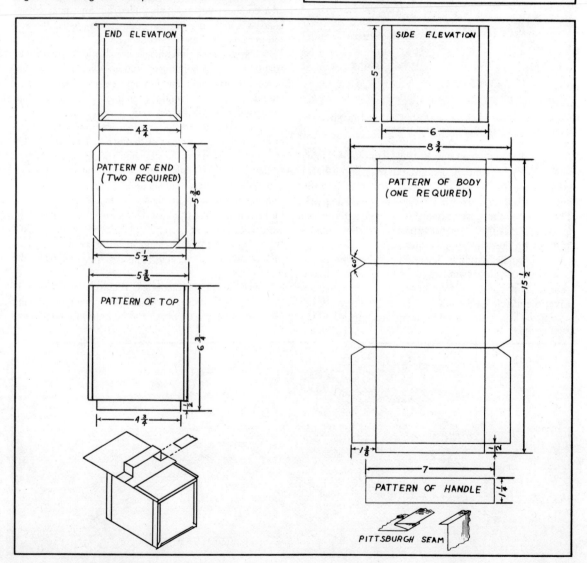

Fig. 3-8. Tote design details.

Fig. 3-9. A completed sheet-metal shell tote that incorporates many basic operations in its construction.

on each side. Do the same for the back of the cover. Notch the back of the cover to fit inside of the seam at the end of the box. Fold the back of the cover 3/16 of an inch to 180 degrees and then bend it 3/16 of an inch to 90 degrees. The sides of the cover are made following the same procedure, making the last break past 90 degrees to about 150 to form the hook to fit on the slide.

The handle should be located near the front of the box so that it will remain closed when it is carried. You should allow space for four fingers under the handle. Rivet the handle to the top.

If the shell tote is going to be used in a hunting skiff—that's what it was designed for—the inside seams and corners have to be soldered to make the container water proof.

To cut down glare and reflection, the tote can be painted either dead-grass green or a dead-grass brown.

A SHEET-METAL BRAKE FOR THAT SPECIAL JOB

While organizing a unit on mass production in a general-metals class, a problem was identified in folding a patio lamp top. The difficulty centered around bending the sheet metal into a pyramidal shape with all faces meeting at a common vertex. This called for four neat corner beads without creasing the opposite triangular faces of the pyramid.

The cornice or box and pan breaks did not seem to be adaptable for this bending operation. A special brake was needed with an open end or some means of bending that would not crease beyond the common vertex of the four triangular faces of the pyramid.

The solution to the problem was to make a small brake without a stationary clamping bar. This allowed the sheet-metal parts to be clamped to the brake using a C-clamp and a triangular piece of steel plate for the upper leaf. The triangular piece of steel plate was cut to a size that permitted it to fit inside the faces of the pyramid during the bending process. This allowed the metal to be bent with four neat corners and reduced the operational time required for each lamp top to 1½ minutes. This included the attaching and removal of the C-clamp for the four bends.

The design of the brake requires two pieces of 3-×-3×⅜-inch angle iron hinged with two pieces of crs 1½ inches long. The brake can be held in a bench vise

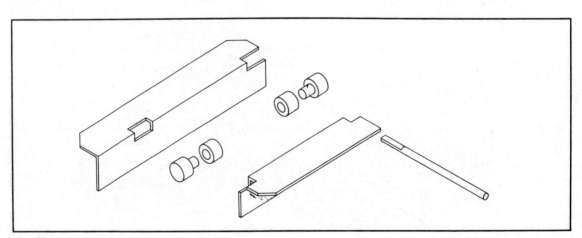

Fig. 3-10. Hinges.

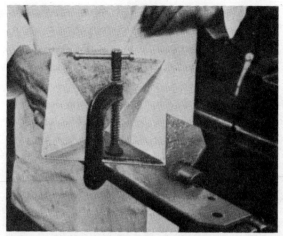

Fig. 3-11. A C-clamp is used to clamp sheet-metal parts to the brake making bending more accurate and operational time shorter.

while being used or placed in the bench drawer for storage. The hinge strength is critical and is obtained by reducing half the length of each piece of crs to ¾ of an inch d, and fitting it into a 1¼-inch steel collar ¾ of an inch long containing a ¾-inch center bore.

Two sections are then removed from each piece of angle iron to allow space for the assembled hinges as shown in Fig. 3-1. The female portion of the hinges is then welded to the angle iron representing the bending leaf and the male part of the hinge is welded to the opposite piece of angle iron.

This brake (Fig. 3-11) is also useful for such opera-tions as bending the ends of boxes which had too great a depth to allow the full use of the box and pan brake. Advantages of this brake include saving time by eliminating hand bending operations, reducing tool marks often caused by hand bending, and permitting a greater degree of accuracy in producing the bends.

BUILD A SHEET-METAL PLANTER

Projects should have a practical purpose in order to ac-quaint metalworkers with the basic processes, tools, and equipment common to the shop.

The planter shown in Figs. 3-12 and 3-13 provides you with experiences that lead to a better understanding of many fundamentals of sheet metalwork. The finished piece is functional, and you will derive personal satisfac-tion from making a product you can proudly display.

☐ Lay out the 28-g stock for the sides and bottom of the box as shown in Fig. 3-14.

☐ Cut stock to size, and notch.

☐ Make a 3/16-inch hem on all edges of the side unit. *Do not* close the hem. Make certain it is reversed on the opposite edges of the side unit.

☐ Fold the side into its rectangular shape using the box and pan brake.

☐ Make the grooved seam on the side. Be sure the seam is on the outside of the box.

☐ Cut metal for the bottom and make a 3/16-inch flange on all edges as noted.

☐ Fit bottom in place and set seam.

☐ Solder all seams inside the box.

☐ Wire the top edge of the box.

Fig. 3-12. The completed planter.

Fig. 3-13. The completed planter.

☐ Deburr the corners of the box and polish the outside faces.

☐ Cut a piece of perforated metal to size (as shown).

☐ Lay out and notch the perforated stock.

☐ Bend the ⅝-inch flange on the perforated metal.

☐ Fold the perforated metal to its rectangular shape using the box and pan brake.

☐ Lap the ends of the perforated shell ⅛ of an inch and spotweld. (Interlace the ends to center the seam.)

☐ Cut two pieces of copper-coated welding rod ⅛ × 18 inches long.

☐ Lay out 3 inches in the center of each rod.

☐ Make a 90-degree bend at each end of 3-inch section (as shown).

☐ Finish shaping the handle bracket as shown in Fig. 3-14. This can be done in a slip roll (see Fig. 3-15) with a wooden jig, or by bending over a piece of pipe and fitting to a template.

☐ Center the handle brackets on the ends of the perforated-metal shell and spotweld them in place (see Fig. 3-16).

☐ Clean the shell and prepare it for finishing. A commercial metal conditioner is recommended.

☐ Mask the portions of the handles and feet which are to be left a copper color.

☐ Spray the shell with a good enamel suitable for use on bare metal.

☐ Unmask the handles and feet, and spray or brush coat these portions with clear enamel or lacquer.

☐ Place the plant box in the completed shell.

BUILD A SHEET-METAL STOVE

A metal project of great interest to sports-minded metalworkers is the fish house or camp stove described here. This project is ideal because it provides experience in basic sheet metalwork, soldering, brazing, and a small amount of basic pipe work. In Minnesota, and in many of our northern lake states, ice-shanty angling and spearing are major winter sports; therefore, the main use for this stove is heating an ice house. It can also be used as a camp heating stove.

The first step is to lay out and cut the body, top, baffle, and bracket from 22-gauge galvanized iron. Variations in seams may be used if desired. All parts are then formed as indicated on a box and pan brake.

The pilot holes for ¼-inch No. 6 sheet metal screws may then be drilled with a ¼-inch portable drill or the drill press.

The burner is laid out next and cut from 18-gauge black annealed sheet metal. The vent holes are drilled; the seams brazed. Care must be taken to assure a minimum of warping due to excess heating by the welding torch. The burner, when completed, is fitted inside the bracket and attached with sheet-metal screws as shown

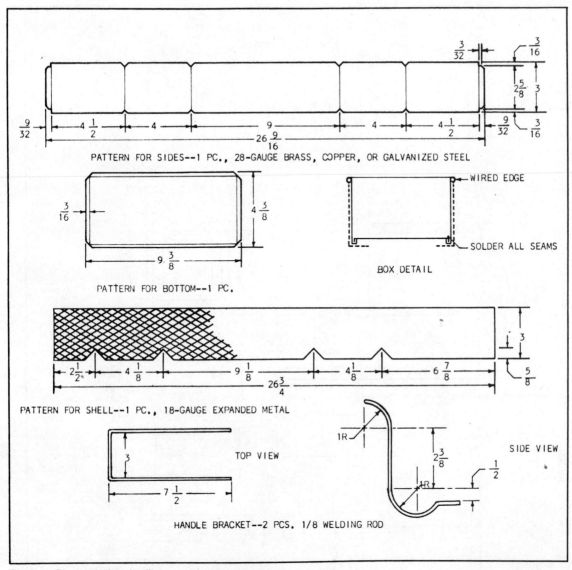

PATTERN FOR SIDES--1 PC., 28-GAUGE BRASS, COPPER, OR GALVANIZED STEEL

PATTERN FOR BOTTOM--1 PC.

WIRED EDGE

SOLDER ALL SEAMS

BOX DETAIL

PATTERN FOR SHELL--1 PC., 18-GAUGE EXPANDED METAL

TOP VIEW

SIDE VIEW

HANDLE BRACKET--2 PCS. 1/8 WELDING ROD

Fig. 3-14. Planter design details.

Fig. 3-15. Forming handles on slip roll.

Fig. 3-16. Welding handle on shell.

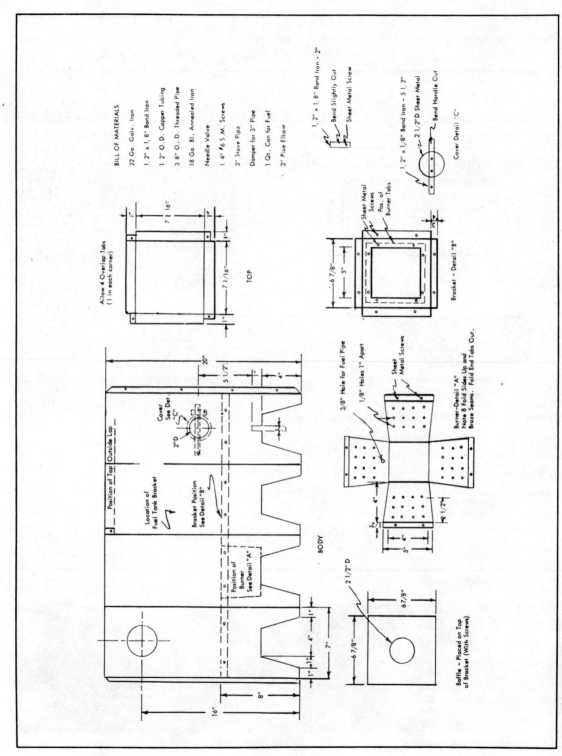

Fig. 3-17. Stove design details.

in Fig. 3-17. The baffle is placed on top of the burner. This cuts down on excess draft and helps contain a maximum amount of heat within the body jacket.

The bracket with burner and baffle attached is then placed in position within the body and attached with sheet-metal screws.

The cover and latch are now attached to the body and the top is last to be put in place.

There are many variations possible in the fuel supply system. The one we found satisfactory is a 1-quart can strapped to a sheet-metal bracket to hold it away from direct contact with the stove body. A length of ½-inch o.d. copper tubing and an air-conditioner needle valve to regulate the flow of fuel oil into the burner were used and found to be very satisfactory.

The finished stove takes up a minimum of space, is light and portable, and will serve to heat many a homemade "wigwam" during cold winter months. See Fig. 3-18.

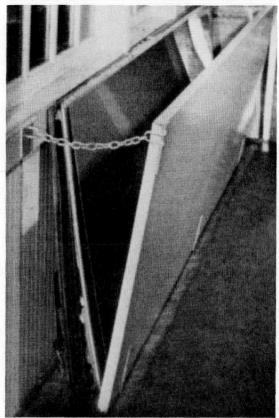

Fig. 3-19. A sheet-metal storing device open to the position where it is a simple matter either to store more metal or take some out. It is made of a piece of wood, some hinges, eyes, and chain.

STORING SHEET METAL

The storing of sheet metal so that it is available for immediate use, and has an attractive arrangement, is a problem in those shops using this material. A solution to this storage problem is shown in Fig. 3-19.

The rectangular wooden piece is hinged at its base so that it may be pulled from the wall to permit the removal of the sheet desired. After the sheet is replaced, the hinged piece is then pushed back into place.

A chain is used to restrict the movement of the hinged piece and it is fastened to the wall and the piece by means of the two eyes shown. The dimensions of this rectangular piece will, of course, depend on the size of the sheets being stored.

Fig. 3-18. The completed sheet-metal camping stove.

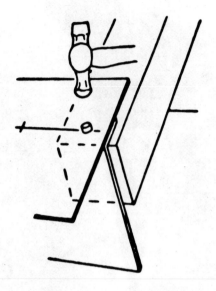

Chapter 4
Metal Sculpturing

STRIP SCULPTURE ALLOWS YOU THE OPPOR-
tunity to design an unusual project and to learn some
simple metalshop operations. The design can be either
traditional or contemporary. Traditional subjects usually
are suitable or you might prefer to create or adapt a new
design to the medium.

The width and thickness of the metal vary with the
specific uses made of it, and wire can be substituted for
sheet metal, in part, or totally. If wire is used, the soldering operation can best be performed with a torch.
Objects can be made to stand or hang. They can be
finished with flat black paint or left in the natural metal
color.

The technical aspects of the project are simple.
Shaping can be done with a mallet on a stake and sharp
bends can be made in a vise or with pliers. The major
objective of the project is not to learn many difficult
operations, but rather to improve the position of sheet
metal in the minds of metalworkers and to make more
difficult and attractive projects. See Figs. 4-1 and 4-2.

WIRE SCULPTURE

Creativity and individuality of design are easy to overlook
in the metalshop. Many projects involve large pieces of
machinery or standard equipment. One of the obvious
benefits of a project in wire sculpture is that you have a
chance at creative design.

Ideas for wire sculpture are constantly around us.
We have only to notice and discover them. The idea for
this project (Fig. 4-3) came from a tomcat. Mild steel rod
is formed into a creative design that would enhance the
wall of any home.

The starting point of this or any design worth its salt
is considerable sketching. Experimentation is the basis of
learning good design, so a large volume of paper is usually
required.

Once the design has been completed, following a
period of trial-and-error sketching, layout work of the
mild steel can begin. A 3/16-inch diameter mild steel rod
is excellent for this type of project. The use of mild steel
instead of cold roll steel makes a simple task of the
bending process.

If the same diameter rod is used for the entire project, however, a bulky appearance will result. The cat's
whiskers, in this case, offered an opportunity to add
another diameter of steel welding rod for variety and a
more pleasing appearance. The runs of the lines should be
kept short because it is difficult to bend long pieces of
either diameter of mild steel.

Fig. 4-1. Strip sculpture allows you to exercise your imagination over a wide range of design and in a variety of motifs.

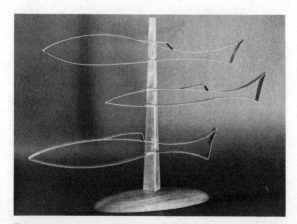

Fig. 4-2. An example of strip sculpture that requires learning the basics of shaping and joining metal, combined with imagination, to produce a pleasing and creative project.

When the design has been completed with the steel layout, the joining process follows. The easiest system is to build the figure in sections, then construct the final form. Using the brazing rod, the joining process is an interesting experience.

The bending process is done mainly by hand, but parts of it would easily be done by a metal bender. The secret here, of course, is the use of mild steel instead of cold roll steel.

To add a touch of individual design to this project, two metal washers were used for the eyes, with marbles glued to the holes of the washers. A bracket was formed on the metal bender and brazed to the cat, to hold it several inches away from the wall.

The finish of such a project can be left to individual choice. The tomcat shown here was finished in flat black. See Figs. 4-4 and 4-5.

Fig. 4-3. After much trial-and-error sketching, the final design is achieved. (Squares equal 1 inch).

Fig. 4-5. The finished sculpture can be brazed to a bracket and hung up.

Fig. 4-4. The pattern is developed by making short runs with the metal.

STRIP-METAL DESIGNS

Another design project that is useful is the creation of decorative wall pieces. The project is a good introduction to strip metal and sheet metal.

The results can be varied and interesting. The design can come from a picture, a magazine, or your own sketches, and is limited only by imagination.

Before starting construction, it is helpful to make planning sheets on which you sketch designs and specify the materials you will need. At this time, go over the list of materials available: strip metal (⅜-inch widths of 22-gauge black iron), sheet stock (brass, copper, aluminum, stainless steel, expanded steel, and perforated steel), acrylic, rivets, solder, tacks, brazing rods, washers, and glue. Using a combination of materials not only adds to the variety of possible designs, but also helps use up small pieces that would otherwise be wasted.

By filling in the strip metal, a foundation is added to which details can be glued or soldered. Construction of a project similar to the ones shown in Figs. 4-6, 4-7, and 4-8 involves—in addition to drawing or selecting a design—cutting sheet into strips; cleaning the strips; bending;

Fig. 4-6. The shelf bracket is slightly more difficult to make than the others.

soldering; cutting, shaping, and fitting detail material inside the strip design; and painting and finishing.

A SCULPTURE PROJECT

Attractive metal sculptures can be modeled from birds, plants, and animals to the less obvious but no less interesting geometric patterns of orbiting electrons and lattices of crystals and viruses.

While steel is usually thought of as a hard, strong, rigid material, it will yield willingly into the desired shape in the hands of a sensitive and knowledgeable metalworker. All it takes to start is some basic planning and development of full-size patterns to work out proportions and locations of assembly. The planning can be kept simple because the sculpture will evolve as the material is worked and shaped.

The various parts for the sculpture shown in Figs. 4-9, 4-10, and 4-11 required both hot and cold forming techniques, along with a variety of machine operations. Flat stock took on a new dimension by being drawn,

Fig. 4-7. Beginners are introduced to a variety of materials, processes, and tools with these wall pieces.

Fig. 4-8. Repeated hammer blows on the steel help to create the appearance of bird plumage.

Fig. 4-9. Full-size patterns help in proportioning the sculpture properly (grid squares above represent ½-square inches). The duck feet must be flared, filed, and formed to shape.

beaten down, and/or raised to shape with a hammer, and an assortment of textures and surface decorations on the metal were created as the material was worked. Left unpainted after these working operations, parts of the bird sculptures we made took on a strikingly natural appearance. Using the lathe to knurl made it possible to achieve an appealingly realistic texture on the cattails of the sculpture.

You can express a variety of emotions in sculpture.

Through suspended or cantilevered forms, other geometric planes are transgressed, creating a feeling of grace, flight, or escape.

Simple heat coloration on the metal surface can produce a distinctive quality in the sculpture. Allow the metal to heat up and progress through the various temperatures to provide a richness of tonal beauty in the metal surface. Once the desired coloration is achieved, the heating-colorating action can be stopped simply by

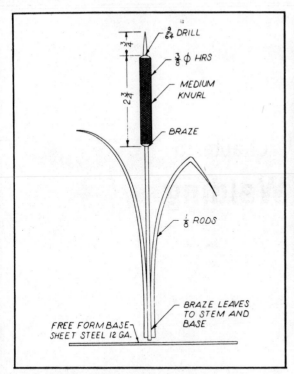

Fig. 4-10. Cattails for the duck sculpture (or as part of a plant sculpture) can be made at random lengths.

Fig. 4-11. Weathered wood was simulated for the pier posts of this sea gull sculpture by using weld bead.

quenching the metal in water; then, a clear finish can be sprayed on the sculpture as a protective coating.

The equipment and materials in your shop are probably all you need to create a metal sculpture.

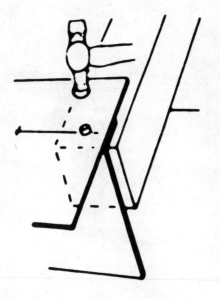

Chapter 5
Welding

WELDING IS A TERM USED TO DESCRIBE THE many metal-joining processes used in making welds. There are approximately 40 welding processes, and they can be grouped under the following major headings: arc welding, brazing, flow welding, forge welding, gas welding, induction welding, resistance welding, and thermite welding.

Man's progress through the ages has been contingent, to a greater or lesser degree, on his ability to join metals. Brazing is mentioned in the Bible and forge welding has been known and used since earliest time. Despite the antiquity of the process, there has been greater development during the last 50 years than in the previous 2,000 years.

The value of a metal today is in direct proportion to its weldability. Alloys are constantly being developed in the laboratory, with a view to improving their properties, but if they cannot be welded, or are difficult to weld, their use becomes distinctly limited. A notable exception to this rule is the metal titanium. This metal was extremely difficult to weld when conventional processes and techniques were used because it reacts with atmospheric gases, hydrogen, and all common refractories. Because of titanium's light weight, excellent corrosion resistance, and potentially high strength, it had many applications in military and chemical engineering fields. It was essential, therefore, that welding techniques be developed to enable this valuable metal to be used commercially. A research program was instituted and, after a great deal of time, money, and effort were expended, welding methods were devised whereby this valuable metal could be used commercially.

The advent of nuclear power and the requirements of our space and missile programs have all contributed to the almost fantastic speedup of technological developments. High-temperature operations have called for materials that will withstand high-service temperatures. These materials, in turn, had to be welded.

No one welding process can satisfy all industrial demands. This is why there are so many processes in use today. When a new process is developed, it does not necessarily mean that it will replace an old process. It is a system of addition rather than replacement. Arc welding did not replace oxyacetylene welding, and gas shielded-arc welding did not replace conventional arc welding. Each process has its place in the over-all picture of metal-joining operations and each has advantages and limitations.

Choice of Process

There are many factors involved in the choice of a welding process, not the least of which is the equipment available in the plant or shop. Economical factors can prevent the purchase of certain desirable welding equipment, and welding personnel will have to use their ingenuity to adapt existing equipment to serve a similar purpose.

In the automotive industry, for example, there is equipment available that will complete a multiweld operation in a matter of seconds. This might be considered desirable welding equipment wherever a multiweld operation is involved but, because the equipment can cost up to a million dollars, the cost factor would rule it out for any but the largest operations.

Arc Welding

Many of the new processes are developments of established processes and have either specialized applications or are used mainly to exercise greater control, such as heat intake or atmospheric contamination.

Among the new arc welding processes is one that relies on the shorting out of the arc for its effectiveness. The principle is simple. The wire is fed at a speed that causes it to come in contact with the work. This causes a short circuit and a sudden surge of current. The increase of current finds resistance in the wire, and the tip of the wire melts and is deposited on the work piece. Contact is broken, the current immediately falls, the voltage increases, and the wire again is fed forward to contact the work piece and start the cycle all over again.

This is a gas shielded-arc welding process and can be used with CO_2 or, for some applications, with mixtures of argon-oxygen or argon carbon dioxide shielding gas.

CO_2 welding gives a high degree of penetration and usually operates with high currents, high travel speeds and wire-feed rates. With the use of this new process, greater control over travel speeds can be exercised and the current can be reduced.

Claims for this process include: less heat intake, reduced operator skill needed, increased speed for vertical and overhead welding, and reduced current and welding time.

The manufacturers of this process have named it "short-arc process," the "dip-transfer process," and the "microwire process."

Plasma Arc

The plasma arc, or plasma jet, has been known for many

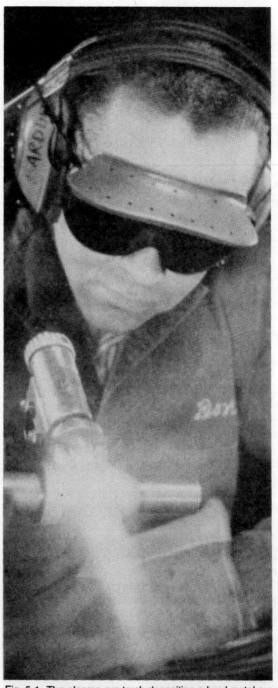

Fig. 5-1. The plasma-arc torch depositing a hard metal surface on machine components. It is capable of producing temperatures up to 50,000° C., more than eight times as hot as the surface of the sun.

years. The principle involved is not new but commercial applications are comparatively recent. See Fig. 5-1.

The intense heat produced by this process is obtained by feeding a stream of gas at high velocity through an arc. There are two basic methods of utilizing this process: by means of the transferred arc and by means of the nontransferred arc. When the arc is maintained between the electrode and the work, it is called a *transferred arc*. When the arc is maintained between the electrode and the nozzle, it is called the *nontransferred arc*.

The arc temperature is much higher than for any other process, reaching 30,000°F with the nontransferred arc and possibly double this temperature with the transferred arc. The highest temperature reached with the oxyacetylene flame is approximately 5,600°F and with the conventional electric arc approximately 12,000°F.

The chief uses for the plasma arc in the welding industry are for cutting and spraying. The jet emitted from a constricting nozzle is quite stable and can be directed in a desired direction. For cutting purposes, the transferred arc usually is used because the objective is to heat the work piece. High cutting speeds are obtainable with narrow cuts, thus keeping the heat affected zone to a minimum.

Because the heat developed with the plasma arc is sufficient to vaporize any known element, the process becomes an ideal medium for spraying metals or ceramics. The nontransferred arc is used because it is not desirable to heat the work. The material—powder or wire—is fed into the arc and sprayed onto the product. High-melting-point metals, such as tungsten, are drawn, in powder form, into the arc and used to coat rocket nozzles and similar parts which require a surface to withstand high operating temperatures.

Ultrasonic Welding

There is a great similarity between ultrasonic welding and resistance welding. With each process the parts are clamped together and the energy is introduced by means of an electrode with resistance welding and a sonotrode with ultrasonic welding.

In resistance welding, electrical energy is introduced through the medium of the electrode, and the resistance of the parts to the flow of current generates the heat required to weld the parts together. In ultrasonic welding, vibratory energy is introduced instead of electrical energy by means of a device called a sonotrode, which is similar to the electrode in resistance welding. The tip, clamped against the work pieces, oscillates in a

Fig. 5-2. Welding metals using high-frequency vibrations. The sheet metal is joined by a circular transducer designed to do seam welding.

plane parallel to the weld interface and the vibrations effect the weld.

Unlike most welding processes that rely on heat to melt the contracting surfaces, ultrasonic welding accomplishes the weld by vibratory energy alone, without melting the parts. The weld is achieved by solid-state

86

Fig. 5-3. A machine that uses the concept of developing heat by using forces of friction. The metals are rubbed together under pressure and at high speed. The contact surfaces melt, then fuse.

bonding and the interpenetration of the material from one part to the other. See Fig. 5-2.

All commercially available metals can be welded by the ultrasonic process and it is particularly suitable for the following: similar and dissimilar metals which do not bond readily by other welding processes; metals that become brittle when heated; and metals that lose valuable properties or suffer a reduction of desirable properties when exposed to the high heat of other processes.

Ultrasonic welding is finding many applications in the welding of foil; in the proposed welding of reactive metals; in seam welding; and in the electronics industry where the finest wires and thinnest foils can be welded to pieces of almost any size or shape.

The maximum thickness in which high strength welds can be produced in aluminum at the present time is approximately 0.10 of an inch. For some of the harder

metals the limit is nearer 0.05 of an inch. This limitation, of course, applies only to the thinner member of the weldment, the other member may be of greater thickness. No lower limit has yet been determined. Wires of less than 0.003 of an inch diameter have been welded satisfactorily and foils as thin as 0.00017 of an inch have been joined without rupture.

Electron Beam Welding

Electron beam welding (Fig. 5-4) operates on the same principle as the picture tube in a television set. A heated tungsten filament emits electrons which are propelled at high speed. For welding purposes, the electrons are focused into a small beam ranging in size from approximately 3/16 of an inch in diameter for heavy material, to as small as 0.010 of an inch in diameter. The welding is carried out in a high-vacuum chamber.

This electron-beam welding process was developed at a time when the welding of reactive and refractory metals presented a problem. Metals such as titanium, zirconium, and molybdenum became so easily contaminated with oxygen, nitrogen, and the like, when conventional welding processes were used, that even an inert atmosphere did not give the results desired. With electron beam welding, the properties of weldments can be improved to match the improved properties of the base metal.

A zirconium-tin alloy, used in the reactor industry, was welded previously with the gas shielded-arc welding process with satisfactory results. The properties of the weld were comparable to those of the base metal. The properties of the base metal, however, were improved by vacuum melting and no advantage was gained from this improvement until a high-vacuum welding process was developed.

It's advantages are:

☐ the elimination of harmful contaminants.

☐ extremely deep penetration.

☐ minimum amount of material heated.

☐ metals with high thermal conductivity are welded more easily.

☐ exceedingly narrow heat affected zones are possible.

☐ less distortion because less material is heated.

Its disadvantages are:

☐ equipment cost.

☐ size limitations of work that can be handled.

☐ part might require simple geometry because of the fixturing and handling problems.

☐ precision fit-up and locating necessary because of the precision of the electron-beam focusing system.

Friction Welding

Basically, the friction-welding process involves the rotating of one part against another to generate frictional heat at the interface. See Fig. 5-3. When a suitably high

Fig. 5-4. The electron-beam welding technique is used to weld refractory metals and in cases where weld reliability is of great importance. A high vacuum chamber (the cylinder with inspection plate at right center) performs the dual functions of conducting the electron beam and protecting the weldment from atmospheric contamination. Fusion is produced by converting electron energy from kinetic to thermal.

temperature has been reached, the motion ceases. Pressure is exerted and a weld results. Pressure can be held contant during the entire cycle or it can be exerted at a given moment. When the motion between the two parts has to cease, it must be done rapidly or the bonds will be broken. Relative motion can be stopped by applying a brake or by releasing the part which had been held stationary during the heating cycle.

The same effect is produced when a bearing seizes through lack of lubrication. The heat generated by the friction of one part against the other causes the bearing to seize, thus producing a friction weld.

High-quality butt welds have been obtained in many metals; these include low carbon steel, alloy steels, gray iron, copper, aluminum, titanium, and brasses. Dissimilar metals have also been welded. Among these are: stainless steel to plain carbon steel, copper to brass, brass to steel, pure aluminum to aluminum alloys, and others.

Its advantages are:

☐ high efficiency, requires only a percentage of the energy needed by other welding processes.

☐ heat affected zone is narrow.

☐ cost of equipment is relatively low.

☐ condition of surfaces unimportant because friction and centrifugal force will break up and disperse oxides.

☐ readily converted to automatic operations.

☐ equipment can be used in the field.

Its disadvantages are:

☐ maximum diameter of bars may be limited.

☐ thermal conductivity of material may dictate application because no heat is generated at the center because the relative motion is at its maximum at the od. The center is heated, therefore, by conduction.

Conductivity is important when welding dissimilar metals because the metals with low thermal conductivity will reach its melting point while the high conductivity metal is still relatively cold at the interface.

Electroslag Welding

This process was developed in Russia and exhibited at the Brussels World Fair in 1958. It is a resistance heating process, the heat being generated by the resistance of the passage of a current through a molten flux between the electrode and the work. The start of the weld corresponds to that of a submerged arc weld but, as soon as the pool of molten slag is sufficiently large, the arc is extinguished and the heat is generated by resistance heating. The joint must be capable of vertical positioning because electroslag welding is a vertical process. See Fig. 5-5.

Its advantages are:

☐ it is a very economical process; welds being made in one pass even in plate up to 14 inches thick.

☐ duty cycle is 100 percent, with the exception of set-up time.

☐ deposition rate is high, up to 45 pounds per hour per electrode.

☐ joint design is relatively simple, a plain butt joint being used, spaced at least 1 inch apart.

☐ less joint preparation.

Its disadvantages are:

☐ it is claimed that the best mechanical properties are not obtained with this process, (further development

Fig. 5-5. An electroslag welding rig that is particularly suitable for welding thick plate materials. The electrode is fed under a thick layer of molten slag to the weld joint which is usually vertically oriented and requires water-cooled back-up fixtures.

will undoubtedly bring about the necessary improvements).

☐ vertical positioning is necessary.

High-Frequency Resistance Welding

This process is being applied to the welding of longitudinal seam tubes and butt welding of strip, plate, and sheet material. The principle of high-frequency heating is used. The behavior of electrical currents changes to some extent when frequencies of 500,000 cycles per second are involved. Normally, electrical current will take the path of least resistance but, when high frequencies are used, the current is attracted to its own return path.

This principle enables the heat to be concentrated on the surface of the edge. Thus, the heat affected zone is very narrow and welding speed very high.

A large variety of metals have been welded with this process including: aluminum, steels, copper, brass, nickel, titanium, silicon bronze, Monel and Inconel alloys, and zirconium.

Summary

The universal filler metal that can be used for all purposes, on all metals and for all processes, has not yet been developed—and probably never will. The same applies to

Fig. 5-6. A flanged reactor component—its reliability can be no less than 100 percent—illustrating the advantages of welded design essential to nuclear reactor fabrication. This is the only way this assembly can be produced.

Fig. 5-7. A unitized automobile body has solved many car-production problems. Several welding processes—seam, spot, and projection welding—are essential to its production.

welding processes. Each new process is in use because it contributes something that other processes lack. It might bring increased speed, protection from atmospheric contamination, or economy in operation. This is why a working knowledge of each process is so essential if efficient weldments are to be produced at an economical figure.

If oxyacetylene welding, for example, were the only process available, the unitized automobile body with its 10,000 or more spot welds, would be impractical. Automatic resistance welding equipment has made this possible. When 100 percent weld efficiency is required in nuclear operations, a gas-shielded process or a high-vacuum process will meet the required standard.

Our standards are being raised to meet the demands of space, missile, and nuclear operations. It is becoming increasingly necessary, therefore, that the latest developments in welding technology be made known so that these higher standards can be met. See Figs. 5-6 through 5-9.

SELECTING ELECTRICAL WELDING EQUIPMENT

Selecting a welding machine for your shop can be a very trying experience. The welding-trade literature is replete with many proprietary terms and specialized jargon that will confuse anyone except those intimately associated with the welding industry. In addition, many technical terms such as *duty cycle, power factor*, etc., are employed. To select the most suitable piece of welding equipment for your shop, take the time to learn the

Fig. 5-8. An operator feeding an automated line of welding presses to weld the inner and outer center-pillar panels of an automobile body.

meaning of these and other terms so that you can properly evaluate the various welding machines available today.

First of all, what is the function of a welding machine? Its primary purpose is to supply electric power to maintain an arc. Figure 5-10 shows the welding arc in detail and illustrates the various conditions that contribute to a successful weld. It generates extreme heat, requires power, but requires power of a special type. It is impossible to obtain power for an arc merely by plugging the electrode holder and ground connections into an electrical outlet. We need the welding machine to change the power made available by the electric utility to the current and voltage required for the arc.

There are many different ways of classifying welding machines; one of the basic classifications is the type of control. There are two basic types: the single-control machine and the dual-control machine. Single-control machines have just one dial that changes the current output of the machine. Dual-control machines have two controls, one for fine and one for coarse current adjustment.

The single-control welding machine is designed to produce a number of characteristic output curves similar to Fig. 5-11. The characteristic curve is obtained by plotting the terminal voltage when loading the welding machine with varying amounts of pure resistance load. You will notice that as the amperage output of the machine increases, the voltage of the machine decreases. The "open-circuit" voltage is a fixed figure based on the design of the machine and is usually in the neighborhood of 75V. The single control of the machine changes the current output and is adjustable from a minimum figure to a maximum figure that is usually greater than the rated output of the machine. The shaded area on this particular curve is the output voltage or "arc voltage" of the machine during welding. By adjusting the current control output a great number of curves can be obtained. The dotted line shows the machine adjusted to 150 amps. On tap or plug-in machines, there will be a number of curves corresponding to the number of taps that are on the machine.

Dual-control machines are normally direct-current generator-type welding machines. Dual-control machines offer the operator much more flexibility in selecting conditions for making different types of welds. These machines, in effect, have what is known as "slope control." A welding machine produces two types of voltage. One, known as "open-circuit" voltage, has the voltage produced when the arc is not in operation. The other, known as "arc voltage," has the voltage output of the machine while the arc is in operation. A dual-control machine has two control adjustments: a coarse adjustment and a fine adjustment. The coarse adjustment sets the current output of the machine and varies the output from the minimum to the maximum current. The fine control actually changes the current setting between the coarse control setting points.

On motor generators, however, this fine control has an additional function. Under nonwelding conditions, the fine control also changes the "open-circuit" voltage of the machine. This relationship is shown in Fig. 5-12. Note that the open-circuit voltage can be changed from approximately 60V to 100V. This is accomplished by the fine adjustment dial. While welding, this same dial has *no* effect on the welding-arc voltage. It is only controlled by the length of the welding arc.

The higher no-load, "open-circuit," voltage provides for easier arc starting with all types of electrodes. It also provides a steeper curve through the arcvoltage range. The change of slope, which is controlled by the open-circuit voltage setting, does have an effect on arc characteristics.

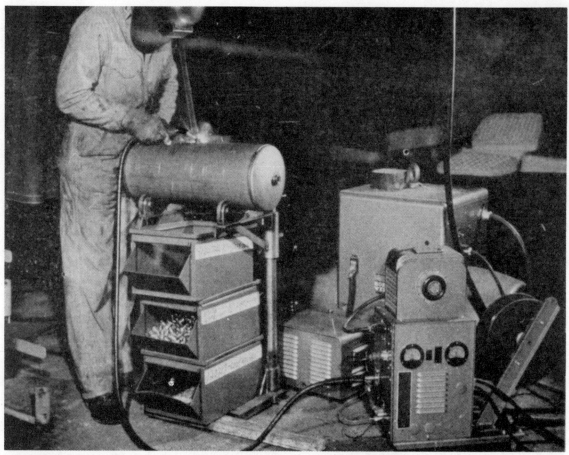

Fig. 5-9. Micro-wire welding thick to thin metal. A fitting with a heavier wall thickness is welded to the 14-gauge steel shell of an air tank.

A study of Fig. 5-13 will help to illustrate this situation. A *short arc* is a lower-voltage arc; with the same settings of the machine, it is a higher-current arc. This is shown by the meters and the diagram of the short arc.

On the other hand, the *long arc* is a higher-voltage arc, but the current is lower, at the same machine setting. The slope of the characteristic curve, which is changed by changing the open-circuit voltage, actually changes the characteristics of the arc.

It can be seen that with the flatter slope an equal change in arc voltage will produce a greater change in welding current. This produces the harsh or digging arc. This type of arc is popular for pipe welding. With the steeper curve, produced by the higher, open-circuit voltage, an equal change in arc length will produce less of a change of current output. This is a softer or quieter arc, and is more useful for sheet-metal welding. Thus, the

dual-control generator welding machine allows the most flexibility to the welder. *Note*: Transformer welders with coarse and fine adjustment knobs are not considered dual-control machines because the open-circuit voltage is not changed.

Welding machines can also be classified as motor generator, ac transformer, ac-dc rectifier welders, engine-driven welders, and many, many more. The direct-current rotating generator was the earliest type of welding machine and still enjoys a very favorable reputation. Generators can be driven by electric motors, gasoline engines, diesel engines, or even from power take-off shafts of any type of rotating device.

Another very popular welding machine is the transformer welder. It is usually the least expensive, lightest, and smallest of any of the various types of welding machines. The transformer welder takes power directly

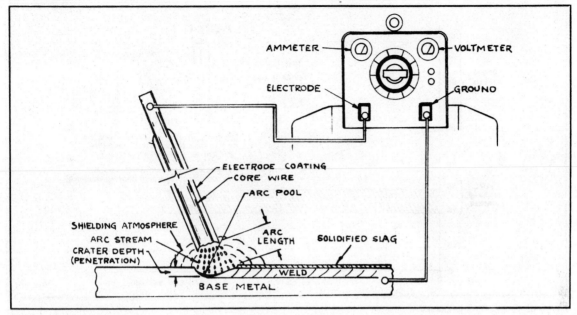

Fig. 5-10. Welding arc details.

from the utility lines and transforms it to the voltage required for the arc. Then by means of various magnetic circuits, inductors, etc., it provides the voltage and ampere characteristics necessary for welding. In alternating-current welding, the polarity of the welding current changes 120 times each second. This cannot be seen, of course, and is not noticeable by the welder.

The welding current output of a transformer welder.

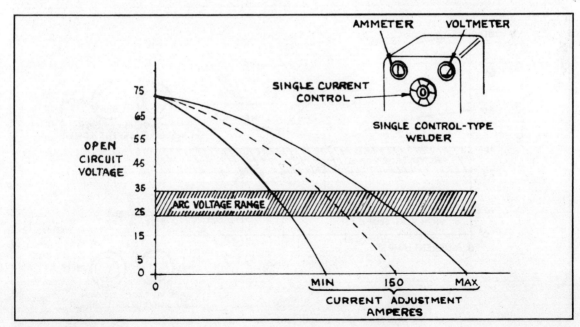

Fig. 5-11. Output curves.

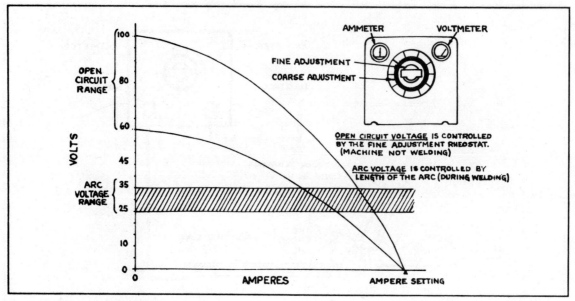

Fig. 5-12. Fine control function.

can be adjusted in many different ways. Perhaps the simplest method of adjusting output current is to use a tapped secondary winding. Plugs or a tap switch can be used. This is a popular method employed by many of the limited input welding transformers. Exact current adjustment, however, is not possible. This type of machine is rarely used in industry.

The advantages of the transformer and rectifier have been combined into machines known as ac-dc welders. By means of a special switch, the output terminals are con-

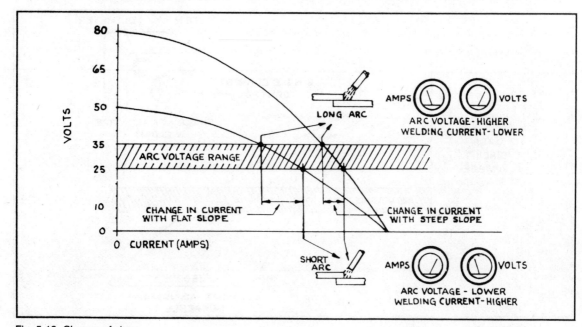

Fig. 5-13. Change of slope.

nected to the transformer, or the rectifier, so the operator can select either ac current or dc straight or dc reverse-polarity welding current to satisfy his welding requirements. In some types of ac-dc welders, high-frequency oscillators, plus water and gas control valves, are installed. This then makes the machine ideally suited for tungsten inert-gas welding as well as for manual, coated-electrode welding.

Semiautomatic welding equipment utilizes the gas shielded or the submerged arc process. The electrode filler wire is fed automatically and the travel speed is handled manually. The gas shielded process, wherein the gas shields the arc from the atmosphere, is the most popular. The most popular unit of this type is shown in Fig. 5-14.

This is the micro-wire package, which contains the generator power source, the wire feeder, and the cable and torch assembly.

The wire size is in the order of .035 of an inch to .045 of an inch, but the welding currents employed are similar to those used for $1/8$ inch or 5/32-inch electrodes. CO_2 gas is the most common gas used for shielding the arc area. It is readily available and is very inexpensive. All-position welding can be accomplished on material as thin as 20 gauge and up to unlimited thicknesses. The gas shielded process is popular for welding pipe.

"Which machine to buy?" The following is a summary of the advantages and disadvantages of each. The dc motor generator welding machine is the most flexible of all welders available. It has the disadvantage of a higher noise level output, and it is somewhat less efficient electrically, but it does employ 3-phase input power and provides welding current unaffected by input line voltage variations.

The ac transformer welder has the advantage of high electrical efficiency, low initial expense, and usually a

Fig. 5-14. Semiautomatic welding equipment.

low noise level. The disadvantages are that it cannot be used for all types of welding electrodes, and it is impossible to shift from the digging to the soft type of arc.

The dc rectifier welder has many of the advantages of the ac transformer welder. It is more expensive, but it does have a high electrical efficiency, and it is quiet. It uses a 3-phase power input.

The ac-dc machine has many of the advantages of the transformer and rectifier welder. When equipped with the high-frequency oscillator, and with appropriate valves and timers, it is one of the best methods of providing power for coated electrodes and tungsten gas welding. The disadvantage of the ac-dc is, again, that it does operate from a single-phase input.

In considering your welding-machine requirements, it is well to analyze your welding-training program. This will enable you to determine the best types of machines required. In other words, are you concerned primarily with an industrial-arts program, evening courses, trade and industrial welding programs, vo-ag programs, apprentice-training programs, adult training, or combinations of all these? Consider also the local community requirements and conditions in local industry. For example: Is TIG welding the predominant type of welding in your community? Or is much of the welding done in the field application where gasoline driven welders are quite common? Does local industry utilize ac transformers?

Consider the advantage of each of the different types of welding machines. In general, it is best to select one predominant type and then supplement it with one or two of the other types. Many shops have generator welders, transformer welders, and one or two ac-dc welders equipped for TIG welding, plus one semiautomatic machine.

After deciding on the proper type of machine, it then becomes a problem to select the proper size of machine. To properly specify the size of a machine, you should become familiar with the way welding machines are rated. Most manufacturers rate their machines according to specifications prepared by NEMA (National Electrical Manufacturers Association). In this official rating method, it is necessary to consider the *welding current,* the *welding voltage,* and the *duty cycle* of the machine.

The following is the recommended type and size of machines for a welding laboratory:

A dc motor generator welding machine—200-amp size, at 30V and 50 percent duty cycle. It should have dual controls to provide for most flexible operation.

An ac transformer welding machine—200-amp size at 30V, and 50 percent duty cycle. It should have continu-ous current control, using the electrical system. The machine should have power factor correcting capacitors.

An ac-dc transformer-rectifier welding machine—200-amp size at 40V and 60 percent duty cycle. It should include a high-frequency oscillator and gas and water valves making it suitable for TIG welding. It should also have a switch to change from ac operation to dc straight polarity and dc reverse polarity operation. The machine should have power-factor-correcting capacitors.

Semiautomatic welding, a packaged unit including the welding power source, wire feeder, and torch and cable assembly should be selected. Choose a 200-amp machine with 25-V output, but at 100 percent duty cycle.

To obtain the type of machine required, you must give complete specifications for the equipment. Consult the various welding manufacturers' catalogs, and list the following information:

—Rated current.
—Output voltage.
—Duty cycle.
—Primary input—voltage, frequency, and number of phases.

Check with building facilities or power company for voltage of power to be supplied to the welding shop. Most machines are manufactured so that they can be interchanged from one voltage to another with a minimum of effort. In the United States, 60 cycle is practically universal.

Manufacturer's catalog number. Include the manufacturer's catalog number so that you will receive the machine you desire, even though the above information is listed.

Accessories and related equipment. Indicate the equipment that will come with the machine, based on manufacturer's literature, and any other equipment or accessories that you will require with the machine. This can include electrodes, holders, helmets, gloves, cable, ground clamp, power line connectors, etc.

Selecting the proper machine, after arriving at the specification, is not too difficult. The following points are made to aid you in obtaining the best machine value for your requirements.

☐ Select industrial type of welding equipment. The equipment need not be the heavy-duty industrial machine. It should, however, be of the same general type as the machines used in industry.

☐ Select top-quality equipment produced by an established manufacturer with a reputation for producing high-grade equipment.

Fig. 5-15. A pipe-welding setup consisting of turntable, gear, rack assembly, and cutting torch.

☐ Purchase your equipment from a reputable local representative who has an established service policy.

☐ Compare value of competitive machines. Remember that it is necessary to consider all of the above factors—current, voltage, duty cycle—in comparing machines.

By following the above information, you should be able to obtain the most value for your money.

PIPE WELDING

In order to bevel pieces of pipe efficiently and quickly, you can use an electrically-driven turntable, rotating from 1 rpm to infinite speed which enables us to cut and bevel a 4-inch to 6-inch diameter pipe at a 90-degree or 180-degree angle in about 1 minute. Most of the pipe is 4-inch diameter and ⅝ of an inch in wall thickness, but larger sizes can be accommodated with our equipment and any beveling device can be used. This equipment, and hold-down clamps and Y-yokes for support, are shown in Figs. 5-15 through 5-21.

A WELDING WORKSHEET

The successful learning of welding is dependent on prac-

tice and repetition. Each weld should first be practical after research on methods and procedure. If you can incorporate your work into one solid example of workmanship, it then gives you a goal to work toward for perfection. The worksheet shown in Fig. 5-22 serves several purposes. It is economical, it covers the basic welds which should be learned, and gives you something from each basic area to compare at one time.

COST-CUTTING WELDING TIPS

Excellent welding booths can be constructed from salvaged restroom stalls or partitions (see Fig. 5-23). When constructing the booths, a center partition works out nicely for placing arc welding machines on the back side; in this way non-welders are shielded from ultraviolet rays. The front or outer booths are used for oxyacetylene welding.

It is not difficult to construct an angle-iron frame on top of the booths with galvanized steel forming a hood. The hood must be ducted into an existing exhaust fan, or a new one should be installed. If the existing fan is found to

Fig. 5-16. Four hold-down clamps on the turntable enable the operator to mount the 4″ pipe in the 180° vertical position or the 90° horizontal position. The alignment is almost perfect and only minor tolerance adjustment is necessary.

Fig. 5-17. For welding two pieces of pipe in the horizontal position, fashion two Y-shaped yokes, each with two 2″-d roller bearings mounted in adjustable slots and tacked on a ¼″ × 4″ × 8″ channel iron. The slots are 4″ × ⅝″ and allow the roller bearings to be adjusted to fit the pipe.

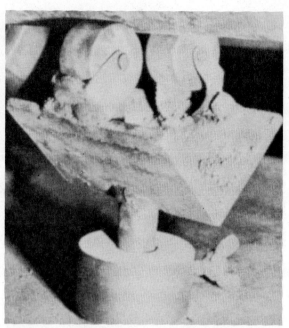

Fig. 5-19. A Y-yoke with two rollers acts as a rotating support for a long pipe.

Fig. 5-18. The roller bearing serves as a rotating table and ground for the vertical pipe. The two pieces of pipe are separated with a hairpin welding rod, enabling the worker to tack the pieces together for the horizontal fillet weld.

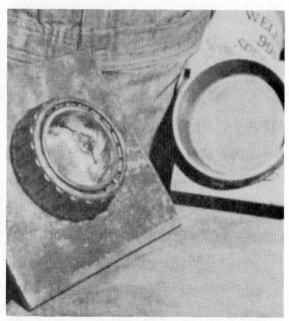

Fig. 5-20. To facilitate welding two pieces of pipe in a vertical position by hand, use this 6″-d tapered roller-bearing assembly. The bearing ring is tacked onto a ¼″-×-4″-×-8″ channel iron (right). The race is tacked onto the underside of a flat piece of steel plate, ⅜″ × 8″ × 8″ (left).

Fig. 5-21. The pipe is rotated by hand for completing a vertical fillet weld.

hooks with a hammer. Then cut off the straps that are for fastening underneath the bottom of the shoe. These straps can be sewn or riveted on in a new position to serve as a means of holding the leggings in position to protect the ankle and top of the feet from hot sparks and slag. The strap gives a much faster and better means of fastening the legging around the leg than the lacing method.

To help cut the cost of practice metal in arc welding, you can run beads on a piece of 4-×-4-×-¼ inch flat steel. On this piece of metal you can run a solid surface of beads in one direction and then they run a solid surface of beads in the opposite direction. This crisscrossing of layers results in a solid build-up in the thickness of the metal.

It is possible to obtain enough practice on one piece of metal to be able to run a fairly good bead before trying to weld two pieces of metal together. It is also possible to use the 4-×-4-×-¼ inch flat steel for oxyacetylene puddling practice—if you do not burn up the metal with an oxidizing flame. The beads are run in one direction until the surface is covered and then they can be run across the other beads. Don't forget that these pieces of metal have two surfaces that should be used.

INERTIA WELDING

If you ever have had the misfortune of freezing a piston or joining a dull drill bit to the metal plate you were working on, you already know about inertia welding. Oddly enough, it was only about 20 years ago that anyone thought to harness and commercially exploit this phenomenon. Now you can employ this simple technique using a conventional lathe or drill press. By doing so, you'll be taking advantage of a new learning experience in metallurgy, with its singular physical and mechanical properties. It might open up a whole new dimension of welding for you.

Inertia welding is a process in which stored kinetic energy is used to generate a sufficient amount of heat for fusion. The kinetic energy is stored in a rotating mass such as a flywheel or chuck. When this rotating mass is forced against a stationary object, the kinetic energy is converted to frictional heat. The heat developed is sufficient to soften the workpieces and forge them together.

Using a Lathe

This technique involves mounting a piece of stock in a universal chuck and another piece in a tailstock fitted with a Jacobs chuck. For initial shop projects, it is best to use short pieces of rather small diameter. The chuck is revolved at the highest speed obtainable. The stationary

be inadequate, small, kitchen exhaust fans can be hung in over the booths to serve as exhaust boosters. It is best to have the exhaust fans set to come on when the welders are turned on.

An excellent method for keeping welding equipment in its proper booth is to color code it. Color coding is most effective if you paint large areas of color on each object, such as all glove tops, all hood or goggle frames, etc.

For safety I have found that arc welders need to wear their safety glasses under the hoods so that, when the hoods are raised for chipping off flux, the glasses are in position and not forgotten. To prevent from burning the tops of your feet when arc welding and cutting, you can modify short army leggings.

First remove the laces and flatten down the string

piece in the tailstock chuck is advanced until light contact is made with the revolving piece. The advancement is slowly continued until good, solid contact is felt between the two pieces. If excessive chatter results, too much pressure is being applied: back off slightly and advance the piece again. The amount of friction produced causes the two pieces to turn to a plastic state (red hot for ferrous metals). At no time does the metal reach its melting point. Shut off the motor and advance the tailstock spindle until the universal chuck comes to a complete stop. The weld is now complete. Depending on the material's physical properties, the entire process will take an aver-

age of 20 seconds to perform. Figure 5-24 shows fusion occurring on a 13 in., 2 hp lathe at 1300 rpm.

Using a Drill Press

You can also use a drill press, but its reduced rigidity and lower chuck mass create certain problems. These can be overcome by using a higher rpm, because less spindle thrust is needed to ensure the proper amount of frictional heat buildup. Although the rod-to-rod weld is easier on the lathe, the rod-to-plate weld works better on the drill press. Caution must be exercised when clamping the plate to the work table; and much better results can be

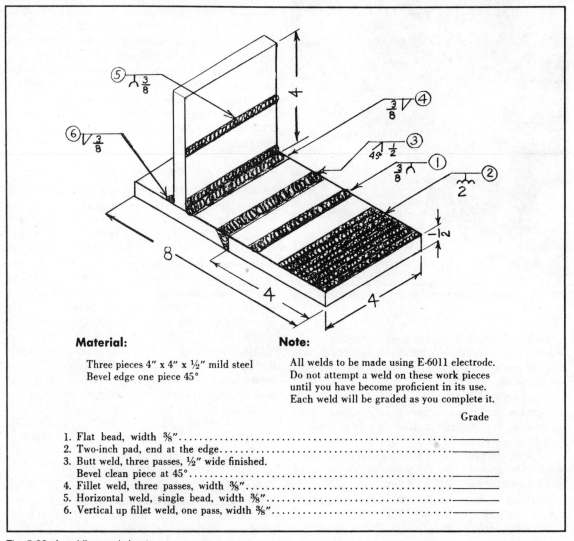

Material:

    Three pieces 4″ x 4″ x ½″ mild steel
    Bevel edge one piece 45°

Note:

All welds to be made using E-6011 electrode. Do not attempt a weld on these work pieces until you have become proficient in its use. Each weld will be graded as you complete it.

                                     Grade

1. Flat bead, width ⅜″.._____
2. Two-inch pad, end at the edge.._____
3. Butt weld, three passes, ½″ wide finished.
    Bevel clean piece at 45°.._____
4. Fillet weld, three passes, width ⅜″.._____
5. Horizontal weld, single bead, width ⅜″.._____
6. Vertical up fillet weld, one pass, width ⅜″.._____

Fig. 5-22. A welding worksheet.

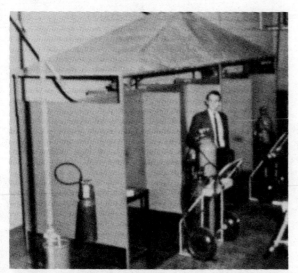

Fig. 5-23. Note the addition of galvanized steel hood over welding booths.

achieved with wood blocks placed between the plate and the work table, to minimize heat loss from interthermal conductivity between the work and the table.

In either the lathe or drill press operation, you will produce better welds when your setup is rigid and properly aligned. For instance, the shorter the piece extending from the chuck or tailstock, the less the vibration and the better the weld. Vibration is also decreased by applying a slight amount of pressure to the spindle locking lever or nut on the tailstock.

Weld Characteristics

Inertia welding produces a small heat-affected zone that can be seen easily with the naked eye. By grinding a flat across the weld, filing and polishing, and then applying an etchant of 2 percent nitric acid to 98 percent ethyl alcohol, the flow line pattern is revealed. These flow lines are both circumferential and radial, producing a very strong weld. Heat treatment is preserved and almost no distortion is produced.

Fluxes and filler materials are unnecessary because the bond is achieved while the metal is still in its solid state, thus eliminating gas absorption and cracking common to conventional welding. Dirt and oxide flow out into the outlining flash.

Dissimilar metals are easily welded with this process; but cast iron should be avoided because of its inherent brittleness and its excess carbon in the form of graphite, which acts as a lubricant and limits friction.

Testing for Weld Strength

Of the many metals you can try (Fig. 5-25), 1095 high-carbon steel, ⅜ of an inch in diameter, produced the best results. The weld achieved should always be stronger than the metal itself, as can be proven by a tensile-strength test.

With 1045, ⅜-inch diameter medium carbon steel and 1018, ¼-inch diameter low carbon steel, it will be a different story. Although the welds will withstand tensile pressures of the *minimum* amount stated by suppliers for that type of steel, failure will occur at the weld.

The weld point of 2024-T4, ⅜-inch diameter aluminum rod will withstand about 60 percent of the tensile strength of the metal itself. However, the 2000 series of aluminum is not noted for its weldability.

Copper rods of ½-inch diameter will not work well at all. This is due to the large diameter of the rod and the rapid heat transfer going on. Thus, because of the low rpm capability of the machine, it could not produce enough frictional heat to keep up with the thermal conductivity of copper.

When attempting to weld dissimilar metals, take care that the diameters of the metals are coordinated to develop equal heat buildup in both pieces at the same time. If not, the stock with the lower melting point will deform considerably, before both pieces are ready to be joined.

You can experiment with different joint designs. Although the most unstable, the butt joint (A of Fig. 5-26) is the most effective. Other designs, such as the concave-to-convex, produced more stability and less chatter; but the heat buildup was not equal throughout the joint because of the varying thicknesses of the metal (B of

Fig. 5-24. Completed weld spins to a stop. The joint is neat and strong, with no gas absorption or cracking.

Fig. 5-26). The thinner metal deteriorates before the rest of the weld area reaches its proper plastic state. A plug joint (C of Fig. 5-26) is effective for metals with varying melting points and conductivity factors. It should be noted, however, that the larger mass must be the metal with the lower melting point and higher thermal conductivity.

If you are looking for some uses for this technique, you might try welding extensions to screwdrivers or drill bits, joining sections of pipe, gears to rods, threaded bolts to rods, and studs to plates.

OXYACETYLENE WELDING AND FIRE

A metalworker lights an oxyacetylene torch, adjusts the mixture of acetylene and oxygen, and becomes the master, at least temporarily, of a 6,000° F flame. It is a wonderful tool. It can cut, weld, and melt most metals with ease. That same type of flame has also started some of the most spectacular and disastrous industrial and marine fires in recent history.

Yet, far too many metalworkers seem curiously unconcerned about the problem of fires. Possibly it is because the materials with which they work—metals—are not readily flammable, and this can lead to a false sense of security. However, there is no lack of either good fuels or sources of ignition in the welding area of a metalworking laboratory.

It is felt that no safety program for an instructional area is complete unless full attention is given to fire prevention and control in that area. A positive approach must include identification of the hazards and reduction of them to the greatest extent possible. The most effective time to fight a fire is before it starts, for then it can be done calmly and objectively. Fires do start, however,

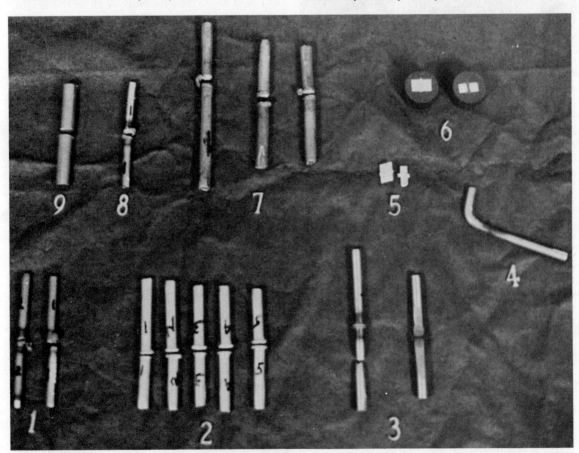

Fig. 5-25. Tensile strength test: 1. Medium carbon steel, 2. Aluminum, 3. High carbon steel, 4. High carbon steel bend test, 5. High carbon steel cut and etched, 6. High carbon steel mounted on Bakelite for microscopic inspection, 7. Low carbon steel, 8. High carbon and low carbon steel, 9. Copper.

1. Medium carbon steel
2. Aluminum
3. High carbon steel
4. High carbon steel bend test
5. High carbon steel cut and etched
6. High carbon steel mounted on Bakelite for microscopic inspection
7. Low carbon steel
8. High carbon and low carbon steel
9. Copper

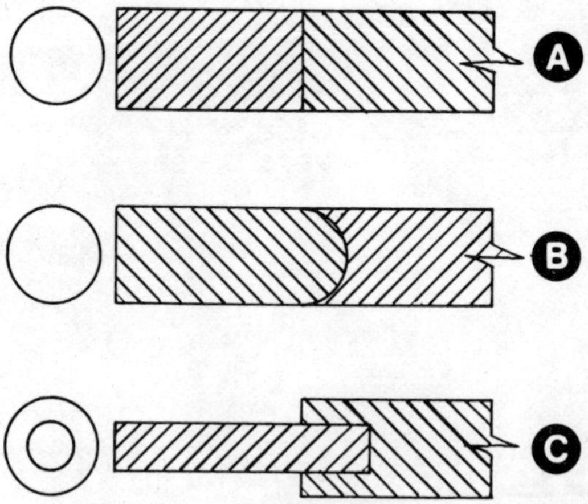

Fig. 5-26. Applicable welding joints: Butt weld (A), Concave to convex (B), Plug weld (C).

regardless of the best laid plans of men, so the means and techniques of fire control cannot be ignored in either safety instruction or facilities design.

Welding and flame-cutting operations have been a prime cause of metals-area fires. The 6,000°F temperature oxyacetylene flame is capable of bringing a wide range of materials to the kindling point almost instantly. Wood, leather, rubber, most plastics, natural and synthetic fabrics, paints, oils and greases, solvents, and some metals, in finely divided form, which may be set afire by this tool.

Another aspect of the hazard is that the gases used are under pressure and that damage to the tank, regulators, hoses, or the tank safety devices will release the gases, thus setting the stage for a violent fire or for feeding an existing blaze.

You must look at all three aspects of the problem:

☐ the design and condition of the physical facilities for welding and cutting.

☐ the fire-protection and fire-fighting devices.

☐ safety instruction.

Nonflammable welding benches and wall sheathing, manifolded multistation welding areas must be fitted with safety equipment other than that found on the tanks. This includes a flashback arrestor and relief valves vented to the outside for the acetylene circuit, as shown in Figs. 5-27 and 5-28 as well as rupture disks on the oxygen regulator at each station.

The flame-cutting torch operates at the same heat and presents the additional hazard of ejecting a stream of red-hot slag globules while operating. Another factor is that the equipment is portable and it might be used in close proximity to flammable substances during dismantling or repair operations.

Inasmuch as flame-cutting operations are a major hazard, the design and construction of a cutting table that will minimize the danger, without restricting cutting operations, is a major step in making this area safer. The table shown in Fig. 5-29 has been developed and used in the metals laboratories at California State College, Long Beach, and in this state it meets the conditions set forth above. In addition, it is easy to maintain and clean and actually facilitates the maintenance of the surrounding area.

It becomes evident that equipment selection, design, and installation are potent factors in developing an oxyacetylene welding and cutting area that is as immune to fires as possible. Proper performance of the functions slated here requires a fairly detailed knowledge of welding equipment.

While this section has emphasized the role of the physical setting and equipment construction and selection in fire prevention, the role of safety instruction and enforcement of regulations is not minimized. None of the classic three E's of safety—engineering, education, and enforcement—can be neglected. Nevertheless, due to the nature of the processes involved, the engineering aspect seems to provide a most fruitful pathway to follow.

ELECTRICAL TUBING FOR WELDING PROJECTS

Thin-wall electrical tubing is inexpensive, lightweight, easy to bend and braze, and will open up a whole new area of design for interesting projects.

There are several good ways of bending this tubing. A commercial bender and standard thin-wall electrical bender are shown in Fig. 5-30. A radius as small as 3

Fig. 5-27. The flashback arrester (arrow A), two pressure relief valves (arrows B and C), and two pipes (arrow D) venting the acetylene circuit to the outside air. Note the use of tank safety chains and coils in the tubing to minimize crack tendencies.

Fig. 5-28. The large pressure relief valve (left) for the acetylene system near the ceiling is at the end of the acetylene manifold opposite the tank. This allows a massive escape of gasses in case of fire in the acetylene manifold and prevents pressure build-up to the dangerous levels.

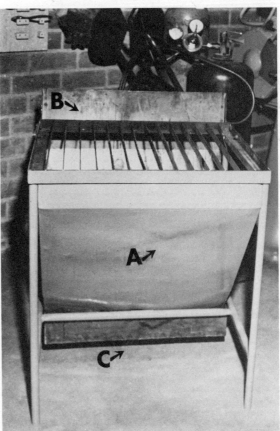

Fig. 5-29. This oxyacetylene cutting table (right) was designed and built in the metals laboratories at California State College at Long Beach. The front deflector pan (arrow A) protects the operator. The rear deflector (arrow B) protects the surrounding area. The catch pan (arrow C) is easily removable for cleaning.

inches can be obtained easily with such a bender. If the tubing tends to buckle on the smaller bends, try packing it with dry sand before the start of the bend. A larger radius is made more easily with the conduit bender. The ½-inch thin-wall tubing is practical for most projects and the ¾-inch thick-wall tubing is used when more rigidity is required.

When tubing intersects at angles, the ends can be concaved on a grinder in a matter of seconds. This provides for a good fit. Once the area to be brazed is cleaned with emery cloth, it is ready for brazing. Any standard-brand brazing rod works well.

Other special brazing rods will cost a little more, but usually result in an excellent job. Many of the special rods are free-flowing rods and a small amount goes a long way. 3/32″ rod or even a 1/16″ rod is recommended for this type of work.

As well as being exceptionally strong (in short lengths), inexpensive for projects, and easy to work with, there is practically no end to the applications you will find for this tubing as a metalworking material. Only a partial listing includes desk frames, bar stool frames, a child's table and chairs, many styles of room dividers, a basketball rack, and a mini-bike frame. You will surely find a multitude of uses for this material. See Figs. 5-31 and 5-32.

Fig. 5-30. A commercial bender and standard thin-wall electrical bender open new avenues to metalworking design.

Fig. 5-31. The tubing used in this mini-bike frame was welded by Mig process. Other uses include furniture and room dividers.

BUILD A WELDING TABLE

Purchasing new arc-welding tables means a considerable dent in your budget. You can build your own. Here's the procedure.

Use a grill top rather than the costlier conventional solid steel, which has a tendency to warp. The grill alsc makes it easier to catch and contain the inevitable buildup of weld deposits and spatter. Make the grill from ¼- × -1¼ inch flats fitted into slots that allow the pieces to be easily turned over or replaced when the need arises. This top design also encourages you to strike the arc on the work instead of on the table top. You can place scrap sheet or plate on top of the grill if needed.

Place the sheet-metal tray underneath the top. This serves a dual purpose: it shields your legs, and, in sloping to a rear opening of 8 inches, it allows dross and electrode stubs to funnel into a 5-gallon pail. The triangulated tray should be pop riveted into place and then painted to help prevent anyone from inadvertently striking an arc on it. The tray helps immensely in keeping the shop clean.

Make the glare shields from ¼-inch tempered hardboard. Sheet-metal angles should be made and then pop riveted at intersecting corners to prevent glare leakage. Bolt the shields to the table using 3/16-×-¾ inch flat head machine screws and finishing washers. The advantage of the hardboard are that it costs less than steel.

Finally, make an electrode storage holder from 1-inch square tubing with a grounding lug on the bottom, and tack it on the left front side of the table. See Figs. 5-33, 5-34 and 5-35.

BUILD A WELDING CART

Gas welding tanks are cumbersome. When you combine them with the usual small wheel dolly, that's a mighty heavy proposition to lug. To design a mobile, heavy-duty welding cart to fit medium-sized (about 122 cubic feet) tanks is an excellent exercise in metal fabrication, bending, forming, and welding. See Figs. 5-36 through 5-39.

Cart Construction. The main construction evolves around the fabrication of ⅛-inch steel plates. Start by cutting a plate a little wider than your two tanks side by side. Lay out all construction lines with welding crayon. Then, using a straight edge, cut all parts and grind edges of welding slag. Fabricate all steel parts taking care to line parts squarely, and avoid buckling by using proper welding techniques.

Before plates are welded, drill holes to accommodate wheel axles. You can use two heavy-duty 10-inch ball bearing rear wheels and a heavy-duty caster fitted with a brake up front.

Add a metal strip to the back of the frame to support the tanks. We attached a chain with a quick release connector to the backing strap to hold the tanks securely.

The Handle and Supports. Mark and bend 1-inch black iron pipe. The ends of the pipe should be fitted as close as possible to the pipe's mating parts and welded to the base and each other. Drill cotter pin holes in the outer part of the axle shaft, and add two pipe spaces for the wheels.

Storage Attachments. You can make a sheet-metal carry-all box and fit it to two hose brackets welded to the pipe frame. Welding rods can be stored neatly by welding short lengths of thin-walled tubing to the inside of the frame. Welding tips can be stored also by bolting a piece of angle iron—drilled to accommodate tips—to the sheet-metal box.

Fig. 5-32. Electrical tubing, inexpensive and easy to work with, can be used in dozens of projects. This basketball rack illustrates but one way to use the tubing as project material.

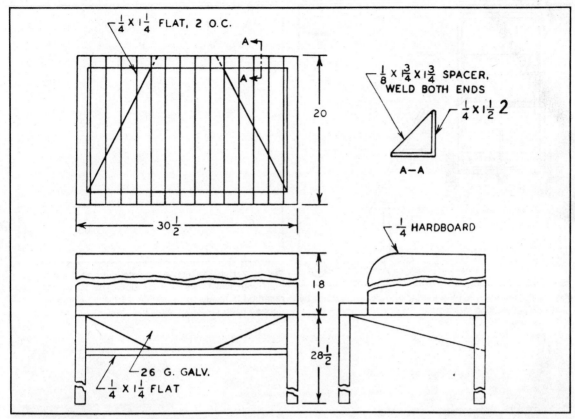

$\frac{1}{4} \times 1\frac{1}{4}$ FLAT, 2 O.C.

$\frac{1}{8} \times 1\frac{3}{4} \times 1\frac{3}{4}$ SPACER, WELD BOTH ENDS

$\frac{1}{4} \times 1\frac{1}{2}$ 2

A—A

20

$30\frac{1}{2}$

$\frac{1}{4}$ HARDBOARD

18

$28\frac{1}{2}$

26 G. GALV.

$\frac{1}{4} \times 1\frac{1}{4}$ FLAT

Fig. 5-33. Diagram of arc welding table.

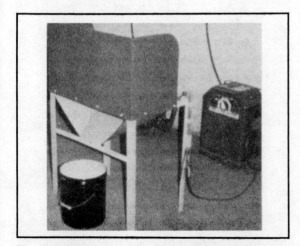

Fig. 5-34. Advantages of this table design are that the grill, left, encourages striking the arc on the work instead of on the top.

Fig. 5-35. A sheet-metal tray slopes to the rear, allowing dross and electrode stubs to funnel into a pail.

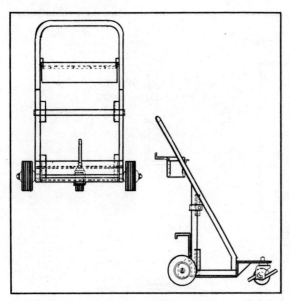

Fig. 5-36. Line steel parts squarely and avoid buckling by using proper welding techniques.

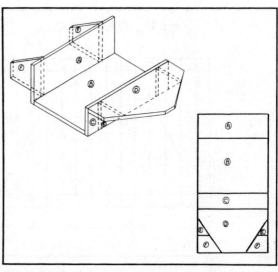

Fig. 5-37. Using ⅛-inch steel plate, cut part B a little wider than your two tanks side by side. The proportions represented here are for a *sample* cart only. Dimensions will depend upon your own particular needs.

Fig. 5-38. The rear view shows the carry-all box. It is fitted to the hose brackets and welded to the pipe frame.

Fig. 5-39. Tanks are held securely in the cart by a chain and backing strap. The low center of gravity and use of caster and ball bearing wheels make the cart stable and easy to maneuver.

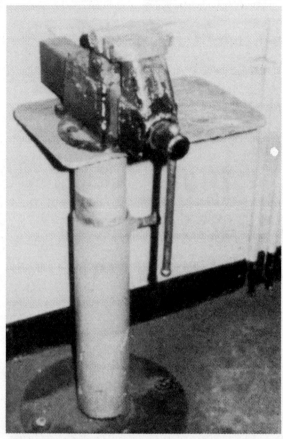

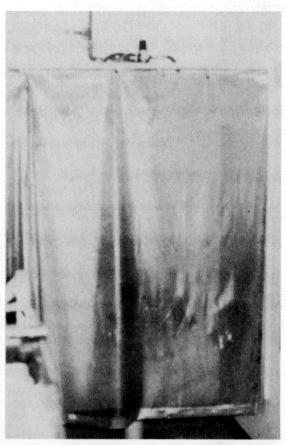

Fig. 5-40. The vise is mounted on an adjustable stand topped with a ½-inch steel plate grinding table.

Fig. 5-41. This grinding booth features an amber plastic curtain to allow light to enter.

The cart offers good stability because it has a low center of gravity, yet at the same time it is easily tilted back and transported over rough ground.

A GRINDING BOOTH FOR WELDING LAB SAFETY

Hand-held grinders can throw sparks many feet in any direction, creating a safety hazard to others as well as the operator. Even an experienced operator can be so engrossed in his work that he does not notice in which direction sparks are flying. To reduce the hazard, you can build grinding booths.

The booths can be used in the preparation of welding samples for the guided bend method of testing welds, and for many small grinding jobs.

Booths should be at least 4×4 feet, with walls of noncombustible materials—sheet metal works well—and about 6 feet high. Amber plastic welding curtains

provide a good entryway and allow light to enter the booth. See Figs. 5-40 and 5-41.

Direct overhead lighting is most desirable, and air or electric receptacles should be placed for easy use. Position eye and ear protection equipment in the most visible location.

Provide a vise to hold the work. Vises can be mounted on adjustable—or nonadjustable—stands, topped with a 12-×-15 inch grinding table made of ½-inch plate. A good working height for the top of the vise is 34 inches. Two pipes that telescope together, each 15 inches long, can be used for the upright leg. The base is made from ½-inch plate, 15 inches in diameter. A ¾-inch nut and bolt provides the tightening device for the telescoping pipes. Mount the vise to the left side of the grinding table. Provide copper or aluminum covers for the vise jaws. Mount the stand to the floor with four ½-inch anchor bolts.

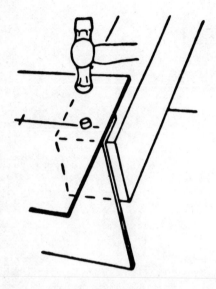

Chapter 6
Dies,
Patterns,
and Castings

MANY METALWORKERS WHO HAVE ADVANCED to die designing have little knowledge of the theory, construction, and operation of a die. Their main sources of information have been what has been written in drafting texts. References, which include die design, often cover the broad field of die operations in many different industries. This results in the information not being directly applicable.

The purpose of the learning aid, shown in Fig. 6-1, is to identify and describe the fundamental principles of dies used in industry so that you will have a basic understanding of die terminology and die operation. Furthermore, because this aid is made from transparent plastic, you can actually see the die do its work.

This aid was designed to:

☐ develop an understanding of the theory and operation of a die.

☐ provide an opportunity for you to familiarize yourself with principles of die construction in a technological society.

☐ foster appreciation of good workmanship and good design in industrial tools.

☐ develop those reasoning powers needed to visualize intricate processes one cannot see.

☐ promote wholesome work attitudes that lead to safe work practices and a systematic approach to complex design problems.

This lightweight scale model is made from clear plastic and tool steel so that it can be moved easily from one situation to another. It is constructed according to standard practices in industry and incorporates three basic principles of die theory: pierce, cut-off, and form. See Figs. 6-1 through 6-8.

Its features are:

☐ it functions like an industrial die.

☐ a section view through the center of the die can be had by unscrewing four brass knobs and removing the front portion (Section A-A of Fig. 6-7).

☐ you can be involved in its operation by using a thin strip of aluminum or heavy paper (to simulate stock) and feed and cycle the die through its basic operation.

The following procedure is recommended for those who want to make this aid. Purchase the stock, as per stock list. To reduce the cost of the plastic, and if you have your own sawing facilities, combine all of the different thicknesses into the least number of pieces. This will save you the cutting charges. Machine, drill and

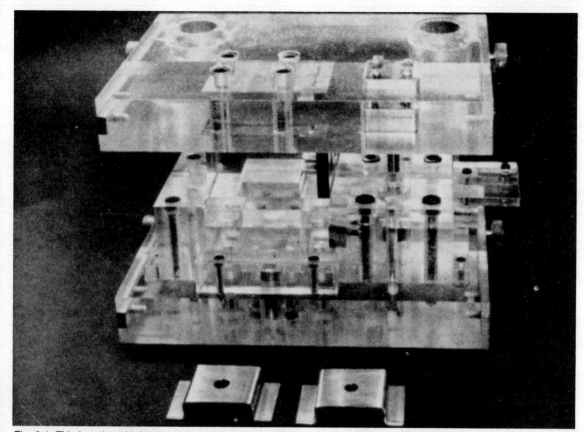

Fig. 6-1. This learning aid demonstrates the piercing, cutting off, and forming process of materials.

counter-bore, and grind all the plastic as indicated on the drawings. Machine, drill and counter-bore, and harden and grind details 9 and 10.

Purchase two pierce buttons (detail 12) and grind or rubber wheel in half so that each button will produce one true half. Purchase two ball lock retainers (detail 14) and repeat as per instructions for the pierce buttons. *Caution:* Remove the ball and spring before cutting in half, and be sure that you cut through the ball seat of the retainer as shown in Section A-A.

Glue the punch (detail 13) and the ball and spring from the retainer (detail 14) in the rear part of the retainer (Section A-A). Screw the tool-steel, cut-off blades (detail 9) to the plastic (detail 8) and cut-off inserts (detail 10) to detail 15.

Lay out and mill the pockets in the punch and the die holders (details 1 and 2) for: (*a*) ½-×-½ inch pocket for keys (detail 3) in the die holder; (*b*) ½-inch deep × 1¾-inch square pocket for the punch retainer (detail 14)

in the punch holder; (*c*) ¼-×-½-inch slots for the tie bars (detail 16) in the punch and die holder.

Drill and counterbore the tie bars (detail 16) and insert them into details 1 and 2. Bore the punch and die holder (details 1 and 2) for the guide pins and bushing (details 21 and 22). See Section B-B of Fig. 6-7. Assem-

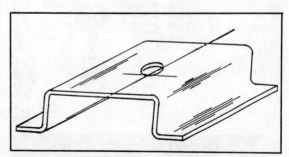

Fig. 6-2. The type of work piece turned out by this learning aid.

111

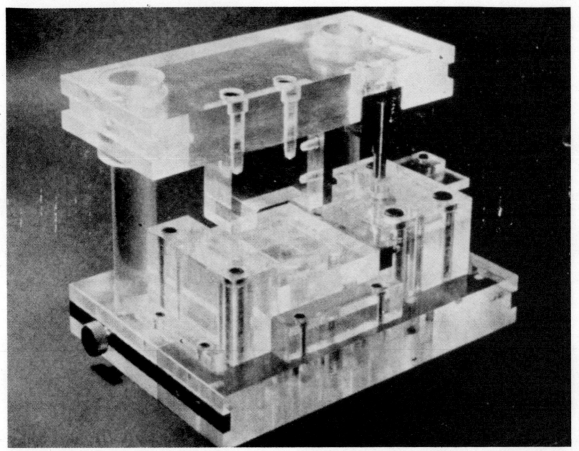

Fig. 6-3. A model of the teaching aid with the front half of the top removed for easier identification of the parts.

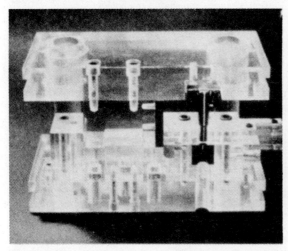

Fig. 6-4. The teaching aid with all of the front half removed.

Fig. 6-5. This is the bottom part of the teaching aid.

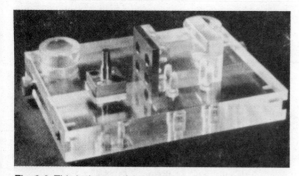

Fig. 6-6. This is the top of the teaching aid. It should be noted that the picture here is inverted.

ble, screw, and dowel all of the details on the die shoe. (See "Plan of Die.") Bore a 7/16-inch diameter hole into the stripper (detail 11) going through the button retainer (detail 15) and the die holder.

Remove the stripper (detail 11) and open the hole to .9375 of a inch in diameter by 15/16 of an inch deep in the button retainer (detail 15) for the die button (detail 12).

Install the die button (detail 12). Assemble, line up, and screw and dowel all of the details on the punch holder (see "Plan of Punch"). (*Note:* The punch holder must be placed on the guide pins of the die holder and made parallel for accurate lining up.)

Assemble the stripper (detail 11).

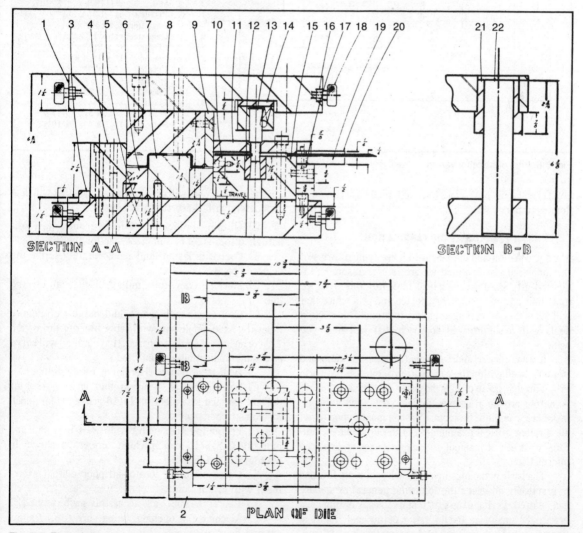

Fig. 6-7. Plan of die.

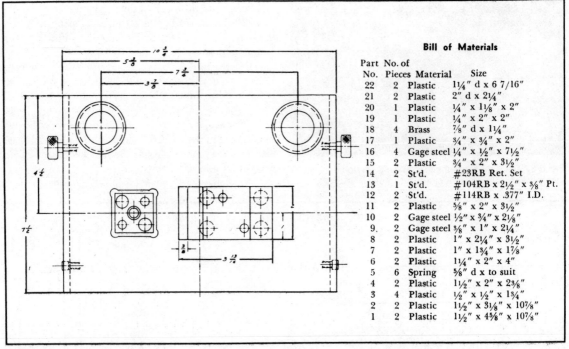

Bill of Materials

Part No.	No. of Pieces	Material	Size
22	2	Plastic	1¼" d x 6 7/16"
21	2	Plastic	2" d x 2¼"
20	1	Plastic	¼" x 1⅛" x 2"
19	1	Plastic	¼" x 2" x 2"
18	4	Brass	⅞" d x 1¼"
17	1	Plastic	¾" x ¾" x 2"
16	4	Gage steel	¼" x ½" x 7½"
15	2	Plastic	¾" x 2" x 3½"
14	2	St'd.	#23RB Ret. Set
13	1	St'd.	#104RB x 2½" x ⅜" Pt.
12	2	St'd.	#114RB x .377" I.D.
11	2	Plastic	⅝" x 2" x 3½"
10	2	Gage steel	½" x ¾" x 2⅛"
9	2	Gage steel	⅜" x 1" x 2¼"
8	2	Plastic	1" x 2¼" x 3½"
7	2	Plastic	1" x 1¾" x 1⅞"
6	2	Plastic	1¼" x 2" x 4"
5	6	Spring	⅝" d x to suit
4	2	Plastic	1½" x 2" x 2⅜"
3	4	Plastic	½" x ½" x 1¾"
2	2	Plastic	1½" x 3⅛" x 10⅞"
1	2	Plastic	1½" x 4⅝" x 10⅞"

Fig. 6-8. Plan of punch inverted.

The die is now complete and ready to use in a demonstration.

TEMPORARY DIE FABRICATION

Mass production and die fabrication are typical terms of the industrial age in which we are living. Assuming industrial arts should reflect and interpret this age, we must take advantage of every device and procedure that will aid in this reflection and interpretation. This section deals with a shop-tested approach that will help you achieve this objective.

A temporary or short-run die (500 to a few thousand items) is well within the capabilities of most metalworkers. Through its use, it is possible to "mass produce" numerous art-metal shapes, project parts, and, in some instances, complete projects. Perhaps most important of all, a rather critical examination of the procedures indicates a wealth of manipulative experiences and related information.

The basic principles involved are relatively few and in practically all cases the following general procedure can be used. Perhaps the greatest handicaps of this project are the small size and limitation of intricacy. Fabrication of a simple shape first, and the application of "common sense" second, will provide experience that will deal adequately with these two problems.

☐ Obtain a piece of ⅜-inch ground-flat, oil-hardened tool steel of sufficient size for the punch.

☐ Coat with layout fluid and accurately scribe the desired shape.

☐ Machine (saw, turn, mill, drill, file, etc.) to the line.

☐ Coat edges with layout fluid and file a 5-degree taper (by hand, on jig saw with sabre file, etc.) to within 1/64 of an inch of scribed surface. (Layout fluid will serve as a guide indicating amount filed.)

☐ Heat treat punch. (Harden and draw temper.)

☐ Select piece of ¼-inch ground flat tool steel for die and a similar size piece of No. 16-gauge crs for punch locator-stripper plate.

☐ Fasten together with two ⅛-x-⅜-inch pins and four 10/32-x-5/16-inch machine screws as shown in photograph and drawing.

☐ Coat surface of locator-stripper plate (assembled) with layout fluid.

☐ Center the punch and accurately scribe around it.

☐ Machine the opening, being sure to *just* allow scribed lines to *remain*.

☐ Disassemble; coat inside edge surface of die with layout fluid and file ½ degree to 1 degree taper to within 1/64 of an inch of top surface. Use layout fluid to guide amount of filing.

☐ Make sure punch will pass through die. (.001-.002 clearance).

☐ Heat treat die.

☐ Surface grind or hone *cutting surfaces* of both punch and die.

☐ Cut and drill stock guides (1/32″ thicker than stock to be punched).

☐ Assemble.

☐ Test in arbor press or large vise. See Figs. 6-9 through 6-11.

THIS DIE IS A SNAP!

If you believe that die making is too expensive, takes too much time, requires equipment you don't have—in short, is impossible: don't you believe it! You can make blanking and embossing dies out of heavy-gauge sheet metal using only a jewelers saw, a soldering torch, and a vise. These are snap dies.

The beginner often has difficulty getting a close fit between the female and male components of a die. The snap die gives you the chance for early success because when the male section is cut out, the remaining section is actually the female part of the die. The method also lets you try your own designs and has the additional benefit of moving you from a jewelry/fine-arts frame of reference to an industrial one.

Cut two pieces of 16- or 18-gauge sheet metal about 2½ × 10 inches. On one piece, draw the shape you want to emboss or blank (A of Fig. 6-12). Drill a 1/32-inch hole off the design to allow the jewelers blade to be inserted (B of Fig. 6-12). Use a 4/0 or 6/0 blade to cut the design (C of Fig. 6-12). Saw the line. Remember, you can't make a double pass. Remove the shape (D of Fig. 6-12), and rivet the ends of the two pieces of sheet metal as in E of Fig. 6-12. Tin the back of the cutout with solder and put it back in the hole it was cut from. Make sure the clearance is the same all around the cutout. Clamp in place and sweat solder the cutout to the second piece of steel (Fig. 6-13). The die is now ready for use.

Insert the metal to be embossed between the leaves of the die and apply pressure in a vise. A few tries will let you feel the pressure needed for a professional-looking embossing job.

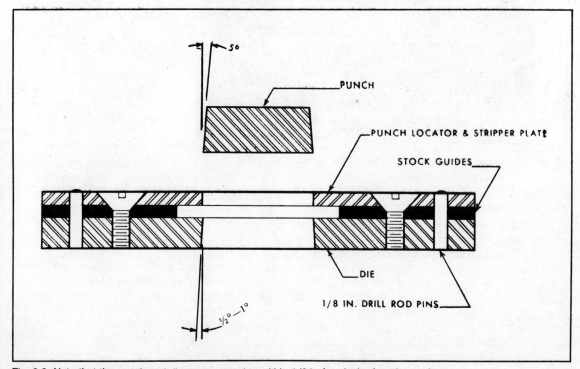

Fig. 6-9. Note that the punch and die taper extend to within 1/64 of an inch of mating surfaces.

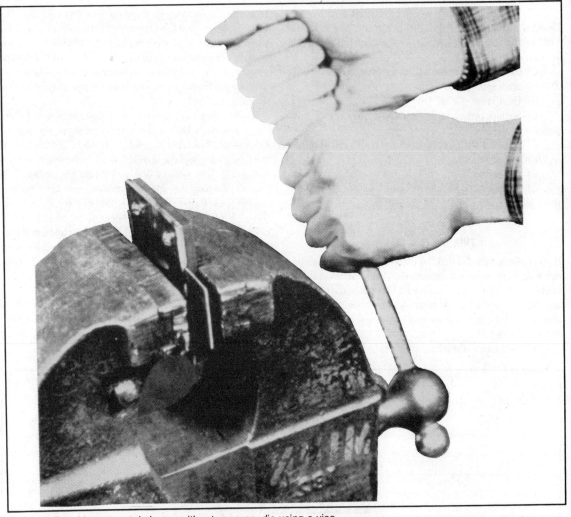

Fig. 6-10. Punching art-metal shapes with a temporary die using a vise.

If the die is made from 18-gauge material, it will emboss IC tinplate and cut thin aluminum flashing.

☐ Using a template, trace the design on the metal.
☐ Emboss the design with the snap die.
☐ Scribe the hems with a metal-marking gauge.
☐ Bend the hems in a brake or bar folder.
☐ Bend the sides up.
☐ Press a mask for the embossed design out of oaktag, using the snap die (die will emboss IC tinplate and cut oaktag).
☐ Spray paint the design and let dry.
☐ Cover the design with the oaktag mask, using rubber cement.

☐ Spray paint the rest of the napkin holder and let dry.
☐ Remove the mask and the product is complete.

BUILD A DIE HOLDER

Have you ever had to chase threads in hard-to-reach locations, such as on exhaust manifold studs? This die holder will make that job easier. Although there are hex-squared dies made especially for chasing or renewing damaged threads, you might not have such equipment. In that event, the die holder will be a handy tool-box accessory.

The holder can be used with standard 1-inch diame-

Fig. 6-11. The temporary die, scrap, and finished shapes.

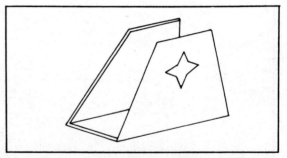

Fig. 6-13. Here's a simple napkin holder that you can mass produce using the snap die.

ter dies. it is machined from mild steel and features a ½-inch square broached hole, on the end opposite the die, for a ½-inch drive ratchet. If a square broach is not readily available, weld an old ½-inch socket with an outside diameter of 15/16 of an inch to the stock; machine finish for a smooth surface. See Figs. 6-14 and 6-15.

If thread damage is not severe, the ratchet might not be needed, and threads can be renewed by turning the die holder by hand.

FORMING METAL WITH A HARDBOARD DIE

The use of hardboard nonconforming dies to form metal is well worth exploring by metal craftsmen. The use of hardboard dies provides an interesting exercise with materials of modern technology applied to an ancient craft. And the hardboard dies provide a fast and economical means of forming metal. A variety of complex curves and forms that are difficult, time-consuming, and expensive to achieve are easily achieved with hardboard dies. The method also offers a means of achieving desirable esthetic effects, which are indicative of the craftsman's

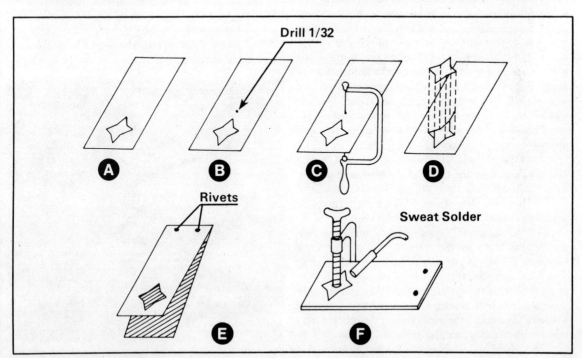

Fig. 6-12. Die design details.

117

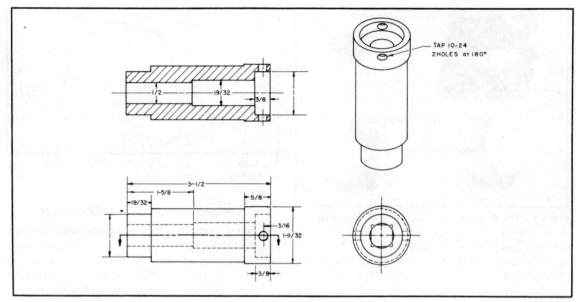

Fig. 6-14. Die holder construction dimensions.

methods of using the process and materials to best advantage.

The following will trace the development of a simple hardboard die that was used to make a sterling silver paten. See the chalice and paten in Fig. 6-16. The first step was to measure the diameter of the cup on the chalice and determine that the depression in the paten would measure 4½ inches in diameter by ½-inch deep. A simple die was then made by gluing together two 8-inch squares of ¼-inch tempered hardboard ¼-inch thick. It was necessary to use tempered hardboard because the untempered material will break down under repeated hammer blows. See Figs. 6-17 and 6-18.

After the glue dried, the band saw was used to cut a 4½-inch circle from the center of the hardboard square. The hardboard was then drilled, countersunk, and screwed to a back plate of pine. This completed preparation of this simple die. It was ready to use.

A 7-inch square of 18-gauge sterling silver was then clamped to the die and the assembly was placed over a spreading T-stake in preparation for the initial sinking.

A 2½-inch diameter round stake was selected as the positive element to dap the metal into the depression. In this case, the entire sinking was done without annealing the metal. Thus, after the initial sinking the relative form was complete except for planishing and finishing.

The advantages of using the hardboard die in this instance included:

□ having dimensional stability as opposed to the instability of the sand bag, maple block, or stake methods.

□ increased speed in manufacturing and using the die.

□ low cost for the die.

□ simplicity of operation for a small budget shop, as opposed to spinning.

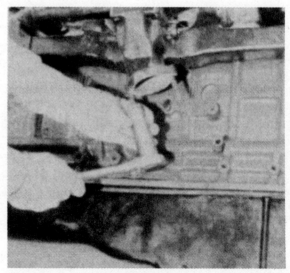

Fig. 6-15. Renewing threads becomes an easy job with this die holder.

118

Fig. 6-16. Sterling silver chalice and paten made during experiment with forming metal with hardboard dies.

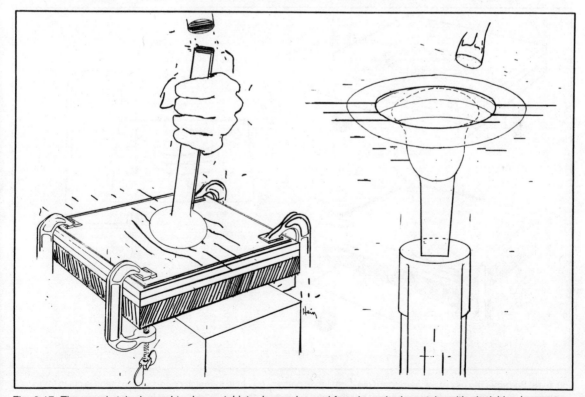

Fig. 6-17. The round stake is used to dap metal into depression and form is worked on stake with plenishing hammer.

The same advantages hold for more complex forms. One of the prime characteristics of the depressed metal form is the flange, or the flat area of metal horizontal to the top surface of the die. This flange can either be utilized as an integral part of the design, or it can be completely removed in an object where a butt soldering joint is needed.

The hardboard-die method can also be used to form such items as a set of salt and pepper shakers. This applies the method to multiple production of parts, flange joining as an integral part of the design, and addition of casting to the project, as the bottoms are cast and added.

In designing salt and pepper shakers, an oval form is preferred as opposed to a round one. The outline of the form must be determined and cut out of ½-inch glued, tempered hardboard, as in the case of the die for the paten. Following this, 18-gauge sterling is clamped to the die and by using sized dapping punches the basic outline of the form can be achieved.

Because the dapping process is worked partially on the blind, it is strongly advisable to select dapping punches that conform closely to the opening in the die

before clamping. One of the hazards of dapping with a punch that is a little too large is the breaking down of the sharp corners of the die. In most instances, this is not desirable. The die used for multiple production of parts will break down much faster than the single or opposed side die.

After annealing, the salt and pepper shakers are once more clamped on the die, and the final sinking course is completed. The two halves are cleaned, fluxed, wired together, and soldered. The bottoms of the pieces can be cast from a sheet of 16-gauge wax. These objects represent a combination of sinking and casting.

The cordial cups shown in Fig. 6-19 were selected as a project to test the hardboard dies in shaping a more difficult form. The elliptical form is an excellent example of the advantages of using this method. The materials and time spent making the dies were much less than if the cups were formed by casting. The cups were made from 18-gauge sterling, the transition pieces cast, and the bases turned on the lathe from black nylon.

The few examples used are the results of one year's experimentation with hardboard dies as a means of man-

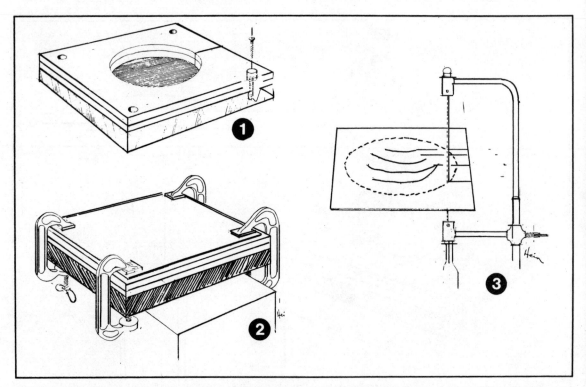

Fig. 6-18. Step-by-step use of the hardboard die. Left, top to bottom, (1) circle to match depression in metal is cut in tempered hardboard; (2) sterling silver is clamped over hardboard die which is backed (3) form is cut from work piece, with ½'' pine.

Fig. 6-19. Elliptical forms of cordial cups were shaped with hardboard dies. The dies work well to produce multiple identical shapes, which would probably have to be cast if this or a similar method was not available. Use of the hardboard dies saved considerable time in this instance.

ipulating sheet metal. The metalsmith, to be able to represent his ideas concretely, must continually search for new apparatus which will accelerate his productivity, thus helping him survive in a technically oriented society. The hardboard-die method successfully lends itself to the development of complex curved forms and shapes that are not easily duplicated by any other means.

PRODUCTION MOLDING PATTERNS

One of the finest metalworking activities is developing and building machine projects that are comparable in size and quality to similar products made in industry. Admittedly, these "live" projects demand a great deal of effort, but the results are well worth any amount of effort.

Such a program has, of course, its inception in the drafting room. From that point it becomes a pattern-shop problem.

It is the purpose of this section, to discuss some of the procedures that have solved, after many years of use, the problem of providing, at a reasonable cost, a considerable number of metal castings necessary to supply a machine-shop with raw material.

Many metalworkers think only in terms of the traditional pattern materials—white pine and Honduras mahogany—for building molding patterns. They think, too, of patterns in the sense of the single-unit pattern that makes one casting to a mold. This is all well and good when only a few castings are required. If an ambitious production program is planned, however, it will require a

continuing supply of castings over a long period of time. This requires you to regard patterns the same way industry does. The single-unit wood pattern still has its use as a master pattern and for use in making larger castings. For small-sized and medium-sized work, though, the single-unit pattern has given way to various types of multiple patterns made of metal and arranged to be used in molding machines. This practice is almost as important in the shop as it is in industry.

Like other industrial operations, costs are billed largely on the amount of labor involved in making the molds. Raw materials and the melt of the metal are only minor parts of the total price of small-sized castings. All of this means that hand molding, and molding of single-unit patterns, is apt to make the cost of your castings—unless you are fortunate enough to have your own foundry—prohibitive.

Wood patterns will, after long use, deteriorate and require periodic rebuilding, refinishing, or replacement.

Besides paying for themselves over and over again because of faster production of molds and negligible maintenance, metal patterns, particularly those mounted on plates or otherwise designed to fit molding machines, have several other advantages worth considering seriously. They will produce castings with higher surface quality with sharper defined detail. Machine-molding methods always produce castings of greater uniformity due to more precise control of mold ramming. Fragile, thin-walled patterns will, if made of wood, inevitably be

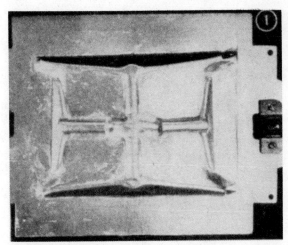

Fig. 6-20. Tool rests.

broken or damaged badly in the "rough and tumble" of a production foundry. An example of patterns of this type are the tool rests in Figs. 6-20 and 6-21.

Although carefully made of laminated mahogany, these patterns can be badly battered and broken after constant use. After being rebuilt and refinished several times, they are finally cast integrally into an aluminum match-plate type of pattern. No further damage or wear is anticipated even from the roughest sort of use in the foundry. Had this been done in the beginning much time and effort would have been saved, to say nothing of the lower cost that results from machine molding the match plate.

There are three methods used commonly in industry for making production molding patterns. All of these are adaptable to machine molding and all may be, and, indeed, have been, made in shops.

The Mounted Pattern. One or more patterns are mounted on a metal plate. The plate is usually equipped with guides called "match-plate lugs" that fit the guide pins of the molding flask. Patterns mounted on these plates (they are usually made of aluminum) will almost always be joined by permanent gates and runners so that the molder is not required to use costly time to cut these into the mold by hand.

Gated Patterns. Two or more metal patterns, not necessarily from the same casting, are joined together with permanent metal gates and runners, but not mounted on a plate. This process is particularly adaptable to un-parted, one-piece patterns that are not of the flat back type, or are not split in two halves and which often have an irregular part line between the drag and cope halves of the pattern. Gated patterns are usually bedded down for molding the drag (first operation) in a sand or plaster "match" that has been cast to fit up to the irregular part line on the cope side of the pattern. An example of a pattern and match of this sort is seen in Fig. 6-22. When the drag side of the mold has been rammed, the match remains behind and the mold is turned over for the ramming of the cope.

The Match Plate. This production pattern consists of one or more master patterns molded integrally with the pattern plate rather than being secured to it with screws, as are the mounted patterns. The match plate is poured with gates and runners cast in place to join the battery of patterns. Cast-metal match plates can be the most dif-ficult of the three types to construct in the shop, and it is necessary to have molding facilities and aluminum melt-

Fig. 6-21. Tool rests.

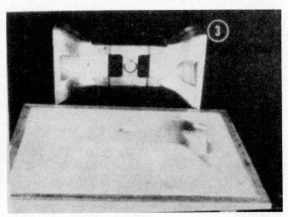

Fig. 6-22. A pattern and match.

Fig. 6-23. The woodworking lathe.

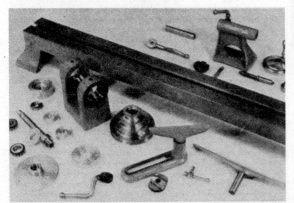

Fig. 6-24. The components of the lathe. The lathe bed is of rolled-steel angles that are secured to cast-aluminum legs.

Fig. 6-25. Four aluminum face-plate patterns mounted on an aluminum plate (drag side) for machine molding.

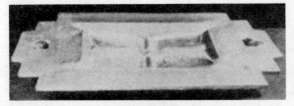

Fig. 6-26. The cope side of the tool-rest match plate.

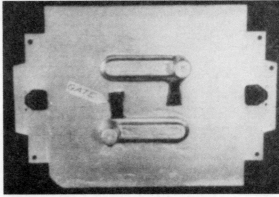

Fig. 6-27. A cast aluminum match plate for a pair of tool-rest sides.

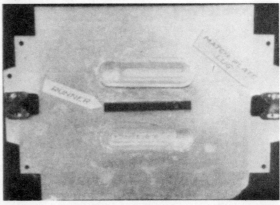

Fig. 6-28. The cope side of the cast aluminum match plate for the tool-rest slides. Note the runner that connects the two gates in the drag side.

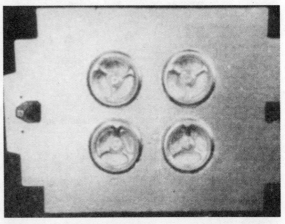

Fig. 6-29. The cope side of a handwheel matching plate.

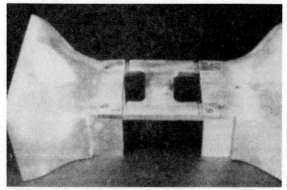

Fig. 6-30. Two aluminum patterns for lathe legs secured to the pattern by machine screws.

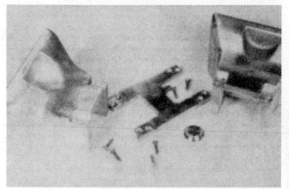

Fig. 6-31. Components of the gated pattern for the lathe legs.

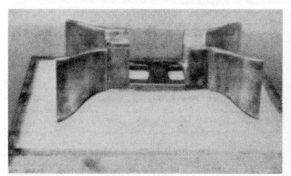

Fig. 6-32. The gated pattern for the lathe legs is set up and ready for molding.

Fig. 6-33. A pair of casting for lathe legs made from the gated pattern, still joined by gates, runners, and the sprue.

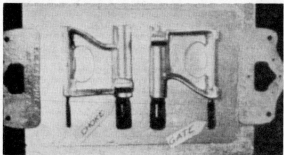

Fig. 6-34. The cope side of the mounted pattern for the tailstock of the lathe.

Fig. 6-35. The drag side of the tailstock of the pattern. Note how gates are narrowed down where they attach to patterns.

ing equipment to make them. The techniques can, however, be learned from several texts on pattern making, and, because they are one solid piece, they are extremely durable. Figures 6-19 and 6-20 are examples of patterns of this kind.

An example of a machine-shop project is the small woodworking lathe shown in Fig. 6-23. The various types of production patterns used to mold the castings in its construction are shown in Figs. 6-24 through 6-39.

For the benefit of those who might not be familiar

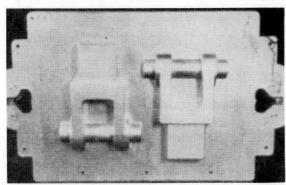

Fig. 6-36. Two aluminum patterns for the headstock of a lathe secured to a 5/16-inch aluminum alloy plate by machine screws.

Fig. 6-38. The core box for the lathe headstock.

Fig. 6-37. The cope side of a plate-mounted headstock pattern.

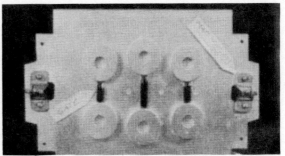

Fig. 6-39. A group of six large grease-seal patterns for the headstock. Note the match-plate lugs at the ends of the three plates.

with some of the principles and procedures involved in the type of pattern-making illustrated, here are some tips.

Your present wood patterns can, in many cases, be used as master patterns to mold and cast duplicates in aluminum. You must, however, take care that additional material is added to the pattern on its important machining surfaces to compensate for the double shrinkage that will result from the intermediate step involved in casting the aluminum pattern. If the pattern is not an overly large one, the dimensional change (3/16 of an inch per foot) might not be significant and can be compensated for by careful rapping of the master pattern in the mold. Of course, the best procedure is to make a wood master pattern on which shrinkage and finish allowance is figured at the rate of 5/15 of an inch per foot if the final casting is to be of iron.

Patterns of large bulk should, when casting the aluminum pattern, be cored out to provide a wall thickness of 3/16 of an inch to ¼ of an inch. If cast solid, it

would be very difficult to prevent deep shrinks in the heavy portions. This will require making a special core box used only for this purpose and discarded after the pattern casting is poured.

After the pattern castings have been molded and cast, the next step involves proper surface finishing. A smooth finish is necessary if the pattern is to draw from the mold properly. This means that side surfaces—those surfaces on which the pattern slides in the sand mold when it is removed—should be cleaned of all roughness and tool marks. Several methods can be used to do this finishing. Scraping is most often used on surfaces not readily accessible to a file. Filing, followed with finish by abrasive cloth, is also popular. Only a few thousandths need be removed if the molding has been carefully done.

Curved or bent files called *rifflers* are very useful for small inside corners or other pockets not accessible to other tools. Make sure that all file and scraper marks run in the same direction in which the pattern will be drawn from the mold in order to prevent undercuts that will cause the pattern to hang up and break the surface of the sand mold.

The two halves of a split pattern should be doweled together after flat machining the joint faces of each half. They are then surface finished as a unit to ensure matching of all edges of the two halves. This method was used for finishing the headstock and tailstock patterns illustrated in this section. After finishing, the two halves should be pulled apart and mounted in this same alignment on the two sides of the pattern plate.

A high-speed hand grinder equipped with rotary files is also useful for finishing certain small details such as the trademark lettering on the lathe headstock. The high-speed hand grinder, equipped with a felt disc or felt "bobs" impregnated with oil and abrasive powder, can be used for the final finish. Abrasive cloth is an old standby for the same purpose.

Some of the denser hardwoods, such as hard maple, make a very satisfactory substitute for metal patterns if they are plate mounted.

Construction of production coreboxes is as important as the pattern because they are subjected to an equal amount of use and abuse. You can often protect the strike-off edges of the box with brass or aluminum edging. Hardwood usually has a long life expectancy and the working of it involves much less time and effort.

CUTTLEBONE MOLDS

Cuttlebone, the calcareous internal shell or plate of true cuttlefish, used in cages of canaries and parakeets to polish their bills and to supply them with necessary calcium, can also be used to form molds for small cast pieces (Fig. 6-40). Cuttlebone molds can produce fine detail for jewelry or other small items. The process involved in making a cuttlebone mold is relatively simple and inexpensive. You can obtain cuttlebone in most pet shops. The mold, if properly cared for, will be usable time and again.

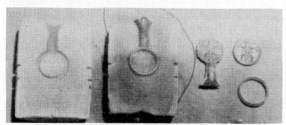

Fig. 6-40. From the bird cage to the foundry area, this soft and pliable bone can be easily shaped to serve as a mold for small, detailed items.

Because most foundry areas have equipment for melting the metals used for the casting, the only cost will be for the cuttlebone and possibly for the mold surface-treatment material. Other materials are those found in most general-metals shops.

The pattern used to form the mold can be shaped from wood or metal and finished to the texture desired. If you choose, you can use an already established shape to form the impression in the cuttlebone. Whichever way you decide to form the mold, care must be taken to keep the size of the pattern small enough to fit well within the limits set by the measurements of the cuttlebone. *Caution*—avoid undercuts on the pattern.

Select two pieces of cuttlebone as thick and as nearly perfect as possible. One bone can be used for small objects by cutting it in two across its length.

Saw with a jeweler's saw blade through the soft part of the cuttlebone across the one end; remove the saw when it reaches the hard part of the bone, and break off the piece. Repeat the same process with the opposite end of the cuttlebone. Next, turn the bone and saw along its length to remove the slight bow formed by the edge of the bone. Repeat this process on the opposite side. A rectangular shaped piece of cuttlebone should be the result. Repeat the above process with the second piece of cuttlebone, sawing it to match the size of the first one.

Saw off part of the bow on the soft side of each piece. Next, rub the surface on a smooth flat board to get a larger flat area. This flat surface can also be obtained by sanding off the bow.

Prepare the impression surface by rubbing a small amount of graphite on both smooth surfaces. Lampblack or soft soot can also be used in this dry method. If you prefer, a wet-surface preparation can be applied to the impression area. Mix equal parts of silicate of soda and borax into a solution and apply to the area with a camel's hair brush. If this method is used, apply a strong solution of borax to the impression area after the pattern depression has been formed.

Hold the cuttlebone in the palm of the hand. Place the pattern near the end of the cuttlebone on the flat surface prepared for it. The thinnest end, which will hold the smallest depression, should be at the top. This is where the funnel will be cut later.

Press the pattern half way into the cuttlebone. Place the other piece of cuttlebone on top. Press slowly until the two flat surfaces of the cuttlebone meet. It should fit well into the palms in order to provide uniform pressure over the pattern.

Use the saw blade to mark several lines on the ends

and the sides so the two pieces will register exactly when put together again. Register pins can be used, but they should be inserted to the outer edge of the cuttlebone as far from the location of your pattern as possible. These pins can be made by cutting pieces of 14-gauge wire into lengths of about ⅜ of an inch.

Separate the two pieces of cuttlebone. Remove the pattern and examine the mold. Be sure the mold is clean.

Cut a funnel-shaped opening in both pieces of cuttlebone with a knife. Next, cut a small sprue extending from the bottom of the opening to the pattern cavity. Avoid cutting the sprue too small because it will form a bottleneck and the molten metal might tend to solidify in this area before it reaches the pattern cavity.

Use either a saw or a sloyd knife to cut light lines across the pattern cavity. These will serve as vents and allow air and gases to escape from the mold as the metal is being poured.

Bind the two pieces of cuttlebone together with a light-gauge binding wire (26-gauge wire works well). Be sure that the cuttlebones are in register. Place the mold on firebrick to protect the bench top when pouring the mold. *Caution*—allow the mold to dry if the wet method of surface preparation is used.

The metal for casting the mold can be heated in a small, clean ladle that can be placed inside a soldering furnace for melting a metal such as pewter. If you use silver, or any metal with a higher melting point than pewter, the oxygen and acetylene torch can be used in addition to the soldering furnace to supplement the heat supply. In the latter case, care should be taken to keep the flame directly off the metal being melted to prevent needless oxidation. Pour the metal into the mold as quickly as possible to avoid having the metal solidifying in the sprue.

The casting can be finished in the usual manner by cutting off the sprue and filing the area to conform to the desired shape. Buff the surface or use a fine grit emery cloth to produce the desired surface texture.

By following the procedures, you can produce a good cuttlebone mold that is reusable. In doing so, you can better appreciate this substance as a medium for learning in the foundry area and for the satisfying and rewarding experience achieved.

TAKE ADVANTAGE OF SHELL MOLDING

Foundry processes have always been among the most stimulating activities conducted in the metal shop. The intrigue of opening a mold in hope of finding a good casting never seems to be lost regardless of the foundry process used. Shell molding can both broaden the scope of a foundry program and develop new insight into precision-production foundry methods.

Since its inception, this molding technique has been widely publicized, and rightly so. It is capable of producing consistently clean and smooth precision castings of complex shape. Shell molding readily lends itself to semi- and fully automatic multistation machines and such problems as the handling and storage of flasks is eliminated. Castings produced by shell molding are generally under 25 pounds, but on rare occasions, some as heavy as 800 pounds have been produced.

Production rates range from 30 to 200 complete molds per hour, depending on the size and shape of the pattern and the equipment available.

The Process

Shell molding is a relatively quick and simple casting process once the pattern plates have been completed. The mold is made in four brief steps:

☐ the resin-coated sand is invested over a hot metal pattern plate.
☐ it is cured in an oven.
☐ the shell is ejected from the pattern plate.
☐ the two shells are fastened together for pouring.

Fig. 6-41. Single pattern plate used for both halves of shell mold.

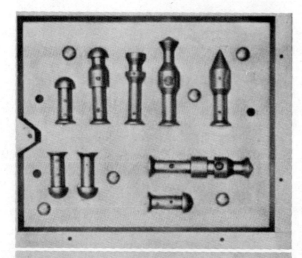

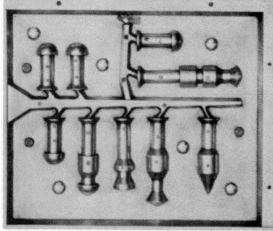

Fig. 6-42. Matching halves of split-pattern plate for chess set.

plate is carefully removed with the shell and cured in the oven. Temperatures in excess of 1,200° F are sometimes used to shorten the curing time to less than 30 seconds. Elevated temperatures are not recommended because of the added handling problems. The curing process can be checked visually by observing the shell's change in color from a yellow to light brown.

The last step in making a mold is to eject the cured mold from the pattern plate with the ejecting pins. Dropping the pattern plate about 1 inch onto a flat, smooth metal-top table will usually give an even ejection.

Split patterns will require two different shells and likewise two different pattern plates. In the case of a flat-back pattern, only one pattern plate is necessary (as shown in Fig. 6-41). A flat-back pattern can be molded on one-half of the pattern plate with a breaker strip molded in the corner. After curing, the shell is broken across the center and the two halves clamped together to make the mold. See Fig. 6-42.

Adopting Shell Molding to the Shop

Shell molding equipment can be constructed in a shop at a nominal cost. The most expensive piece of equipment will be the oven. Ideally, the oven should have quick-recovery characteristics and should be able to maintain a relatively constant temperature between 400°F and 750°F. The higher temperatures will speed up curing time and, consequently, the time per mold and casting will be reduced. The oven can be of the electric or gas-fired type. Gas-fired ovens generally have a quicker recovery and are capable of higher temperatures. One should not be discouraged by the crudeness or smallness of the oven. An old kitchen oven will suffice. A small electric ceramic kiln with settings of low, medium, and high also works well.

The construction of the dump box is relatively simple. Larger units (Fig. 6-43) can be constructed from ¾-inch Douglas Fir plywood, and small units (Fig. 6-44) from ½-inch sugar pine. The mounting apparatus can be made from pipe flanges, a suitable bearing, and ¾-inch to 1-inch angle iron. Wheels on the larger units add portability and will not interfere with the dumping action. The frame on the top of the dump box can be made from ¾-inch angle iron and must have a flat surface to allow an acceptable seal with the pattern plate. A clamping device can then be fastened to this frame to hold the pattern plate onto the box for the investment operation. The depth of the dump box will be determined by the amount of reserve sand preferred and, to some extent, by the size of the pattern plate. Usually, 14-inch to 24-inch depth is

The first step in the molding process is to heat the pattern plate to approximately 500° F. The pattern plate is then clamped securely to the dump box and inverted. The function of the dump box is to cover the face of the pattern plate with the resin-coated sand for a given length of time. From 20 to 40 seconds is usually sufficient, depending on temperature and desired shell thickness. As the sand comes in contact with the hot pattern plate, the resin is activated and begins to flow. The amount of resin activated is a function of both time and temperature. Shell thickness should be at least 3/16 of an inch to ¼ of an inch for aluminum castings and slightly thicker for bronze or higher-temperature metals.

After the investment procedure, the dump box is quickly returned to the original position. The pattern

Fig. 6-43. Large dump box made from ¾" plywood (10" × 12" × 24" id).

sufficient. A minimum of 6 inches of sand must cover the pattern during the investing operation to obtain optimum results.

The most time-consuming operation will be construction of the pattern plate. Aluminum (6061-T6) is a suitable free-machining material for pattern-plate parts. It is very important that the plate on which the pattern is to be mounted is flat because this will determine the flatness of the shell produced. The pattern and gating system can be fabricated or cast and mounted onto the plate with screws. The lip around the plate that prevents peel-back and warpage of the uncured shell should be machined and also attached with screws. Normal shrinkage and draft rules should be followed (Fig. 6-45). The ejection pins can be made from standard ¼-inch carriage bolts. A nut and washer can be used on the back to hold the ejection-pin springs in place. The spring functions only after the shell has been ejected, to pull the pins back into position.

Before the first trial run, coat the plate with a good quality silicone mold-release agent. Periodic recoating of the plate will be necessary and will depend on the number and complexity of the shells to be produced.

Optimum pattern-plate sizes for shapes with limited space should not exceed one square foot. With longer pattern plates, the cost of each shell and casting begins to become unreasonably high for an instructional situation and ease of handling is reduced. Minimum-pattern plate sizes should not be less than 50 square inches, as casting sizes become too small.

Size-Determining Factors

The size of the operation will be determined by a chain of factors. The oven will limit the size of shell that can be cured, and this, in turn, will again determine the pattern and dump-box size.

Two basic supplies are needed:

—a tube of silicone mold-release agent.
—premixed resin-coated sand.

There are two forms of the release agent, the liquid type which is sprayed or brushed on, and the gel type which is rubbed on by hand. Both work equally well.

Prior to ordering sand, you should consult with a

Fig. 6-44. Small dump box made from ⅜" pine (7" × 8" × 18" id).

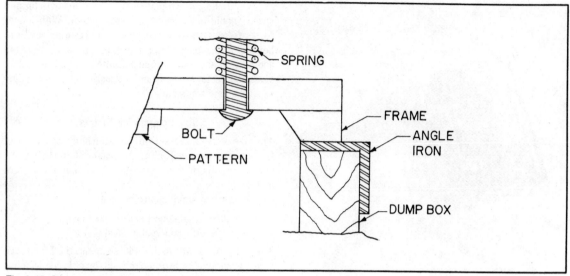

Fig. 6-45. Cross-section detail of pattern plate and dump box.

local foundry supplier. Round sand grains are preferred over angular and sub-angular shapes for small, precision operation with nonferrous metals. A round sand grain will require a higher resin content, which, in turn, will give better surface quality and higher shell tensile strength. Increases in resin content will also decrease permeability. Permeability will not be a major problem in small castings. Shell-molding sands will cost approximately $5 per 100 pounds depending upon the mix and brand. For all practical purposes, it is not reusable in the shop.

Here are several guide posts for troubleshooting:

☐ Draft angles of 0° to 1° are usually sufficient.

☐ Allow the oven and pattern plate to seek a temperature level by producing at least two shells before attempting to set cycle times.

☐ Improper curing will cause shell warpage—result of insufficient heat.

☐ To remedy sticking shells, clean the pattern and add more release agent. Slightly undercure mold for deep draws.

☐ Avoid excessive oven-pattern temperature differences.

☐ Avoid over-baking of the shells.

☐ Position molds horizontally, when possible, to avoid a high metal head.

Since its introduction to the United States, it has grown into a major segment of the precision-casting industry. Shell molding is interesting, exacting, inexpensive, and most of all, rewarding to those who pursue it.

SIMPLE MOLD FIXTURE MAKES SLIP CASTING EASIER

Ceramic slip casting can be frustrating. When the molds are large, you might have difficulty in setting up and filling them, agitating them to remove air bubbles, and pouring out the slip. In addition, the mold must either be held upside down or supported in some way for extended periods in order to drain. The weight and bulk of the molds make them difficult to handle. These problems are particularly troublesome with multicolor pours using different slips.

You can use a slip casting fixture to alleviate these problems. Basically, it is a shelf with threaded retainers and with an axle shaft mounted to it. The axle is fitted to a convenient vertical support, and is free to rotate the shelf and molds to the fill and pour positions. Once the mold is in place and the retainers are tightened, the mold need not be handled again until it is time to separate the pieces.

The fixture is easily constructed (see Figs. 6-46 and 6-47). Mark and bore the plywood base for the retaining rods. Mount the shelf to one end of the base with screws and glue, and mount the pipe flange to the back of the base with four wood screws.

We secured the threaded rods with double nuts and washers, and found a suitable vertical support in the side of our bench-mounted drying rack (very convenient for drying cast pieces). We used an expansive bit to bore through the side of the vertical support and through an additional block of wood that had been previously fas-

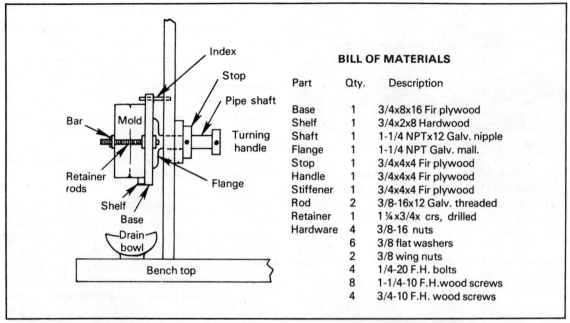

BILL OF MATERIALS

Part	Qty.	Description
Base	1	3/4x8x16 Fir plywood
Shelf	1	3/4x2x8 Hardwood
Shaft	1	1-1/4 NPTx12 Galv. nipple
Flange	1	1-1/4 NPT Galv. mall.
Stop	1	3/4x4x4 Fir plywood
Handle	1	3/4x4x4 Fir plywood
Stiffener	1	3/4x4x4 Fir plywood
Rod	2	3/8-16x12 Galv. threaded
Retainer	1	1 ¼ x3/4x crs, drilled
Hardware	4	3/8-16 nuts
	6	3/8 flat washers
	2	3/8 wing nuts
	4	1/4-20 F.H. bolts
	8	1-1/4-10 F.H. wood screws
	4	3/4-10 F.H. wood screws

Fig. 6-46. Construction details.

tened to the support with screws, which provided extra stability. We fitted the pipe shaft tightly in the hole. With the bit still set at the pipe diameter, we bored holes in two more blocks of wood, one to be used as a stop and the other as a turning handle.

Next, we assembled the pipe to the flange and placed the unit into the pivot hole in the support. Allowing about a paper thickness for clearance, we secured the stop with ¼-inch 20 screws. We then shaped a handle grip from the remaining block and secured it with flat-head ¼-inch 20 screws.

The completed fixture worked beautifully, but we also added a rapid indexing system which consisted of dowels and bored holes to locate the fixture in the fill, pour, and intermediate positions (for filling an appendage). By making a spacer or shim for the shelf, we could accommodate shorter molds.

METAL FREEFORMING

The metal craftsman need not be bound by traditional, conventional designs. Many limit their work largely to round or symmetrical shapes when forming and, if they prefer an irregular shaped piece, make a mold and shape the piece over it. The technique for forming an irregularly shaped vessel presented here and referred to as freeforming, allows the metal craftsman almost unlimited

Fig. 6-47. The completed mold fixture.

Fig. 6-48. An example of an art-metal piece.

opportunities for creativity and expression. It is not suggested that this method of forming replace the more traditional techniques, but rather that it supplement them. The craftsman who masters this technique opens new and exciting horizons in the area of art metalwork.

Freeformed pieces can be made of brass, copper, or sterling silver. The metal should be 18 gauge to allow bowls to be formed with appropriate depth. See Figs. 6-48, 6-49, and 6-50.

Designing the Piece

The freeform-design approach is stimulating to craftsman, because it sets few restrictions regarding shape. It is suggested that the craftsman hold a pencil loosely and, with free and easy motion, draw a series of intersecting curves on a sheet of paper without lifting the pencil. From these curves it should be possible to select an appropriate and pleasing form for the bowl portion of the project. The form selected might need slight modification or alteration to serve satisfactorily.

After selecting and refining a design for the bowl, an appropriate border must be developed. Because the bowl is irregular in outline, in all probability the border will not be of uniform width.

Fig. 6-49. Another example of an art-metal piece.

Transferring the Pattern

The design should be transferred to a sheet of tracing paper. The pattern is then glued face down on the center of a rectangular piece of metal an inch longer and wider than the pattern. The piece of metal, paper side up, is then placed on a thick, hardwood board.

The next step is to chisel carefully along the lines of the pattern. The chiseled lines should be deep enough so that a raised line can be seen easily on the opposite side of the metal sheet and yet should not cut into the metal to any appreciable depth. The raised lines serve as guides for forming the bowl and making the border.

Forming the Bowl

The pattern should be cut around approximately ½-inch outside the chiseled line with a pair of tin snips. This results in a piece similar in shape to the pattern. Surplus metal around the border serves as support and prevents the piece from becoming distorted while the bowl is being formed. All metal splinters and sharp edges must be filed away.

The metal is then annealed and cleaned in a pickle bath before being formed. In the annealing process the metal is heated to a cherry red color and allowed to cool in the air until the red color disappears. At that point it is quenched in the pickle or in plain water. (A solution composed of 10 parts of water and 1 part of concentrated sulfuric acid makes an excellent pickle.)

Constructing the Base

Spheres are appropriate and interesting as feet for free-formed bowls. A sphere is constructed by hard-soldering two hemispheres together. There are several easy-flow hard solders available. One satisfactory solder is composed of 65 percent silver, 20 percent copper, and 15 percent zinc. It melts at 1280° F and flows at 1325° F. The hemispheres are formed using a dapping die and dapping tools.

The piece should be studied so a decision can be made regarding the location of the feet. The piece must

Fig. 6-50. Note the hemisphere legs in the free-formed metal dish.

be stable and well-balanced. The location of the feet determines to a degree the size of the spheres. After the size of the spheres and their location is ascertained, the following procedure is suggested for their construction.

From 18-gauge metal, two discs, each having a diameter that is approximately 1 1/5 to 1 1/4 times the diameter of the sphere, are cut for each sphere. Each disc is centered over the appropriate dome depression, and the correct dapping tool for that depression is placed on its center. The dapping tool is struck with the flat face of a ball peen hammer to drive the disc into the depression. The dapping tool is raised and struck again. The raising of the dapping tool each time before it is struck causes the hemisphere to "dance" and permits uniform and rapid forming. Forming is continued until the height of the hemisphere is equal to the radius of the sphere. Finally, the base of the hemisphere is filed flat.

A second hemisphere is formed in the same manner and the two pieces are hard-soldered together to make a sphere. After soldering, the sphere should be allowed to cool in the air and should not be placed in the pickle bath.

To prevent hollow spheres from exploding during heating, it is recommended that a small hole be drilled in the bottom of each. Exploding is most apt to happen when the piece has been cleaned in the pickle and reheated.

After the spheres are constructed, they are hard-soldered into position on the underside of the bowl. To determine if the feet are properly located, the piece is placed on a surface plate and the height from the surface plate to the border is measured. If one of the feet is out of position, the foot and bowl are reheated until the hard solder melts. Using a poker, the sphere is then carefully moved to its correct position.

After the feet are positioned so the piece is level, it should be placed in the pickle bath until clean; then it should be removed, rinsed, and dried.

For use in shaping the bowl, an appropriate forming hammer, having a slightly domed face, and a heavy, hardwood block with a shallow concave top surface and several rounded corners are selected. The piece of metal, with the raised lines up, is placed on the wood block directly over the concave depression and struck with the forming hammer. The first few blows should be in the area that is to be lowered the most.

The hammering is continued in a pattern that parallels the contour of the bowl, working from the beginning point, gradually out, around and around, toward the edge. The blows of the hammer should overlap.

Eventually, forming causes the border to become wrinkled and portions to curl. The border must then be flattened. This is accomplished by placing the piece on a flat hardwood board and striking the border with the flat face of a ball peen hammer. If, during the forming, the metal becomes hard and brittle, the piece should be annealed and cleaned before the border is flattened.

To smooth and flatten the border near the bowl, a slightly beveled, rectangular punch is used. The sharp edge of the punch is placed in the chiseled line and struck with a hammer.

The forming of the bowl is continued, using the concave surface and rounded corners of the wood block. The border is flattened after each series. These procedures are continued until the bowl is formed to the preferred depth and shape.

Planishing the Bowl

Because of the irregular shape, planishing the bowl can best be accomplished by striking the inside of the bowl lightly with a highly polished planishing hammer while moving the piece over a similarly polished curved stake. The curved edge of a large, round surface plate works very satisfactorily as a planishing stake.

Planishing should begin at the line of intersection of the bowl and the border, and progress to the bottom of the bowl. In this manner the entire bowl should be planished.

After completing the planishing it will be observed that the border is not flat or smooth. The piece should be annealed and cleaned and the border flattened and smoothed with the hammer and rectangular punch. After the final smoothing of the border, the area where the bowl and border meet is carefully planished. The line of intersection of these two parts should be sharp.

It is not necessary to planish the border if it is to be covered with stone or mosaic tile.

Constructing a Mosaic Border

If the piece is to have a mosaic border it is necessary that the mosaic surface be confined within metal edging. A rectangular wire, 16-gauge by 1/8-inch, soldered on edge to the border along the bowl and around the periphery, serves very satisfactorily. The wire is bent to conform to the curvature of the border and, with spring clamps, held in position while being soft-soldered to the border. Surplus metal is removed with a jeweler's saw by cutting just outside the wire edge. A file is used to smooth the edge and remove saw marks.

If the mosaic is to be stone, slabs having a thickness equal to the height of the wire edging must be cut. After the pieces have been cut and fitted, they are glued into position with a cement (such as DuPont Duco Cement) that will bond metal and stone. Joints and hair cracks that sometimes occur should be filled with a mixture of glue and pulverized stone. The pulverized stone mixture is driven into the cracks by mild blows of a lightweight hammer. Malachite and lapis lazuli are beautiful stones to use with brass.

After the cement has dried for a minimum of 24 hours, a wet carborundum stone is used to smooth the mosaic surface and bring it level with the wire edging.

The piece is now ready for finishing. All surplus solder is removed with a file. Polishing is done by buffing on an electric buffer, using tripoli as the buffing compound. Jeweler's rouge is used to give a high luster.

If mosaic tile is used to cover the border, the height of the wire edging should be slightly less than the thickness of the tile. The piece should be buffed and polished prior to setting the tile. The tile is glued into position with a cement that adheres metal to ceramic. Grouting and rubbing down the surface are done after the tile has set.

Fig. 6-51. Scribing the shape of the insert.

MARRIAGE OF METALS

Constructing pieces of art metalwork and jewelry from sheets of metal that represent a combination of different metals gives the craftsman an opportunity to use the design element, color, as well as those of balance, form, line, and proportion. The technique of combining metals in this fashion so that they can be used in the construction of jewelry and holloware was perfected in the silver shop of Los Castillo in Taxco, Mexico, where it is referred to as the "marriage of metals."

Fig. 6-52. Preparing the insert for placement in the opening.

Forming a Sheet with Small Inserts

The techniques used in constructing articles made with the marriage of metals are the same as those used where a single metal is involved, except that the several metals must be first hard-soldered together in a sheet. The soldering operation is the same as the hard-soldering that a silversmith does. See Figs. 6-51 through 6-61.

When articles are constructed mostly of one metal, with small inserts of other metals forming the design, the basic metal is first pierced; that is, openings, that will receive inserts, are cut with a jeweler's saw. The metal from which each insert is to be made is clamped to the back of the pierced area, and the exact shape of the opening is scribed on the metal. The insert is carefully cut out with the jeweler's saw so there will be an undercut of 20 degrees to 3 degrees. It is then placed in the opening in the basic metal.

Fig. 6-53. A properly fitted insert.

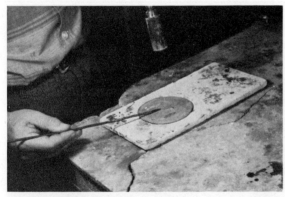

Fig. 6-54. Soldering inserts in position.

Fig. 6-57. Soldering a reinforcing ring in position.

Fig. 6-55. Examples of the kinds of effects that can be achieved with "marriage of metals."

Fig. 6-58. Forming a piece to a desired depth.

Fig. 6-56. Removing surplus solder by filing.

Fig. 6-59. Forming the curved sides of a piece.

The insert should always be put in from the top side, and, if the two pieces are properly fitted, the insert will not fall out when the piece is lifted.

To fit the insert, the basic metal is placed on a surface plate and the insert put in. If the insert does not slip readily into the opening, light tapping with a small hammer will move it into position. It must *not*, however, be forced with heavy blows from the hammer.

Points of interference must be carefully filed until the insert fits properly. When this occurs, a fine line of

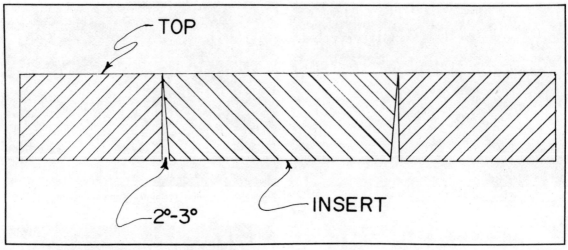

Fig. 6-60. Angle of sawing for marriage of metals.

light around the insert can be seen when the piece is held up to the light. Hard solder will not fill a wide crack but a very fine line should exist to accommodate the solder.

After the inserts are fitted, the top and bottom surface of all joints to be soldered should be fluxed. Pieces of solder are placed along the line, and the entire piece is heated with a torch until the solder flows around the inserts. Following this, the piece should be picked up, turned over, and the soldered joints checked very carefully on the back side.

It is important that the entire piece be heated to the melting point of the solder in order to prevent warpage during the soldering operation. A poker is used to flatten the piece if it buckles during soldering and also for manipulating solder during the operation.

After the inserts are soldered in place, the piece is pickled, rinsed in water, and dried. Next, it is bent over a stake in a large convex curve, and surplus solder on the top surface is removed with a coarse file. After the lumps of solder are filed away, the piece is flattened, reheated to a temperature that is just below the melting point of the solder, pickled, rinsed, and dried.

Forming a Large Sheet

If the design requires the use of a large section of various metals in combination, a slightly different procedure should be followed.

Two edges of different metals should be filed and fitted until they are contiguous and the resulting butt joint fluxed and soldered. It is important to raise simultaneously the temperature of both pieces to the melting point

of the solder to keep the joint straight and sound. The soldered piece is then flattened and another butt joint is prepared by filing and fitting the edges of the pieces. When the second joint is soldered, the craftsman must be careful to heat the original soldered piece and the new piece to a temperature that is slightly less than the melting point of the solder before concentrating the heat on the new joint to be soldered. Occasionally it will be

Fig. 6-61. If you look very closely, you can see the figures, made of contrasting metal, in the sides of this shaker.

necessary to heat the two pieces at positions other than the joint during the soldering to keep the metal expanded and the joint closed. A poker is used to keep the pieces flat during soldering. Other metal pieces are added by fitting, filing, and soldering the butt joints until the sheet is completed. Then it is pickled, rinsed, and dried.

Tray Forming

Before a tray is formed from a sheet of marriage of metals, a reinforcing ring should be soldered to the edge. Usually, a ring of copper or brass (the width and thickness will vary with the size of the tray) is bent to the exact shape and size of the tray. When used on small round trays, such as ash trays, the ends of the ring are soldered together. The ring is then made absolutely round over a large mandrel, placed on the sheet of metals that has a slightly larger diameter than the ring, fluxed, and soldered to the sheet. If the tray is large, the reinforcing edge strip is formed and clamped to the sheet with spring clamps that can be made from 3/16-inch mild sheet rod.

A line is scribed on the surface of the sheet to indicate the flat bottom of the tray. This is accomplished easily with a pair of wing dividers. The dividers are set with the distance between points equal to the perpendicular distance from the edge of the tray to its bottom. Keeping the line between the points of the dividers perpendicular to the edge of the tray, the dividers are drawn around the tray.

For forming, the piece is placed on a surface block or, if it is a large tray, on a flat smooth piece of 2-inch hardwood. The metal is struck along the inside of the scribed line with the flat face of a ball peen hammer. Striking along this line until the bottom has been set to the depth desired. Rather heavy blows are necessary, but they should be equal in weight so that tray depth is kept uniform. Occasionally it is necessary to strike the reinforced edge strip with the hammer to keep the top of the tray flat and smooth.

After the specified tray depth has been reached, the curved top edge of the tray is formed. This is accomplished by striking the inclined surface with the rounded face of a hammer as the surface is rotated over a surface plate. Forming is begun by holding the tray so that the line formed by the inside of the reinforcing edge strip and the tray surface is against the edge of the surface block. The inside of the tray (at point of contact just beyond the edge of the surface block) is struck with the hammer while the tray is rotated slowly. The surface should be curved uniformly from the reinforced edge to the bottom of the tray. If a soldered joint breaks during forming the opening must be closed and resoldered—with more solder being added if necessary.

When the curving of the sides of the tray has been completed, the top edge of the tray should be placed on a flat surface and the reinforced edge strip flattened with the flat face of a ball peen hammer. A chisel is then held inside the edge strip and, with the tray over a steel surface block, a sharp line is chiseled between the flattened surface above the reinforcing edge strip and the curved surface of the sides of the tray.

Finally, the bottom of the tray is flattened, buffed, and polished. Emery paper, or a sewn buff covered with fine emery or carborundum powder, can facilitate the removal of excess solder and the smoothing operation prior to buffing.

HOT METAL CHALLENGE

Molding and casting a two-piece, non-uniform parting line pattern is an excellent project.

The metalworker who has molded flat back, split, and follow board type patterns will learn that this experience requires good sand control, a skill in parting down to the pattern, calculated gating, and good pouring techniques. See Figs. 6-62, 6-63, and 6-64.

☐ Prepare the petro bond sand for molding.

☐ Select a ¾-×-13-×-17-inch molding board and a 4-×-12-×-16-inch flask.

☐ Place the molding board on the molding bench flask support bars.

☐ Place the cope section of the flask, in its natural position, on the molding board. Natural position is as it would sit on the drag.

Fig. 6-62. The finished casting.

Fig. 6-63. The cope shown in natural position. Note parting down.

□ Using a No. 8 mesh riddle, riddle 1½ inches of sand into the cope.

□ Spray a silicon release on the concave side of each split pattern and on the convex surface.

□ Press each half pattern into the sand until it touches the molding board. Center the patterns. From the center of the well, each ingate is 2 inches long, or the patterns at the gating system are 4 inches apart.

□ Riddle additional sand and ram the mold using the peen end of the rammer around the perimeter. Finish ramming with the butt end of the rammer.

□ Using a strike off bar, strike off the surplus sand.

□ Place a ¾-×-13-×-17-inch (or larger) bottom board on the struck off cope top.

□ Roll the mold and remove the molding board and the sand inside the two patterns.

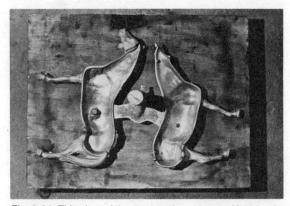

Fig. 6-64. This view of the casting shows tapered ingates to each horse half.

□ Using a slick and spoon, cut or part down to the parting line of each pattern. The oil in the petro bond serves as a lubricant, resulting in an easier operation than in a water tempered sand.

□ Place the cope with the top down against the bottom board.

□ Apply parting compound to the sand and pattern.

□ Place the drag on the cope. The drag will serve as the cope.

□ Riddle sand over the pattern and parted down area of the cope to a height of 3 inches.

□ Press sand down over the patterns with your hand.

□ Riddle additional sand and ram.

□ Strike off the surplus sand with a strike off bar.

□ Vibrate the drag you are using as the cope and remove from the cope and place it top down against a bottom board.

□ Locate and form the well ¾ of an inch deep by 1½ inches in diameter.

□ From the well, cut ingates to each horse. Make the ingates 1½ inches deep by 1 inch wide at the well and taper or choke down to 3/16-×-¾ inches at each casting.

□ Locate and cut the sprue using a ⅝-inch straight sprue cutter. Cut until you hit the bottom board. *Note:* Sprue will align with the well and is smaller in diameter than the well.

□ Vibrate and draw the two patterns.

□ Clean up the gating system and blow off all loose sand using a bellows.

□ Roll up the drag, which you will use as the cope, and cut a pour cup at the sprue top.

□ Blow off all loose sand with a bellows.

□ Close the mold and move to the pouring area.

□ Select an alloy of aluminum with 6 to 7 percent silicon. Allows 356 or 319 work well. Because little machining is required, you can use 356.

□ Charge your crucible and take the metal to 1385°F.

□ Remove from the furnace, flux, degas, use nucleant for grain refining, and pour, using good pouring techniques.

□ After cooling, shake out and cut off ingates. *Note:* If shaken out after 5 minutes, the ingates will snap off; but you might distort the casting and this would result in a poor fit of each half of the casting.

□ Drill boss on inside of casting with a No. 25 drill and tap with 10-24 NC tap.

□ Assemble with 10-24 stove bolts 1½ inches long. The one half of the pattern is countersunk for the stove bolt head.

138

☐ Spray paint with flat black paint or paint to your choice.

☐ Casting can be mounted on a board, if you prefer, by drilling into two legs, one front and one back with a No. 29 drill ¼ inch deep and tap to 8-32 NF. Length of screw will depend on thickness of base.

MATCHPLATE PATTERNS

A perennial problem in most foundry laboratories is the preservation of rather delicate wooden patterns. They are very prone to breaking, denting, chipping, shrinking, swelling, and myriad other ills.

Construction of metal matchplates eliminates or reduces many of these problems but, unfortunately, is often beyond the capability of available equipment. Another prohibiting factor is the inordinate amount of time required to construct good matchplates in the traditional manner. The method described in this section, however, makes it relatively easy to convert your existing wood or metal, one-piece or split patterns to matchplates with a minimum of time and difficulty.

The only items needed that you might not already have available are a large foundry flask, either commercial or homemade, a ¼-inch thick steel spacer plate or frame, and a way to melt a quantity of aluminum sufficient to fill the matchplate mold. The large flask must be at least 1 inch greater in each direction than the width of the matchplate and the center to center index pin distance of the flask with which the matchplate will be used.

The spacing frame can be welded of ¼-×-1-inch strap iron or similar material. The welds should be ground flat and the frame prevented from warping out of the flat plane. See Figs. 6-65 and 6-66.

The split or one-piece pattern to be converted to a matchplate is rammed up in the usual manner in the large flask. After cutting the normal sprues and risers, drawing

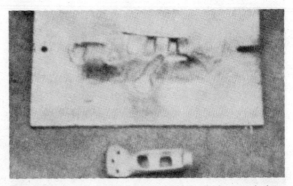

Fig. 6-66. This finished flagpole holder and its matchplate pattern indicate the degree of complexity possible with this method of casting matchplate patterns.

the pattern, and cutting gates and runners, the spacing plate is positioned on the drag half. It can be notched or drilled to accept the index pins as a means of preventing it from shifting position. The cope half of the mold is now placed in position and the mold is ready for pouring. The spacer between the two halves of the mold causes the resulting casting to be a ¼-inch-thick plate that has a half pattern of the desired object on each side. If a one-piece pattern was used for the original, the resulting matchplate will have one blank side.

On cooling, the coefficient of expansion of the aluminum results in sufficient shrinkage to free the casting from the surrounding spacer plate. The new matchplate usually needs only minor trimming, possibly some smoothing, and the addition of a hole and slot at opposite ends to accept flask index pins. If you prefer, pegs can be inserted in the sprue and riser bosses to facilitate the use and positioning of sprue and riser pins. If pins are not used it is a simple matter to mark the top of the cope so that coordinates can be marked on the sand to locate the sprue and risers at the proper points to intersect the runners on the matchplate.

When matchplates made in this manner become unusable, they can easily be cut up, remelted, the wood original can be brought out of honorable and safe retirement, and a new matchplate can be constructed in less than an hour.

METALCASTING TECHNOLOGY

Castings are involved in practically everything we encounter in our daily lives—from the automobile to the artificial heart. In 1973, castings were successfully made for the first time in the weightless vacuum of outer space as part of the Skylab program, thus opening new frontiers

Fig. 6-65. The spacer plate, the original wood split pattern, and the finished project.

Fig. 6-67. Modern foundries use modern equipment such as the control console shown in this melting department.

Fig. 6-69. New processes produce higher quality castings that must meet rigid inspection standards.

of metal-processing technology. See Figs. 6-67 through 6-70.

Keeping pace with a rapid technological growth in our society, the metalcasting industry has introduced countless new processes and innovations to produce castings with higher quality at a lower cost to the consumer, while providing environmental control and a pleasant work place.

High Density and Flaskless Molding. The bulk of casting production is still made in "green sand," that is, silica sand bonded with clay and water. This type of bonding mechanism requires that energy be applied to develop adequate bonding strength. This may be done by hand or pneumatic ramming, or by jolting, squeezing, or a combination of jolting and squeezing.

As casting quality demands increase, so do the demands for highly stable molds—which require more energy input. Sophisticated machines are used to apply pressure to the sand using hydraulic cylinders. These

machines are highly automated, producing hundreds of molds per hour, and are normally found in high production foundries such as those of automotive and farm implement producers. Frequently, automated pouring equipment is used in conjunction with these systems.

With certain types of equipment, the flasks used to contain the sand are eliminated because the mold is stable and rigid enough to contain the metal. These systems are also characteristically high-volume systems.

Because of the sophistication and expense of the equipment involved, this type of molding cannot, of course, be demonstrated in a typical shop. However, since this is the most common system that you will encounter in the industry, plant visitations could be arranged.

Another Approach. Industry also achieves mold stability by the use of chemically bonded molding sands. These are often called self-setting, air-setting, or no-bake systems. There are many different chemical sys-

Fig. 6-68. High-density molding calls for sophisticated, automated equipment for high-volume production.

Fig. 6-70. Accelerating technology in the metalcasting industry has brought with it a clean working environment.

tems available such as furan resins, urethanes, alkyd oils, sodium silicate, and others. All of them, however, work in a similar manner. Sand, binder, and catalyst are all blended in a mixer. A muller, such as is required for green sand molding, is not necessary. The system will have a finite setup time, or "benchlife," during which molding must be completed. The mold will then "cure" itself with the pattern still in place, which gives excellent dimensional accuracy. Benchlife and curing time may be adjusted to suit the application by adjusting the type or amount of catalyst.

These binder systems offer several advantages to a laboratory:

☐ they are relatively inexpensive.
☐ they give more consistent casting quality.
☐ they are clean.
☐ little or no smoke or fumes are generated.
☐ they require no expensive equipment.

Although these binders are not available from the usual supply houses, they can be obtained at any foundry supply house in your area, often at lower costs.

Full Mold Process. This process combines an expendable polystyrene pattern with conventional sand technology. A pattern is prepared from expanded polystyrene, the material used for Christmas decorations. This can be hand carved and finished or made in special injection molds for high production industrial applications. The pattern incorporates the gating and risering system as well.

The pattern is next surrounded by molding sand. Although green sand or oil-bonded sand can be used, more acceptable molding media are the self-setting systems described earlier. Because they require no ramming energy to develop strength, there is no chance for damage to the pattern. The expendable pattern remains in the mold; therefore, extreme overhangs and undercuts are permissible, which makes this process ideal for one-off art castings.

Once the binder has cured, the mold is ready for pouring. The heat from the molten metal vaporizes the polystyrene pattern and allows the metal to fill every detail of the mold cavity. The pattern may be coated with several coats of silica or zircon wash before molding to improve surface finish. If three or four substantial coats of wash are used, the back-up sand does not require any binder at all. A 12-mesh sand, compacted by vibration, will do an excellent job.

The extreme latitude in pattern design for this process makes it ideal for sculpture work. Special textures can be obtained by coating the polystyrene with a thin coat of wax and molding the desired texture in this layer of wax. The wax will vaporize along with the polystyrene pattern giving the desired results.

Because of the high volatility and combustability of the polystyrene pattern, open risers should never be used and adequate ventilation must be provided.

V-Process. A recent (1973) innovation in molding technology is the Japanese vacuum process. This is particularly suited to the casting of flat plate-like casting such as plaques, screens, wall ornaments, etc. The process can best be explained by describing the production of one half of the mold.

A thin plastic sheet is heated and placed over a pattern that has ports and connections to allow a vacuum to be drawn at the pattern surface. The vacuum is applied to the pattern, and the plastic sheet conforms exactly to the pattern contour, similar to the vacuum packaging seen in most hardware and grocery stores. A flask is placed over the pattern and filled with loose, unbonded, dry silica sand. Next, a second plastic sheet is placed over the top of the flask, and a vacuum is drawn on the volume between the two plastic sheets. The vacuum provides a rigid mold half between the two plastic sheets. Because the sand is unbonded, a small amount of flexibility is obtained at the pattern surface, which allows for minor undercuts and backdraft.

When both the cope and drag halves of the mold are completed, they are closed and poured. The vacuum must be maintained to keep the mold rigid until solidification is complete. Casting surface quality is excellent and easily reproducible.

While this molding system might sound complicated for the average shop, it actually is not, and provides an excellent challenge for the innovative metalworker. Vacuum pumps, will provide an adequate vacuum for this process. Flasks can be rather simple because they support no load. Pattern design and porting requires ingenuity, but little expense.

This molding system is relatively new and the technology of the plastic films is far from perfected. Nevertheless, the V-Process offers an excellent vehicle for casting plaques, etc., with superb detail.

An Old Process. Although the investment casting process dates back to about 3000 B.C., it is still relatively new to most shops. Also known as the *lost wax* process, this casting process offers an inexpensive method to produce precision castings. Industrial applications of this process range from jewelry to outboard motor props and jet turbine blades.

The process is as follows: A wax pattern is prepared by hand carving or fabrication, or injection molding to the exact casting shape. Care must be taken because every detail of the pattern will be reproduced in the casting—including nicks, gouges, and scratches. A sprue is attached, and the pattern is thoroughly cleaned to remove dirt and grease from handling.

Next, a slurry of "investment" material (usually silica) is prepared and poured into a flask to surround the pattern. This is allowed to set in a manner similar to plaster of paris. Once the investment is "set," it is placed in a gas or electric "burn-out" furnace to dry the investment and remove the pattern. The mold is slowly brought up to a temperature of approximately 1000° F, which cures the mold and burns out the wax pattern, leaving the mold cavity.

After burn out, the metal is cast using centrifugal, pressure, or vacuum techniques. As soon as solidification is complete, the mold is quenched in water, which causes the investment to disintegrate. This frees the rough casting; it is then cleaned and finished using conventional techniques.

Multiple castings can be made at one time by attaching several patterns to a common sprue, forming a "tree." The only limitation is the size of the equipment and capacity to melt metal. The metal is melted by torch, and common alloys used are jewelers bronze, silicon bronze, silver, and gold.

The required equipment is relatively simple:

☐ a gas or electric burnout furnace.
☐ a casting machine.
☐ a melting torch.

A basic system consisting of a small electric burn-out furnace, a simple vacuum casting machine, a propane melting torch, and all supplies including investment powder, flask, gasket, wax patterns, sprue wax, and miscellaneous items may be obtained for around $130. This is about an absolute minimum system. A heavier-duty system could consist of a larger electric burn-out furnace, a centrifugal casting machine, and an oxy-gas or oxyacetylene torch. Larger castings can also be cast by this process using conventional crucible melting.

Although finished patterns can be purchased, the hand crafting is a fascinating aspect. Wax may be obtained in many different hardnesses and shapes for carving, molding, and shaping, natural objects such as flowers, insects and twigs can be used as patterns, although burn-out time is longer. A classic example is an investment cast thistle.

There are numerous other new processes such as the ceramic molding process, that uses a ceramic slurry similar to investment casting but with a conventional,

reusable pattern, hybrid binder systems, and a fluid sand process, where surface active materials cause a low moisture sand mix to flow like a slurry. Detailed descriptions of these processes are beyond the scope of this section but information can be obtained from the library of the American Foundrymen's Society.

Technical Assistance. The Cast Metals Institute, American Foundrymen's Society, Golf & Wolf Roads, Des Plaines, IL 60016, assists teachers who have cast metals in their labs or are considering adding this important subject. Assistance can be obtained directly from the above address or through any of the 50 local chapters located throughout the U.S., Canada and Mexico.

Assistance includes:

☐ Metalcasting career guidance booklets and free loan of color/sound filmstrip package.

☐ Publications list, including textbook recommendations, i.e. Metalcasting Instructors Guide.

☐ Consultation with teachers and administrators regarding layout plans, equipment, and safety aspects.

☐ Technical talks and assistance for industrial education conferences, seminars, and workshops by CMI staff personnel.

☐ Metalcasting instructors seminars, held annually in June. This is a four-day technical program for qualified instructors and supervisors involved with cast metals programs in secondary schools, technical institutes, and teacher training institutions.

☐ Assistance with free-loan AFS and other supplier films. Contact AFS Film Librarian for free film catalog.

☐ AFS members in local chapters provide unlimited help and give the teacher a chance to communicate better with local foundrymen.

CASTING BRONZE PLAQUES

Several foundry techniques for casting bronze plaques are not commonly used. These are processes that have been handed down from father to son, and which, although little known, are tried and true methods of great value to the metalworker. One such method, described here, is for casting a basic plaque or marker.

Materials

We used Albany #2 (AFS class) molding, but any fine grain naturally bonded molding sand is acceptable. Metal for the melt should be a low zinc content copper alloy. If you purchase material in ingot form from a commercial supplier, use alloy #85-5-5-5 (ASTM class). Another metal source, however, is the local scrap yard where you can purchase old valves and large heating and plumbing

Fig. 6-71. Cut several ingates in the drag for various size plaques.

Fig. 6-74. With the drag half removed, the cast pieces look like this.

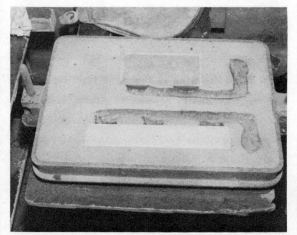

Fig. 6-72. Cut whistle vents in the cope, positioning them as shown.

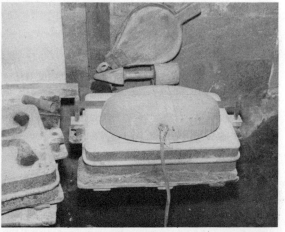

Fig. 6-75. Use a filament wire hot plate to skin dry the mold.

Fig. 6-73. With a trowel smooth around the pattern in the drag.

Fig. 6-76. You can use a blow-type atomizer to spray on the sugar water mix.

Fig. 6-77. Place broken brown bottle glass in a #30 crucible.

fixtures. Alloy #85-5-5-5 has been used many years for the manufacture of these items. You will also need sugar, brown glass (old beer bottle glass is good), a hand insecticide sprayer or a detergent spray bottle, and a hot plate or air-acetylene torch.

For the pattern you will need foundry type, sometimes called marker letters, which can be purchased in various fonts and sizes from foundry supply firms. Other materials needed for the pattern are textured acrylic sheet stock 7/32 of an inch or ¼ inch thick, ⅛-×-¼-inch hardwood stripping, glue, and a small can of colored spray lacquer. See Figs. 6-71 through 6-78.

Pattern Construction

☐ Lay out the desired letters on a work surface to determine the size of your plaque. Allow for margins and border.

☐ Cut the acrylic sheet to dimensions. Drill and tap the backside of the sheet for a 10-32 screw, which will be used as a draw pin. Be careful not to drill through the stock. Use a *bottom tap* for maximum threaded depth.

☐ Cut hardwood stripping to fit around the edge of the pattern. Fit the stripping and determine the inside edges. Bevel the inside edges of the stripping with block sander to allow for draft.

☐ Glue the beveled stripping into position on the sheet. Fill any small gaps with wood filler.

☐ When the glue has dried, sand bevel the outside edges to allow for draft.

☐ Using melted beeswax, form a small radius on the inside edge of the stripping where the wood meets the acrylic sheet. To do this, grind a nail to a taper with a rounded end, and work in small pieces of beeswax by heating the nail over a flame and running it down the inside edges to form a radius with the wax.

☐ Lay out letters on the pattern and lightly spray the pattern with colored lacquer. When the paint is dry, remove the letters. The painting is done to aid in positioning letters when they are finally glued into place.

☐ Before gluing letters to the pattern, smooth off the border with fine sandpaper. Inspect the pattern for proper draft.

☐ Cover the entire back surface of the letters with glue to be sure they will adhere securely to the pattern. After the glue has set, the pattern is ready for molding.

Molding the Pattern

☐ Place the drag portion of the flask on the molding board. Position the pattern on the board and sprinkle with parting compound.

☐ With a fine riddle, apply about a ½-inch layer of sand over the pattern. Fill the drag with a second layer of sand. With the peen end of a ram, compress sand around the edges first; then evenly peen the rest of the mold with a weave pattern sweeping across the drag. Fill the drag with another layer of sand until it is about 1 inch to 1½ inches higher than the drag. With the butt end, pack the sand in the same order as before. Using a strike off bar, strike off the drag.

☐ To set the bottom board after striking off, sprinkle some loose sand evenly across the bottom surface of the drag. Place the bottom board on the mold and move it back and forth until it is in contact with the drag. With the butt end of the ram, hit the center of the bottom board with a firm blow.

☐ Roll the drag over. Using a small trowel, smooth the sand around the pattern with a light pressure and blow the loose sand away. Determine where the sprue is to be

Fig. 6-78. The finished casting, painted and sanded, is ready to be mounted.

located and with your thumb make a sprue witness mark in the drag mold. With vent wire, scratch the center line of the runner in the drag half. After the cope is rammed up, the center line and sprue witness mark will be visible in both mold halves so you can accurately align the gating system when it is cut.

☐ Place the cope on the drag. Sprinkle the mold with parting compound and apply the first layer of sand with a fine riddle. Continue to ram the cope in the same manner as for the drag. Strike off, and with vent wire vent the cope over and around the pattern. The vent wire should touch the pattern.

☐ Remove the cope. Notice that the witness mark made with your thumb and the center line for the gating system are visible in both halves of the mold.

☐ Cut the runner in the cope, extending it ½-inch to 1 inch beyond the end of the pattern impression. This will help to trap the slag from the melt and prevent it from entering the mold cavity. Cut whistle vents. Blow the loose sand away with a bellows. Cut the sprue, and dress off the sprue and runner with a molding tool. Sprinkle the runner with parting compound and brush clean with a camelhair brush.

☐ With the pattern in the mold, cut the runner and ingates. Make the ingates wider than the runner. Blow away loose sand with a bellows; touch up the runner and ingates with a molding tool. Sprinkle with parting compound and brush clean with a camelhair brush.

☐ Insert a draw pin into the pattern. Rap the back of the pattern from the draw pin toward the extreme edges, alternating from side to side. This will help to set the pattern evenly. Next, rap the draw pin side to side and back and forth. There should now be visible a separation line between the pattern and mold. While lightly rapping the back of the pattern, draw the pattern from the mold. Should the pattern lift any sand from the mold letters:

—clean out the sand from the pattern; locate the letter in the mold and add a pinch of sand where needed.

—sprinkle the pattern with parting compound and set it back in the mold.

—rap pattern on the back and draw.

☐ The mold is now ready to be skin dried. Skin drying increases the mold's strength and removes excess moisture, thereby reducing the chances of gas porosity caused by steam when the mold is poured. Mix 2 tablespoons of sugar to 1 cup of warm water. With a detergent sprayer, dampen both the cope and drag faces of the entire mold cavity.

☐ Sprinkle the pattern with parting compound and reset it into the mold cavity. Lightly press the pattern evenly with your fingers. Lightly rapping, draw out the pattern.

☐ Using a filament wire hot plate, bake the face of the mold until it begins to stop smoking. It may be necessary to move the hot plate periodically to cover the entire mold surface. Bake the cope half in the same manner. The surface of the mold can also be dried by using an air-acetylene or oxy-acetylene torch with a heating head attachment. *Note:* If you are using an oil based sand, do not use the sugar water hardening process.

☐ After the cope and drag have been baked, assemble the flask. Cover the flask with the bottom board and weight it down with cinder block to prevent the cope from floating.

The Melt

Select a suitable-size crucible. Put some broken brown glass in the bottom. An old 10- or 12-ounce brown beer bottle will suffice for a #30 crucible. Charge the crucible with small pieces of metal first and then larger ones. Do not overcharge; material can be added later. If metal is to be added to the melt, allow the piece that will be added to lie on top of the furnace so the moisture will be removed. As the charge melts, the glass that is at the bottom of the crucible will float to the top bringing with it impurities from the melt. The molten glass also forms a cover over the melt to help prevent gas absorption into the melt. Recommended pouring temperature for this alloy is 1950-2250° F (1066-1232° C). The melt should not be heated to more than 100 to 150° F (48-66° C) higher than the desired pouring temperature. Skim the slag back from the lip.

Keeping the lip of the crucible as close to the sprue opening as possible, pour in such a way as to keep the sprue full at all times. Do not allow the pouring to be interrupted.

Finishing the Casting

☐ Cut off the gates and runner system.

☐ Face the casting with a belt sander until the letters are distinct with a minimum of pit marks.

☐ Spray the background with dark brown or mahogany lacquer and let it dry.

☐ Face off lightly on belt sander to remove paint on the surface of the letters and border. Clear lacquer can be sprayed over the finished product to prevent tarnishing of the metal.

Plaque Mounting

One method for mounting is to drill and tap blind holes in

the back of the plaque. These should be drilled in the center of the borders. Another method is to use contact cement if, for instance, you want to secure the plaque to a piece of hardwood for a desk marker.

Mounting pins for larger plaques can be cast using decorative buttons as patterns. Ram the buttons in the flask. When the flask is separated, cut the stake portion of the pin in the same manner as for a sprue or riser. Thin wall, small-diameter tubing ¼ of an inch to ⅜ of an inch (depending on the button size) can be used. The button will leave a witness mark for the center from its original securing device. Sink the brass tubing 1½ to 2 inches in the cope and remove the core of sand. Be careful to run gates in the cope so that the design side remains unblemished.

DIE CASTING IN THE GENERAL METALS SHOP

Die casting is an effective and efficient way to produce large numbers of metal parts (Fig. 6-79). Small lathe turnings that often take too much time as a practical learning experience can be produced quickly by die casting. Small knobs are typical of this casting technique.

Fig. 6-79. Die castings.

If the die is carefully made, waxed, and stored in a dry place, it can be used year after year. Metals such as Zamak and Gar-Alloy are recommended for die casting. They require less heat and time. Nevertheless, the inherent qualities of light weight and machinability make aluminum desirable for die casting.

Cold rolled steel is the most practical material for the die because it can be used continually without cooling. Care must be used in the design and construction of the

Fig. 6-80. A die design should allow accurate alignment of the centers of the die parts.

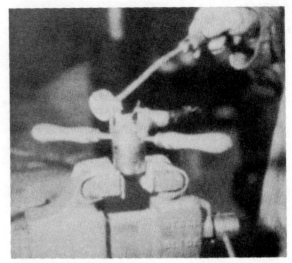

Fig. 6-81. Pouring aluminum.

die to avoid undercuts and negative draft. Depending on the shape of the desired object, some dies can be constructed of two parts. The steel die shown in Fig. 6-80 is made of three parts. See Figs. 6-81 and 6-82.

Making the Die

Machining procedures can vary according to the size and shape of the die. It is essential, however, that the die design and the machining procedure allow accurate alignment of the centers of the die parts during various stages of milling and particularly during the casting process. Procedure can also vary according to the type and availability of basic stock sizes and shapes. For example, the die shown in Fig. 6-80 is made of 2-inch diameter centers. It could also have been made of flat bar stock—two pieces 1-×-2-×-2-inch stock for the split die and 2-×-2-×-2-inch stock for the lower or base unit. The use of flat bar stock would eliminate the need for milling the cold rolled steel to the center line. Separation of the die at the center line is necessary to remove the casting after the molten metal solidifies. An application of a die release compound such as Prodag will aid in removing each casting.

Once the die has reached a relatively constant casting temperature, all casting should be identical. Approximately 8 to 10 seconds should be allowed to permit proper solidification of the Zamak. A gentle tap with a mallet might be necessary to remove the castings.

It would help to make a small steel ladle that would hold just enough molten metal for each casting. This would avoid having to handle and control a large volume

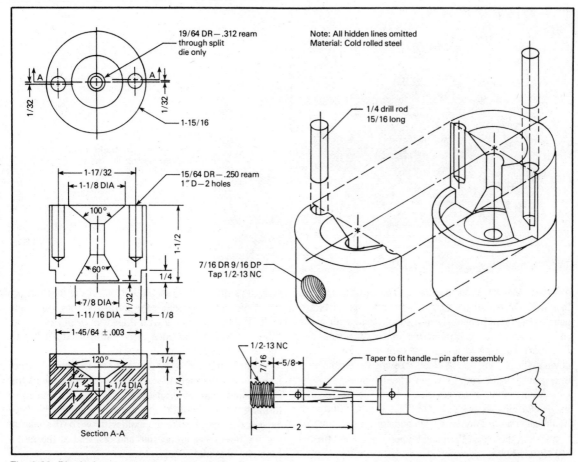

Fig. 6-82. Die design.

of molten metal from larger ladles that could cause overflow and safety hazards. A short piece of 1½-inch black iron pipe with a ⅛-inch flat sheet steel bottom makes an ideal ladle. A piece of ⅜-inch cold rolled steel approximately 8 inches long welded to the side of the pipe serves as the ladle handle. A wooden file handle driven on the end would eliminate using asbestos gloves.

A clamping device should be used to hold the split die together preventing separation of the two parts while pouring the metal into the die cavity.

CASTING ALUMINUM COLLECTOR'S ITEMS

Reproducing cast iron antique toys can provide you with a challenging, worthwhile project. While originals are not inexpensive, they can be bought at auctions or antique stores. Reproductions, which work well for making patterns, can be purchased for much less. The variety of toys

that can be made is endless. See Figs. 6-83, 6-84, and 6-85.

To make a mold, carefully disassemble the toy and save all screws, axles, and pins. Cast aluminum parts

Fig. 6-83. A complete set of wheels can be made from one pour.

147

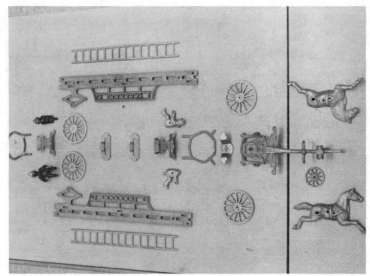

Fig. 6-84. Over 20 parts make up the fire ladder wagon.

from the original toy, and use these as patterns to prevent loss or breakage of the original. Four to six parts are usually cast simultaneously in a small flask, with gates radiating out from a central sprue; no riser is necessary. Due to irregular parts design, use care in removing sand down to the parting line. A small screwdriver works well in removing sand from between wheel spokes.

After casting, parts are cleaned and filed to remove excess flashing. Flaws or small holes can be filled with liquid aluminum. Any holes needed for axles, pins, or screws can then be drilled and tapped. Individual pieces are spray painted and detailed. Parts are assembled with 5/32-inch welding rods used as axles and pins. Rod ends are peened over to lock parts in place.

CASTING AN ALUMINUM INGOT MOLD

Do you use weldments of angle iron or channel iron to make ingot molds for excess aluminum? This is a common practice, but not one that is recommended. Molten aluminum has a high affinity with iron, which dissolves into it readily and has a harmful affect on the metal. Here's how to make a much better ingot mold. It is cast from aluminum and coated with a commercial ceramic coating or with a graphite wash. See Figs. 6-86, 6-87, and 6-88.

The Pattern. Ingot mold patterns can be made of almost any wood. The wall thickness of the pattern should be ⅜ inch to ½ inch and should be constructed with an approximate 15-degree draft. The size of the ingot mold pattern will be determined by the needs of each individual foundry.

You can personalize the mold by placing an emblem or letters (in reverse) in the bottom of the pattern.

Glue and nail together the pattern bottom, sides, and ends. Fill the nail holes with fillet wax or plastic wood. Fillet the bottom and sides of the pattern and finish with shellac or lacquer.

The Casting. Ram the pattern in foundry sand. Draw it from the sand; take extreme care in removing the cope from the drag because the larger green sand core, forming the inside of the ingot mold, can easily be damaged or destroyed. Gate the mold with two or three large ingates intersecting one side and one end of the mold. Pour the aluminum.

Remove the gates and risers from the casting either by hand sawing or band sawing. Now the casting is ready for an insulating coating and subsequent use.

The Coating. The ingot mold must be coated with a ceramic coating or a graphite wash to prevent the molten metal from sticking to the aluminum ingot mold. This coating insulates the mold from the molten metal long enough for the new casting to solidify without sticking.

Fig. 6-85. Antique toys, like this 16-inch long fire patrol wagon, are good objects to reproduce in cast aluminum.

Fig. 6-86. The completed ingot mold and its molded aluminum ingot are flanked here by the wooden pattern (left) and a cast ingot mold with attached gating system (right).

Ceramic coating can be purchased from any foundry supply company, while graphite wash can be made from a mixture of powdered graphite and water. Graphite wash has the advantage of being able to be used on skimmers, plungers, ladles, or any other iron-base tool that will come in contact with the molten metal.

Using either of these coatings, apply two or three thin wash coats to the mold, and allow it to dry thoroughly

Fig. 6-87. Care must be taken in removing the cope from the drag to prevent damage to the large green sand core.

Fig. 6-88. The aluminum ingot mold must be coated with commercial ceramic coating or "homemade" graphite wash (shown) to prevent the ingot sticking to the mold in use.

before using. After 10 to 12 uses, recoat the mold to prevent the molten metal from sticking.

CAST IT IN SCRAP ALUMINUM

This economical clock case, copied from an antique cast-iron clock, is cast of aluminum. This project involves green sand casting four parts, machining, assembling, and finishing. If a mistake is made and a part cannot be salvaged, the material is melted and the part again cast. Because the cast material needs little strength, all types of scrap aluminum can be used.

The single-piece patterns are constructed of wood with ample draft to allow easy removal from the sand. Use an angle plate on a mill or shaper to remove the draft on the front and base. Drill the front and back holes on the lathe or mill. Use small sections of ⅛-inch welding rod in the dowel holes to keep the case parts aligned. When assembling, take care not to strip the threaded holes in the top.

To finish, fill the seams and flaws with a good epoxy filler; continue in the conventional manner, ending with a good coat of gloss black lacquer. You can add pinstriping and other decorating.

Various clock works, faces, and bezels from numerous suppliers or discarded clocks can be adapted to the design. Always examine the face and works before boring the hole in the clock body. See Fig. 6-89.

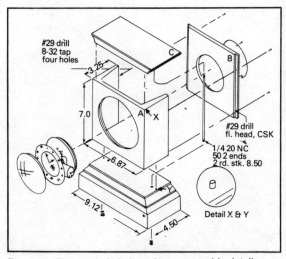

Fig. 6-89. This exploded view shows assembly details.

150

INEXPENSIVE INGOT MOLDS

An inexpensive ingot mold can be made for your foundry from short pieces of angle iron or channel iron. The molds can be used to convert scrap aluminum, lead, etc., into ingots for easy storage. Aluminum left over from a "heat" can also be made into ingots. The size and number of ingot molds can be readily adapted to individual shop requirements.

There are several factors to be considered before proceeding with this shop-improvement project. The height of the crucible should be considered, especially if the furnace has a lid or top. If the ingot mold is too long, the lid on the furnace will not close. Also, individual shop requirements will determine how many ingot molds are needed. The molds can be made as separate units of various sizes and lengths or fabricated with two, three, or

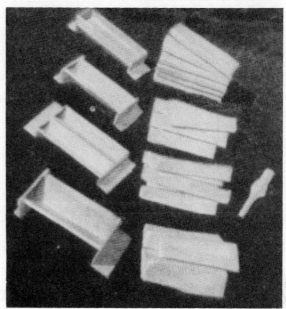

Fig. 6-91. Ingot molds.

more molds as a unit. One-fourth inch thick angle iron works very well for the main body. A short piece of channel iron can also be used for the main body. There should be some draft on the ends of the body to facilitate emptying the molds after the metal has solidified. The angle iron ends are electric welded to the body.

In using these ingot molds, the usual safety precautions should be exercised at all times, as they should whenever you handle hot metal in your shop.

One coat of heat-resisting aluminum paint will serve as a professional finish for these inexpensive, ingot molds. See Figs. 6-90 and 6-91.

CASTING SILVER

Casting sterling silver (Fig. 6-92) in sand molds is similar to the molding and casting in a foundry except that it is on a small scale. The process is intriguing and gives an insight into pattern making, molding and casting metal.

Making the Pattern. Make sketches of the design full size on paper. The design may be an animal head, a letter such as a school award pin, or a design modeled in low relief as the medal shown in Fig. 6-93.

The original pattern can be made of wax, plasticine, wood, clay, or plaster of Paris. The medal pattern shown is carved in plaster of Paris. If a more permanent pattern for the original is desired, a cast of the plaster original can be made of lead in a sand mold. Because lead is soft, the

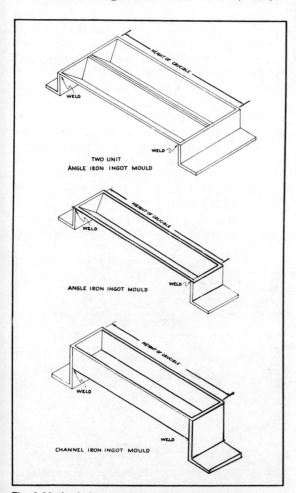

TWO UNIT
ANGLE IRON INGOT MOULD

ANGLE IRON INGOT MOULD

CHANNEL IRON INGOT MOULD

Fig. 6-90. Angle iron can be used to make molds.

151

Fig. 6-92. Examples of cast sterling: Religious design in low relief, colt head, and bracelet of old South American coins and figures.

design can be refined or reshaped by carving and scraping the lead.

Plaster of Paris is a good material to use for the pattern because it can be cut and scraped easily when it is "green" and because it is quite strong and shows shadows and outlines well.

Making the Form. After the design is sketched on paper, draw the outline of the design on a smooth piece of wood and build up a form along the outline lines with plasticine. The plasticine form should be as high as the thickness of the proposed pattern.

Preparing the Plaster of Paris. Prepare the plaster of Paris by placing a small amount of water in a pan and sieving plaster into the water until about half of the water is absorbed. Stir the plaster a little and add water or plaster until a thick creamy mixture is obtained. Next, pour the plaster into the plasticine form and smooth it off flush with the top of the plasticine. Let the plaster set until it is solid; then remove the plasticine form and let it dry. After it is dry, smooth the top surface and the edges with a used file.

Next, sketch the design on the plaster with a pencil, wet the plaster to soften it, and start cutting and scraping the design (Fig. 6-93).

Tools to cut and scrape the plaster can be made of ⅛-×-6-inch tool steel rod by forging the ends to the desired shape. Design and forge the tools as they are needed.

Pattern Draft. All pattern surfaces must taper from base to top in order to permit the removal of the pattern from the sand without breaking the mold. This taper is called *draft*.

To produce a solid sterling silver casting the pattern surfaces must be at least 1/16 of an inch thick. The pattern can have a flat solid base or it can be hollowed out from the back under the raised or high surfaces in the design.

Preparing the Sand for Making the Mold. You can purchase prepared jeweler's sand or you can prepare your own sand. Make your own by sieving fine casting sand through wire-screen netting to remove any foreign matter. Then add glycerine to the sand to hold it together. The glycerine is mixed with the sand by *cutting* the sand. *Cutting* the sand is the term used to describe the mixing and breaking of the sand into fine light particles by cutting off small portions of sand from one pile and scraping it into another pile with the edge of a piece of metal or scoop. After the sand has been cut several times, let it remain in a pile for a day to allow the glycerine to be distributed uniformly. The sand is properly prepared when it remains in a mass without breaking and shows the sharp impressions of the hand after it is compressed in the palm and the hand is opened.

Flask and Sieve. The mold is made in a cast-iron *flask* consisting of two pieces parted in the middle; the half with the pins is the *drag* and the half with the holes is the *cope*. Jeweler's flasks are made in a number of sizes. A sieve to riddle the sand over the pattern in the flask is made by cutting the ends out of a food can and soft soldering a piece of wire screening over one end.

Molding. To make the mold, lay the cope with the sprue hole down on a piece of wood slightly larger than

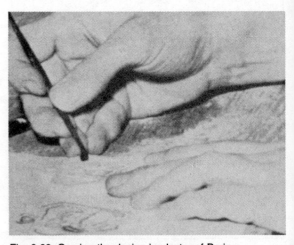

Fig. 6-93. Carving the design in plaster of Paris.

the flask. This piece is called the follow board. Next, lay the pattern in the cope with the base resting on the *follow board* about ¾ of an inch from the sprue hole. The sprue hole in the flask permits pouring the metal into the mold cavity.

Next, place some parting powder—charcoal dust or fine brick dust—in a muslin bag and shake the bag over the flask to cover the pattern with the powder. This powder bag prevents the sand from adhering to the pattern, ensuring easy removal. Riddle sand into the flask (Fig. 6-94), covering the pattern with about ¼-inch of the fine sand. Then fill the flask with the cut sand, compressing it lightly with the fingers. Take care not to compress the sand too hard. If it is compressed lightly, the gases and air can escape through the porous sand when the molten metal is poured into the mold cavity. Scrape the excess sand off the top of the cope with a straightedge, place another board similar to the follow board on top of the cope, and turn the cope upside down. Then remove the follow board and the bottom of the pattern is exposed in the sand.

Next place the drag on the cope and shake a small amount of parting powder on the sand and the pattern. Then riddle sand into the flask. Fill the flask with sand, compress it, and scrape the excess sand off the top of the drag.

Place the follow board on top of the drag, lift the drag off the cope carefully, and turn the drag around laying it down on the follow board. Place a follow board on the top of the cope, turn it upside down and lift the cope from the board. When the cope is lifted, the pattern should remain on the board. If it remains in the sand, tap it lightly with the end of a pair of tweezers to loosen it. Take the pattern out of the sand.

Next, cut the gate; it is a channel in the cope and drag running from the sprue hole in the flask to the pattern cavity for the purpose of pouring the molten metal through (Fig. 6-94). A bent piece of tin plate or rounded end of a pair of tweezers can be used to scrape the channel in the sand.

Large castings might require several gates cut in the sand around the edge of the cavity to act as reservoirs for the molten metal in the cavity. As the molten metal cools, it contracts and draws the molten metal from the gates into the pattern cavity, thus insuring a solid casting.

Next, dust the pattern cavity with fine brick dust or charcoal powder. This produces a smoother surface on the casting. Close the flask, place the follow boards on the outside of the flask, and hold them in place with a C-clamp. Stand the flasks upright on a fireproof table. The mold is now ready to receive the molten metal.

Operating the Furnace. Melt enough sterling scraps for your casting in a No. 0 graphite crucible that is placed in the center of the furnace so the flame can swirl around it. Put a level teaspoon of borax in the crucible to help the sterling melt and the same amount of powdered charcoal to protect the sterling from oxidation (molten sterling absorbs oxygen readily). The borax and charcoal will float on the molten metal in the crucible and will float to the top of the sprue if it is poured in the mold.

Place the nozzle of a furnace blow torch about 2 inches from the furnace opening and directly in line with the opening. Light the torch and turn the gas on full. Then turn the air on gradually. The torch will use from 5 to 10 pounds of air pressure. Adjust the volume and pressure of the air until the torch roars and a white flame comes out the hole in the furnace cover. The "homemade" furnace shown in Fig. 6-95 will melt several ounces of sterling in 10 minutes.

Watch the metal in the crucible and, as soon as it is completely molten, pour it into the mold. To ensure smooth castings, the metal must be poured at the lowest

Fig. 6-94. Riddling sand over the pattern. The opened flask on bench top shows mold cavity.

Fig. 6-95. Pouring the molten sterling into mold cavity. Note homemade furnace and gas torch.

Fig. 6-96. The opened flasks showing the castings. The black sand in the flasks is "dead" sand.

possible temperature. Also, pouring must be done quickly and continuously (Fig. 6-95). The molten flux and charcoal is poured into the mold with the sterling, and it will float to the top of the sprue.

The metal solidifies in several seconds so the flask can be opened as soon as the crucible is returned to the furnace and the lid replaced. Cool the castings in water or pickle immediately after taking them out of the sand to avoid the danger of someone picking them up with the fingers.

You will notice that the sand in contact with the metal is black or "dead" (Fig. 6-96). This "dead" sand should be scraped off and disposed of, and the sand in the flask broken up and cut in preparation for further use.

If the casting is good, clamp the sprue in a vise and cut it off with a hacksaw or jeweler's saw. If the metal is poured at the correct temperature and the mold is good, the surface of the casting will be quite smooth with a uniform texture.

This is the finished surface on some types of castings. Small, intricate designs are smoothed with chasing tools—punches with faces shaped and polished to fit portions of the casting. Large flowing surfaces can be made smooth with needle files and Scotch stone; then they can be buffed with fibre wheels charged with abrasive.

The Melting Furnace. You can purchase a melting furnace or make one yourself. The furnace shown in Fig. 6-94 is homemade. If you decide to make your own, you can make the outside shell of the furnace out of a section of a 5-gallon steel drum. The drum must be at least 12 inches in diameter and 11 inches in height. Use a baby-food can as a form for the hole through the lining. A hole the diameter of the baby-food can is cut in the side of the drum with the center 5 inches from the base. A food can is also used to make the form for the inside furnace wall.

This can must be at least 5 inches in diameter so that the cavity inside the furnace is large enough for the crucible and still allows space for the flame to swirl around the crucible. It must be 8 inches or more in height so the top is as high as the sides of the drum.

Furnace Lining. To prepare the lining, crush several fire bricks to the size of marbles and mix equal amounts of fire brick and fire clay; then add water, and mix until a thick concrete-like mixture is obtained. Fill the base of the furnace shell with 3 inches of the lining mixture and compress it by tamping with a stick. Next, place the inside furnace form (can) on the bottom lining and run the baby-food can through the hole in the drum against the inside form. Fill the space around the forms with the brick-clay mixture. As the lining dries, it will settle so the top edge is built up about ½ inch above the drum wall.

Place the furnace in a dry place to dry for a week; then remove the inside forms to hasten the drying. Several more weeks are required for thorough drying. After the lining appears to be dry, heat the inside of the furnace with the torch, heating for several minutes the first day and increasing the time gradually each day. When you heat it the first time, you probably will observe steam coming out of the lining.

A steel plate with a 2-inch hole in the center can serve as the cover, or you can build up a 2-inch-thick cover out of the clay-brick mixture, using a section of the drum for the outside form and a 2-inch bottle or can for the hole form. Steel reinforcing rods laid in the mixture will strengthen the lid.

CONSUMABLE PATTERN CASTING

Consumable pattern casting is a recent development in one of the oldest metalworking arts. It is also known as "the foam vaporization method," "cavity-less casting," "the full-form foam method," and "replacement casting."

The technique uses a polystyrene foam pattern that is left in the green sand mold to be volatilized by the molten metal. See Figs. 6-97 through 6-100.

This technique offers many applications that are very difficult or impossible with other types of patterns or casting methods. For example:

□ Objects with complicated configurations can be cast with no consideration to draft because the pattern is left in the sand mold.

□ Surface textures can be used that are impossible with ordinary patterns which must be removed from the sand.

□ Separate cores are usually eliminated because

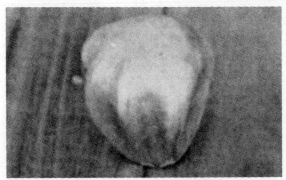

Fig. 6-97. Partially finished aluminum floor shift knob would be extremely difficult to cast conventionally.

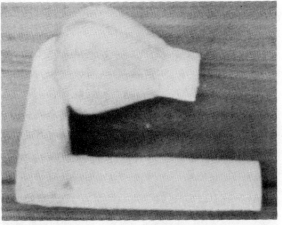

Fig. 6-99. One-piece carved pattern with foam sprue, gate, and blind riser attached with rubber cement and then coated with beeswax.

the hollow spaces can be filled with ordinary sand that will remain in place as the molten metal volatilizes the foam pattern.

☐ Bank sand without a binder can be used because mold strength is not a crucial factor.

☐ Sand with a low moisture content can be used. This results in minimum shrinkage, better surface texture, and more gradual cooling.

☐ Sprues, gates, and risers are made of foam and attached to the pattern. This eliminates disturbing the pattern after it is placed in the mold.

☐ Reinforcement parts such as bolts, nuts, tubes, sleeves, and bearings are put in the pattern and cast in place.

☐ The time required to make a foam pattern is about one-fourth the time needed to make a wood pattern.

There are, however, some limitations that must be considered. Only one casting can be produced from each pattern. The foam must be carved and not molded like wax or clay. Other limitations are inherent in the process, but are minor when compared with the many advantages.

Procedure for Consumable Casting

Obtaining Foam. Polystyrene foam is available locally from florists, lumber yards, and insulation dealers. Its most common trade name is Styrofoam. The shapes and sizes available are quite varied and will usually fit every type of pattern.

Shaping the Pattern. Carve the pattern with woodworking tools (an electrically heated resistance wire cutter can be used). When power tools are required, high operating speeds and low material feed rates should

Fig. 6-98. Examples of carved and fabricated consumable patterns of polystyrene foam.

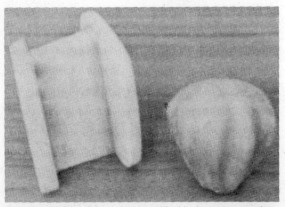

Fig. 6-100. Fabricated pattern with thin beeswax coating. One-piece carved pattern with ⅛-inch beeswax coating permits easy surface modeling.

be used. The pattern does not have to be carved out of a solid block of foam, but can be fabricated out of several pieces using rubber cement.

Preparing the Surface. The surface texture can be left as is or can be made smooth by applying a paraffin or beeswax coating. The paraffin is kept molten in a pan of warm water, and the pattern is dipped into the wax and quickly removed. This can be repeated until the desired thickness of up to ⅛ of an inch is achieved. If beeswax is used, it should be mixed with a small amount of turpentine and heated directly in a pan instead of on water. The turpentine slows the solidification of the beeswax, allowing it to be modeled for finer detail and surface texture.

Attaching Sprues, Gates, and Risers. The sprues, gates, and risers are made of foam and attached either before or after the wax coating. The position of the pattern in the mold should be considered so that the molten metal will enter the bottom of the pattern and proceed to the top. The sprue must be large enough for it to have enough head to fill the volatilized pattern. Extremely fast filling of the mold with molten metal is very important. The risers should not protrude above the sand mold because excessive oxygen causes the pattern to burn rather than volatilize. Nevertheless, small vents can be used. The sprues, gates, and risers should be as smooth as possible to prevent unnecessary turbulence in the molten metal.

Preparing the Mold. The finished pattern should be coated with a refractory material before it is placed in the flask. A 360-to-400 mesh zircon flour refractory mixture using an alcohol vehicle is recommended, but a water vehicle refractory mixture can be used successfully if the coating is thoroughly dried prior to molding. Patterns without a coating can be used, but surface quality is compromised. The coated pattern is placed in the flask and lightly covered with slightly moistened or dry shakeout sand. This is then backed up with low-moisture heap sand that is evenly rammed. Heavy ramming is not required because mold strength is not as crucial a factor as permeability. Improved permeability results from light ramming and low-moisture sand which allows the gases to escape.

Pouring the Metal. The pouring temperature should be slightly higher than with conventional molds, and pouring should be accomplished as rapidly as possible. There are no special requirements for fluxing agents. Ordinary fluxing agents work well with the consumable pattern method.

Flexibility Allows for Individual Needs

This procedure will be suitable for most industrial-arts applications. But after experimentation with the process, you will undoubtedly come up with your own individualized alterations and improvements.

The main factors that make consumable pattern casting so well suited for industrial arts are:

☐ the limitless variety of shapes.
☐ the small amount of time required to make a pattern.
☐ the need for each metalworker to make his own pattern.
☐ the inexpensive materials.
☐ the opportunity to add a new and exciting technique to the foundry area.

GREY-IRON CASTING

Scrap cast iron can be made into finished pieces of equipment such as vises, drill presses, belt grinders, and wood lathe parts. In following one medium (scrap iron) through an entire production cycle, you will be able to obtain a great sense of satisfaction from the finished product. See Figs. 6-101 through 6-106.

Grey-Iron Casting Requirements

The essential requirements for a small, grey-iron foundry are: ferrous sand; a sand muller; a furnace with grey iron melting capability, and metal.

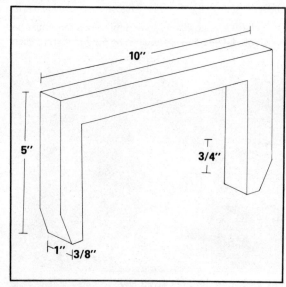

Fig. 6-101. Metal frame for magnet.

Fig. 6-102. "Jolt squeeze" compresses the sand in the casting box.

There are many formulas for mixing ferrous sand, and it is wise to consult a local foundry for advice. One formula is as follows:

100 lbs. #90 silica sand.
4 lbs. western beconite.

Fig. 6-103. This is the way the casting appears after mold shakeout.

Fig. 6-104. Drilling fixture aligns cast elements for machining operations.

3 lbs. sea coal.
1 lb. wood flour.
1-½ pts. ± of water.

These additives have to be replenished periodically, depending upon the amount of use the sand receives. *Foundry Sand Practice* by Clyde A. Sanders. Skokie, Illinois: American Colloid Company, is an excellent reference on ferrous sand.

Mullers with up to a 250-pound capacity, such as the Simpson Porto-Muller, or the #65, #125, and #250 McEnglevan Speedy-Mul mullers, are ideal for the typical shop. Large furnaces are the most practical; the more metal that can be placed in the initial charge of the crucible, the faster the melt.

Most previously machined scrap cast iron will melt down and produce acceptable castings. Old cast-iron automotive bell housings are made of good-quality iron and are easily broken into small pieces for melting. About 1 ounce of ferrosilicon and 2½ ounces of carbon riser should be added to each 30 pounds of scrap iron to maintain the proper carbon content for the cast iron.

The drill press vise described as follows is a grey iron casting.

Fig. 6-105. Finished vise (right) shown with the casting and other machined parts.

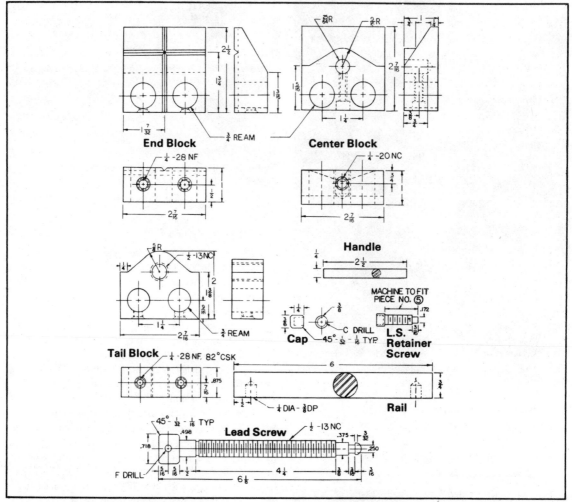

Fig. 6-106. Grey-iron casting design details.

Construction Procedure for
Rail Type Cast Iron Drill Press Vise

Castings

1. Cast up three cast iron blocks using a riser and gating.

2. Load crucible with 20 pounds of iron, 2 ounces of ferrosilicon and 2 ounces of Mexican graphite.

3. Snag, using hammer and grinders.

Machining—blocks

1. Face off front and back of all three blocks using shaper or fly cutters on mill.

2. Lay out and center punch (using template) tail block for drilling; then stack and place in drilling fixture.

3. Drill and ream one rail hole (¼-inch pilot, 47/64 drill and ¾-inch reamer). *CAUTION:* Be sure that table clamp is tight at all times.

4. Place short rail in this hole and repeat process in other rail hole.

5. Place short rail in second hole and pilot drill; drill and tap lead screw hole. *CAUTION:* This is a blind hole; do not go more than ⅝-of an inch deep into the middle block.

Procedure:

☐ ¼-inch bit—drill 1½ inches deep.

☐ 25/64-inch bit—drill 1½ inches deep.

☐ 27/64-inch bit—drill 13/16 inches deep.

□ ½-inch NC Tap—tap ¾-inch deep using tapping head.

□ Remove project from fixture, place block in bench vise and finish tapping by using a tap handle.

6. Install the long rails; using them as parallels, machine off bottom of vise using milling machine or shaper. Dismantle; put two rails in the two jaws and mill top of vise by squaring against bottom of vise.

7. Remove one short rail and install long one. Place in machine vise using long rail as parallel; square up using small square against bottom of the two vises. *Note:* Vise is to be re-assembled for this operation.

8. Machine off one side; check width between rail and side of vise; then repeat step for other side.

9. Install rails in center block using rails as parallels, and machine 1/16-inch off bottom of block (For working clearance).

10. Mount end block on parallels in milling machine and cut V grooves (.125-inch—.325 RPM—2-9/16 inch—feed).

11. Assemble blocks and rails. Drill and tap for 4-¼ 28 NF set screws. *CAUTION:* Wedge blocks so that rails will not turn while drilling and tapping. Be sure all parts remain square.

12. Drill No. 4, counter bore 25/64 and tap ¼ 20 (NC—for lead screw retainer bolt).

13. Break all sharp corners and edges.

14. Paint all unmachined surfaces.

Lead screw

1. Cut off ¾-×-7-inch stock (allow 1½ inches to 2 inches extra for dog and removal of center holes).

2. Face and center drill each end.

3. Mount between centers and turn down to .718.

4. Lay out for handle area and turn balance down to .498.

5. Lay out for threaded area and turn balance down to .375.

6. Machine groove for end of threads.

7. Chase threads, compound rest 30 degrees dial compound in .005 for first four cuts then reduce to .0025 until you have dialed in .058-in. deep. If screw will not fit vise, continue taking light passes (.001) until it does. (Use nut to test.)

8. Cut groove for retainer screw; .060 depth is sufficient.

9. Remove from lathe; cut off each end (hack saw). *CAUTION:* Put waste stock, not lead screw, in vise.

10. Wrap copper around threaded area; face off handle end and turn chamfers.

11. Shape other end round by grinding, then mount in lathe and finish shaping by filing. Polish on buffer.

12. Drill F size hole for handle. (Lay threaded part on a parallel with handle part sticking outside of vise when you drill.)

Handle

1. Cut off a piece of ¼-inch CRS.
2. Face and slightly round each end.

Caps*

1. Cut off 3-inch piece of ½-inch CRS.
2. Face off and spot end.
3. Turn down to .375 and chamfer.
4. Drill a C hole ¼-inch deep.
5. Part, turn around, face and chamfer (no copper, just do not secure too tightly).
6. Repeat steps 1-5 for second cap.

*This operation can be done on a turret lathe.

Assembly

1. Press on one end, using arbor press and a little oil.

2. Place through handle and repeat step 1.

Retainer screw

1. Mount ¼-inch-NC-×-1-inch socket head cap screw in turning fixture (½ CRS × ¾-inch drilled and tapped ¼ 20)

2. Turn end down to .172.

3. Face off end to fit your vise. Use *caution* when fitting.

CAN YOU FIND THE CRACK IN THIS CASTING?

One problem common to both auto and metal shops is that of locating cracks in castings. The casting is usually sent to a machine shop that has expensive special equipment for magnetizing and locating the crack. Most metalworkers cannot afford such equipment, but you can use inexpensive and convenient means of accomplishing the same task. The idea is to place in a magnetic field sections of the casting with conductive particles sprinkled on top. Should a crack exist, the particles will form a line along it. See Figs. 6-107 through 6-110.

To construct the electro-magnet you will need a metal frame, 200 feet of 18-gauge stranded wire, dusting powder, a toggle switch, alligator clips, and electrical tape. Construct the frame to dimensions in the diagram. Wrap the frame center section with wire and cover with electrical tape. Add the toggle switch and alligator clips for correct polarity. Energize the winding with a 12-V

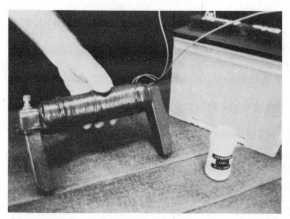

Fig. 6-107. The finished magnet is wrapped with wire and tape, and connected to the 12-V battery.

Fig. 6-109. Outlined by the energized iron filings, the crack is easily detected.

automotive battery. For a weaker or stronger magnetic field, use 6V or 24V respectively.

Place the electro-magnet on the casting and, using a salt shaker, apply either conductive dust or metal filings between the magnetic poles. Now you can detect a crack just like the pros!

PROCESSES FOR PRODUCING CORES

Using a shell core adds greatly to a metalworker's experience and understanding of some of the technology of metal casting. The shell core is versatile, easily made, relatively light, and adaptable to the typical shop. It is made of resin-coated core sand in a metal core box. When the core sand is heated, the resin bonds the sand grains together. The unbonded core sand is dumped out, leaving a hollow shell. We used split-core boxes for the shell core for the bodies of a goblet and mug. These split boxes are

aluminum and are cast from plaster masters. See Figs. 6-111 through 6-114.

Coring the Bases. Bases of commercial castings of goblets and mugs generally are cored, not machined, because machining is time-consuming, costly, and dangerous. Use of a second core, which requires another core print on the pattern, recesses the base of the casting, which then needs only minimum clean-up.

We designed a flat, disk-shaped core to form a flat recess in the bottom of the drinking mug. This core can be made in a one-piece core box. We designed a conical-shaped core for the base of the goblet to recess the base and make the stem hollow, which avoids shrinkage in the stem, provides excellent directional and progressive solidification, and reduces the amount of metal needed to pour the casting. Because of the shape of this core, a split-core box is required.

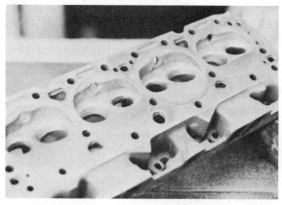

Fig. 6-108. The casting to be checked contains a crack not visible at this time.

Fig. 6-110. The device is used to search for cracks on an automotive engine block.

Fig. 6-111. The split-core boxes with shell cores for the body of the mug and goblet are cast from plaster masters.

The educational advantage of the base core is that, because of its design and function, any type of coring process can be used. Three types, however, are best suited for the typical shop. These are the shell process, the CO_2 process, and the air-set process. Core-making machines or manual methods can be used to produce these types of cores. But because many shops do not have core-making machines, here the manual method only is explained.

The Shell Process. Using the same process and core sand as the body core, this process is well suited for the base cores of the mug or goblet. Make the solid core by pouring or dumping the core sand into the core box. Strike off the excess core sand. Then place the core box into an oven (500°F) and allow it to bake to a yellowish-brown color. Remove the core from the core box. This core is strong and can be stored for indefinite periods of time without picking up moisture.

The CO_2 Core. Make the CO_2 core by mixing sodium silicate binder with round grain, washed silica sand. This silica sand should be 99 percent pure and have

Fig. 6-112. By using a second core, the base of the casting is recessed and requires no machining and minimum clean up.

a grain fineness of 90. Ram the mixture into a core box made of metal, wood, plaster, or plastic. After ramming the core sand so that the grains are brought close together, strike off the excess. At this point, CO_2 gas is passed through the sand mixture and reacts with the sodium silicate, hardening the core. The core is then removed and is ready to use. If, however, the gassing equipment is beyond your shop budget, leave the core sand mixture in the core box overnight. The sodium silicate will react with the CO_2 in the air. This will also produce a good core, but is obviously slower than the minute it takes to gas the core.

If not properly stored, the CO_2 core will start to disintegrate after a few days (and will pick up moisture that could cause blows). After mixing the sand and the sodium silicate, store the mixture in plastic bags. This will help eliminate moisture pick-up and disintegration. For aluminum castings, we use 3 to 3½ pounds of sodium silicate per 100 pounds of silica sand. This provides adequate core strength and excellent core collapsibility.

The Air-Set Core. This core is made by mixing round silica sand with a binder and a catalyst. The type of binder and catalyst will vary among manufacturers. As with the CO_2 core, place the mixture into the box, ram it, and strike off the excess. Leave the mixture in the core box until the chemical reaction is completed between the binder and the catalyst. The core box for this process could also be made of metal, wood, plaster, or plastic.

Additional Hints. All core boxes must be coated with a releasing agent. On the shell-core boxes, you can use a water soluble silicon. On the CO_2 and air-set core boxes, a light machine oil wiped on the box works well. Ejection pins are not needed.

Because the shell core for the body of the casting is an unbalanced type (it is supported on only one end by the core print), you can use pieces of foamed plastic (from a

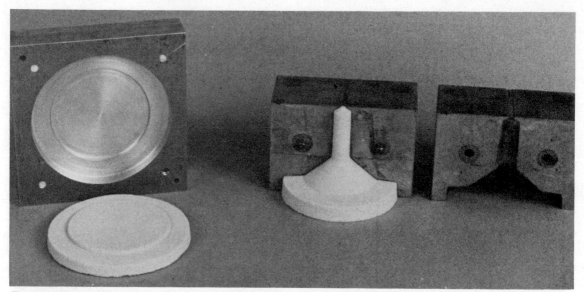

Fig. 6-113. The disk-shaped core (left), designed to form a flat recess in the bottom of the mug, is made in a one-piece core box. The conical-shaped core (right), for the base and stem of the goblet, requires a split-core box.

Fig. 6-114. In this casting with the cope removed, note the sodium silicate core in the base, the shell core in the body, and the attached gating system before shake-out of the drag. Neither of the cores are reclaimed.

foamed plastic coffee cup) for chaplets. These are placed between the core and the mold's surface to prevent core shift. Chaplets should be placed in the drag to keep the core from dropping and in the cope to keep the core from floating. After performing their job, the chaplets will vaporize.

"INDIVIDUALIZED" EXPERIENCE IN THE FOUNDRY

The overall value of a project can be enhanced by adding a bit of personality to its construction. Letters and figures, when used on a pattern, can add distinction and individuality to a finished casting by placing a name, the year of construction, or other identifying data on the pattern before casting.

Investigation might reveal that the purchase price of a substantial quantity of letters and figures may be prohibitive for small foundries. This cost can be greatly reduced by the establishment and operation of a small letter and figure unit within the total foundry area. The necessary equipment can either be purchased or constructed in the shop as projects. The following is a suggested list of the basic tools and equipment, and where to find them:

☐ A small flask can be cast in the foundry.
☐ A pair of matching mold boards can be made.
☐ A small rammer can be turned on a wood lathe.
☐ An ear syringe will serve as a small bellows.
☐ A riddle can be made.
☐ A small trowel can be shaped in the cold metals area.
☐ A strike-off can be made.
☐ A C-clamp can be borrowed from the metals area.
☐ A small ladle can be welded in the welding area (a piece of pipe for the bowl and a rod for the handle).
☐ A sheet of aluminum will serve best for letter plates.

The Flask and the Mold Boards

The shape and size of the flask will vary according to your preferences (see Fig. 6-115). First construct a pattern that will include the core print. This necessitates the construction of a core box. Because both parts of the flask will be the same, it is necessary to construct only one pattern from which two castings will be made. A large baked sand core will be used to produce the hollow of the flask.

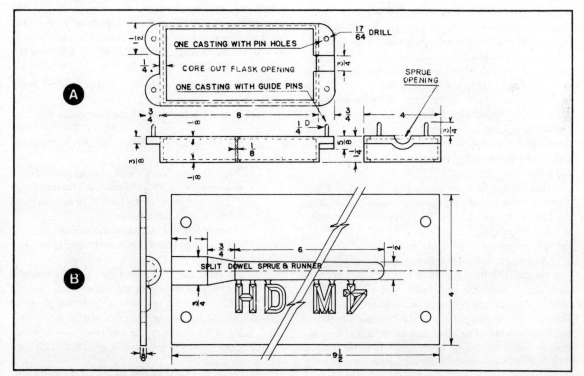

Fig. 6-115. Flask design details.

The two castings can be made of aluminum or iron, transferred to the machine-shop area, and completed as regular foundry flasks. The holes for the guide pins, if they are to be made of solid rods, will be drilled slightly smaller in diameter than the rod so that they can be fastened into the ears of the flask by a force fit. Another effective method would be to drill a smaller hole in the ears and tap them to a standard thread size. A short length of threads on the rods will hold them firmly in place. These pins should have a slight taper from the base to the tip to assure ease of closing and separating the cope and drag of the flask.

The aligning holes in the cope ears will be about 1/64 of an inch larger than the pins to allow for free separation from the drag and must be carefully drilled to assure a precise fit. The halves of the sprue opening should form a circular sprue hole when the flask is closed.

The necessary mold boards can be constructed of a good grade of ½-inch exterior plywood (½ inch wider than the width of the flask and ½ inch longer than its total length). These can be lacquered to eliminate any absorption of moisture that might occur during the molding operation.

Constructing Letter Plates

A good material to use in the construction of the letter plates is ⅛-inch sheet aluminum. These plates should be cut to the same width as the flask and about 1 inch longer (see B of Fig. 6-115). Remove any sharpness on the arises with a mill file. Drill the guide holes in the plate to correspond with those in the ears of the flask. This is accomplished by placing the flask on the plate and scribing the hole positions. After drilling, burrs can be removed with a countersink bit. Some filing with a rattail rasp might be necessary to assure free movement over the pins.

The runner is made by placing one half of a split dowel in the center of the plate longitudinally and fastening with small wood screws. The sprue part of the runner is formed from a larger dowel that is the same diameter as the sprue opening in the flask.

A complete alphabet of letters and figures of varying sizes is available from a foundry supply house. Fine-file each of the characters to be sure that all vertical and oblique surfaces are perfectly smooth. Each individual character becomes a pattern in itself. Place the letters and figures on the plate about ⅛ of an inch away from the runner. Each should be spaced so that the body is positioned in a manner that allows for the flow of metal down into the mold cavity when the mold is stood on end.

It is best to space each character not less than ¼ inch apart. This will provide sufficient sand around each cavity to prevent wash when the metal is poured in.

When the adequate number of characters have been positioned on the plate, hold the plate over an alcohol burner or other form of heat until it has reached a temperature sufficient to melt beeswax. Apply wax at the base of each letter and allow it to flow under each by capillarity. When it is properly cooled, the wax joint is sufficiently strong to hold the letters and figures in place for the molding operation. A beeswax gate is added by melting a small quantity of wax in the space between the runner and legs of each figure using a 12-gauge wire as the planting tool. The size of the letters and figures will determine the number of plates needed to complete a full font of characters.

The type of sand to be used must be of fine texture and of high-molding quality to assure exact detail of each character. This sand should be screened several times through a fine cloth screen. A small quantity of cereal binder, about 2 tablespoons per gallon of sand, should be added to produce a good bond in the sand. Test the tempered sand by using the standard testing method.

The process of molding letters and figures is very similar to that in regular pattern-plate molding. The two major differences are that there are no sprue or riser pins used and the pouring is done at the end of the flask.

Best results will be attained when the following are pursued:

☐ Place the drag of the flask on the molding bench with the guide pins up.

☐ Place the letter plate on the flask with the letters down.

☐ Place the cope of the flask over the letter plate, then invert.

☐ Dust the plate lightly with parting material.

☐ Riddle about ½ inch of sand over the plate.

☐ Fill the remainder of the flask with sand and ram firmly in place around the letters.

☐ Strike off the excess sand on the mold.

☐ Rub the mold board firmly on the bed to assure a smooth and snug seat.

☐ Invert the flask and repeat the operations above.

☐ Invert the entire flask and remove the cope.

☐ With extreme care, remove the letter plate. Be careful not to jar it laterally. This should produce a clean, sharp mold. If necessary, make any repairs—carefully.

☐ Close the mold and place a mold board on each side of the flask.

☐ Clamp the mold boards firmly to the flask with

the C-clamp. Take care not to crush the center of the mold by drawing the clamp too tight.

☐ Stand the flask on end on the pouring bench with the sprue up.

☐ Pour the molten metal into the mold quickly to prevent possible freezing before the mold is filled. This will assure sharp, clean characters.

When the metal has cooled in the mold, the casting is removed and brushed clean with a soft bristle brush. The characters are trimmed from the runner by using an old wood chisel. Make sure, when cutting them off, that the same taper is maintained on each leg as is found on the sides. It might be necessary to fine-file the letters and figures preparatory to using them on a pattern. See Fig. 6-116.

The types of metal most commonly used are those of low melting temperatures, such as babbet, lead, type metal, and zinc.

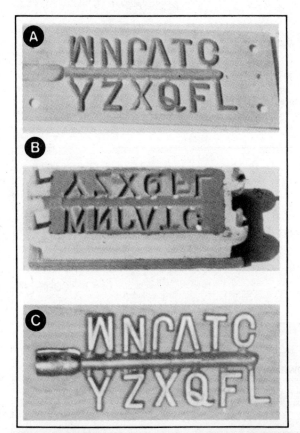

Fig. 6-116. Pattern letters mounted on an aluminum plate (A), a sand mold for pattern letters (B), and a type-metal casting of pattern letters (C).

TRY AIR SETS IN THE FOUNDRY

European foundries have used the no-bake process for many years, but it has been slow to catch hold in the United States.

No-bake or air sets, as it is sometimes referred to, is a process that uses a washed silica sand that has been coated with a liquid binder and a catalyst that set (harden) when exposed to the atmosphere. Thus, it is different than green sand or the waterless (petro-bond) molding process. The no-bake method of producing casting molds is an ideal foundry process. See Figs. 6-117 and 6-118.

The Process

One or more binders are mixed with washed and dried silica sand. A catalyst is added and mixed and a chemical reaction immediately begins between the binder and the catalyst on contact with the atmosphere. The mixed sand is quickly inserted in the core box or mold. This sand does not have to be rammed. The sand is given time to set (harden) completely, setting from the outside to the inside starting with all surfaces in contact with the atmosphere. The cured sand is then removed from the box.

Materials, Pluses, Minuses

To produce air setting molds or cores, you will need: scales to weigh out sand and binders; a bucket, muller, or mixer to mix sand and binder; a wood, plastic, or metal core box or pattern equipment; and a method of holding the core box and placing sand into it.

Advantages of no-bake are:

☐ Core boxes can be made from wood, aluminum, grey iron, or plastic.

☐ Cores are cured in box and are very accurate dimensionally.

☐ May be used for making cores or molds.

☐ Bond strength and curing time may be varied over a range by changing binder additions and catalyst concentrations.

☐ Does not require expensive equipment. Ideal for industrial arts programs.

Disadvantages of the process are:

☐ Depending on the system used and percent of combustibles in the binders, some gases may be produced while pouring.

☐ Some systems use acids that will require protective clothing to be worn by the operator.

☐ Many air setting binders are not water soluble.

☐ Sand mixture is wet and not as easy to insert into core boxes as shell sand.

Fig. 6-117. Material and equipment used, and the results of the air-set system. At lower left is a 3-pound mix of coated 70 GFN silica sand. Sand at the right is not coated. The maple gang core box in the left background shows three cores that were air hardened for 20 minutes before vibration and removal of one-half the split box. An aluminum step core box with two air set cores are in the right background.

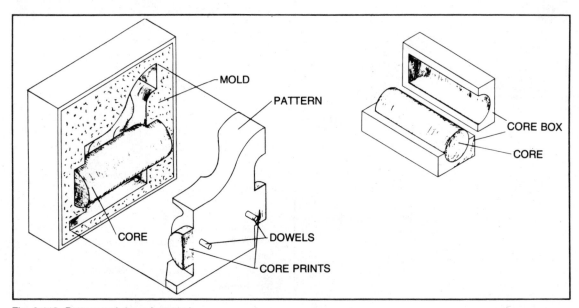

Fig. 6-118. Pattern and core placement.

□ Sand must be mixed immediately before use by the operator.

□ Bench life is short and storage in airtight containers does not help much as even a small amount of air will eventually set a large amount of mixed sand.

□ Binders must be protected from freezing and water.

There are many types of sand that can be purchased and used in the production of cores and molds in the foundry. Sand characteristics such as grain fineness number, grain shape, and impurities in the sand should be taken into consideration.

Grain Fineness Number. This is a system worked out by the American Foundryman's Society to designate the size of the average sand grain. Basically, the higher the number, the finer the sand, and conversely, the lower the number, the coarser the sand. Factors to take into consideration when selecting a GFN are:

—Surface finish desired on the casting; the finer the sand, the smoother the surface finish.

—Metal being poured; gas is produced when molten metal comes in contact with the sand binder. The higher the metal pouring temperature, the greater the amount of gas produced. To omit casting defects, this gas must be removed from the mold through the sand. The coarser the sand, the greater its permeability or ability to allow gas to escape to the atmosphere.

—Type and quality of binder used; almost all binders begin to burn off at around 500°F. Some of the binders on today's market contain higher amounts of combustible gas than others. This should be a consideration for selecting one binder over another. This information is supplied by all manufacturers. The quantity of binder additions also affects gas production. Normally, the more binder used the greater the amount of gas produced when exposed to heat.

Binder Compatibility with Sand Contaminants. Contaminants in sand as well as pH will affect performance of different cinder systems.

Grain Shape. Sand grains, like snow flakes, all have different shapes. Sand shapes are generally categorized into round, angular, and sub-angular.

Suggested sand for school shop pouring aluminum and brass is: 70-95 GFN washed and dried silica sand. Round or angular sand grain 3 to 4 sieve distribution.

Making No-Bake Silicate Cores

Ingredients for 130 lb. muller:

1. 100 pounds of washed and dried 70 AFS-GFN silica sand.
2. 3.6 lbs. of sodium silicate (182-4X-1).
3. 10 oz. of catalyst (192-7X) (Blue color).

Ingredients for 3 lb. sand hand mix:

1. 3 lbs. washed and dried 70 AFS-GFN silica sand.
2. 1.5 oz. of sodium silicate (182-4X-1).
3. .3 oz. catalyst (192-7X).

Procedure for hand mix:

1. Weigh all materials in separate containers.
2. Place the sand in a 3-pound empty coffee can.
3. Separate core box and wipe cavity or cavities with a rag that has a light coating of 10-weight oil.
4. Reassemble core box and clamp together.
5. Pour sodium silicate over the silica sand as if you were putting syrup on a pancake.
6. Mix with a wooden stick until sand grains are coated. This takes about 2 minutes.
7. Pour the blue catalyst in a circular motion over the sand mix.
8. Mix in catalyst until the color disappears. This takes about 60 to 90 seconds.
9. Immediately pack or lightly ram the sand into the core box. All of the sand mix should be used within 10 to 12 minutes.
10. After 20 minutes rap core box, remove clamp, open box, and remove core or cores if a gang box is used.
11. Cores should set one hour before they are placed in the core prints of the mold.
12. *Note:* Set core for vise as set in mold with pattern removed (see drawings).

Safety:

1. Catalyst 192-7X is a very mild acid.
2. Sodium silicate (water glass) is a safe, non-toxic, inorganic binding substance and is a very mild base.
3. Wash hands after using core or mold sand.

The hardening of sodium silicate (a mild base) is accomplished by the addition of the catalyst (a mild acid) that causes some of the water in the silicate to be chemically removed, resulting in a hardened core or mold.

FOUNDRY TRUCK AND CRUCIBLE STAND

Are you hesitant to set up or expand a foundry area because of limited space? Then perhaps a foundry truck can help you. This simple, inexpensive truck serves the dual purpose of transporting molds from one part of the shop to another and provides a fireproof base when you are pouring hot metal.

Among its many advantages is safety. The molten metal need not be carried around the shop to be poured; necessary moving is done by the truck, and spillage during pouring flows harmlessly into its sand bottom. One person can safely handle the metal. This eliminates the possibility of injury to a helper.

The molding bench can be located away from the furnace. Several molds can be rammed up, and then transported to a pouring area on the truck. When not in use, the truck and stand can be placed in a corner or under a bench.

The sand bottom of the truck allows the pouring of molten metals in areas with floors that might be damaged or ruined by hot-metal spillage.

The sand box is made by bending 1/8- × -3-inch band iron to form a rectangle 26 × 36 inches. Ends are welded together and tabs are welded underneath to hold a 3/4″ piece of plywood (same dimensions as metal frame). The box rests on two 1/2- × -2-inch steel bars which are bent up at the ends 6″ to allow room for wheels. This will also raise the height of the fenders so molten metal can be poured into the pigmolds at about the same height as the molds.

Fenders are made from 24-gauge galvanized iron. They protect the wheels from spillage and also form a convenient place to locate the pigmolds when pouring excess metal. Ball-bearing, swivel-type wheels should have at least 5-inch diameters to pass over loose sand or irregular floors.

Dimensions will vary to meet individual needs, but the truck should be deep enough to hold at least 2 inches of sand. Keep the sand box as close to the floor as possible as an added precaution against spilling or splashing.

The truck is placed in front of the stand so that the sprue hole of the sand mold is approximately in the center of the stand. The crucible is then lifted from the furnace with a chain hoist (not shown) and placed into the crucible shank. Minor adjustments are then made in centering the sprue hole with the crucible by moving the truck. The metal is now in a position to pour by tipping the handle on the crucible shank.

At first, there was some apprehension that the movement of the truck would cause the sand to loosen and fall in the molds. In practice, it didn't happen.

Fig. 6-119. Foundry truck and stand, the author claims, not only conserve space in a crowded shop, but also add a dimension of safety to foundry area.

The truck and stand have worked well in fulfilling their purpose. They make a crowded condition more usable and provide a safe method of handling molten metal. See Fig. 6-119.

MODIFY YOUR FOUNDRY
BENCH INTO A CONDITIONER-STORAGE BIN

A commercially manufactured foundry bench can pose constant problems. Proper storage and conditioning of our foundry sand was difficult, especially with contamination from small metal particles, trash, bits of paper, and floor sweepings. Using Petro-Bond sand can mean frequent hand mulling to recoat the burned facing sand particles with oil binder. It can also be difficult to reach down into the bench and scoop up the sand. You can modify your bench. The resulting inexpensive storage bin will continuously sift out foreign matter from the sand, break up

lumps and recoat sand particles with binder and oil, and deliver sand onto a convenient front tray. See Figs. 6-120, 6-121, and 6-122.

Fabrication. The sand hopper bottom was cut on both sides and across the front, bent down to contact the bench floor, and welded in this position. An extended front tray was made from ⅛-×-2½-inch angle iron 2½ feet long and ⅛ inch steel plate and welded to the bench front, extending out about 8 inches. Two 16-gauge galvanized sheet metal sides were made to box in the triangular side openings and direct the sand out into the front tray. The angle iron lip which previously supported the grate at the top was removed and replaced by ½-inch round supports for the vibrating screen.

The vibrating screen was welded from ¾-inch angle iron with several strap iron crosspieces and a centrally located plate for mounting a pneumatic vibrator. We used

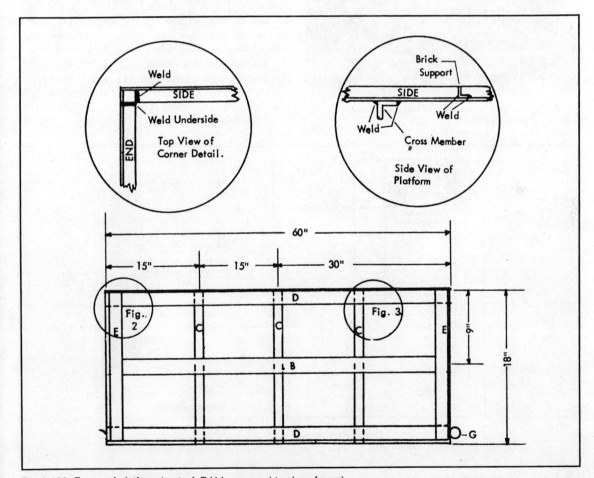

Fig. 6-120. Frame of platform (parts A-F-H-I- removed to show frame).

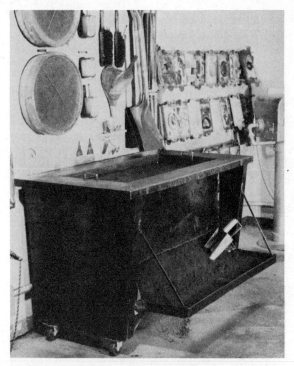

Fig. 6-121. Revised bench features include a shelf for convenient sand scooping.

a Cleveland model VBB rotating ball-type vibrator. Such vibrators are a common foundry supply item and probably can be purchased locally.

The screen angle frame was covered with diamond mesh expanded metal with openings approximately ⅛-×-½ inch. This material was pop-riveted to the frame. The vibrator was bolted to the frame with the exhaust port facing down and connected with flex hose to a lever acting valve on the side of the bench. The hole received 100 ppsi of air from the shop line via a coiled nylon line with quick-connectors. The exact dimensions of the screen are not crucial but ½-inch clearance between the hopper walls and the frame will allow the screen to move on the support pegs without having sand bind between the walls and frame.

Finishing. The removable top grating was welded with a 1¼-inch angle frame and 1-inch angle crosspieces mounted with their apex up in roof-ridge fashion to allow the sand to slide off and into the screen. This grating breaks up large clumps from broken-out molds and keeps tools, flasks, etc., from piling up on the screen.

Bin dimensions are not given as they are not critical. However, several points should be noted. Four round support bars will work much better than a ledge or angle iron support for the screen as the sand will pile up on the ledge and eventually jam the vibrating action. The vi-

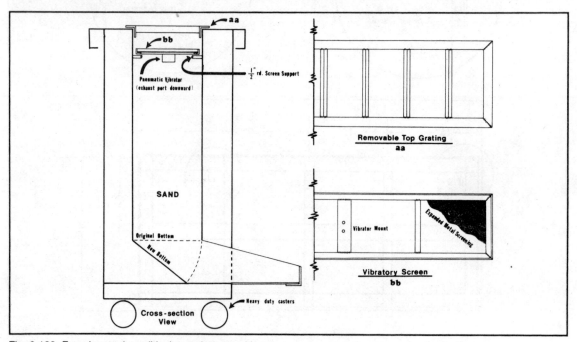

Fig. 6-122. Foundry sand conditioning and storage bin.

brator itself should be mounted as near the center of the screen as possible and with its plane of action horizontal so the screen will shift from side to side rather than up and down.

The price of pneumatic vibrators is proportional to size; purchase the largest your budget allows as it will deliver superior performance. Be sure to direct the exhaust air downward so sand is not blown up or out toward students. Mount the unit on large heavy-duty casters and your clean-up chores will be reduced.

SIMPLIFIED SHELL MOLDING

Shell molding, a foundry method developed in the 1940s but until recently thought too expensive and complex to use in industrial arts, can be employed in any metalshop at minimal cost, given a basic knowledge of foundry fundamentals.

The process involves mounting a metal pattern to a plate and heating to 400-600°F. A silica sand combined with a thermosetting resin binder is then dumped onto the heated pattern and allowed to cure. The cured sand forms the shape of the pattern, and the hardened mold is separated from the pattern by means of ejector pins. The two mold halves are then clamped to make a complete mold cavity ready for pouring the molten metal. See Figs. 6-123 through 6-129.

Shell molding has several advantages over other casting methods.

☐ Tolerances can be more closely controlled; variations as close as .002 are common.

☐ Less draft is required than for other forms of sand casting because the shell sand hardens and the edges of the mold cannot break off easily as in most sand molds; very often, zero draft is used.

☐ Castings with thin walls can be produced.

☐ Metals can be poured at lower temperatures because the shell tends to insulate the metal, causing the metal to solidify at a slower rate.

Fig. 6-124. Silicone spray on the pattern eases removal of mold cavity.

Fig. 6-125. Dump box situated around the pattern confines the resin sand placed on the assembly.

Fig. 6-123. Complete pattern plate assembly has pattern fastened to plate, with sprue removable from pattern; ejector pins on lower plate are easily removed as well.

Fig. 6-126. After curing, dump box and sprue are removed; mold is removed by activation of ejector pins.

171

Fig. 6-127. Complete mold cavity. Notice the ejector pin marks left in the sand.

Fig. 6-128. After mold halves are together, molten aluminum is poured through sprue of one mold half.

Fig. 6-129. Finished casting; comparatively little machining is required to complete the end product.

☐ Sharp contours and small cored holes are possible.

☐ Smooth surface finishes can be obtained.

Used in this type of casting is a high-grade silica sand coated with a liquid resin; the thermosetting resin most often employed is phenol-formaldehyde. The shell sand mixture, as used for the shell molding process, usually has about 6 percent binder.

To plan a shell molding exercise, first select a pattern and design the pattern plate, sprue, dump box, and ejector pin locations. The item chosen for this exercise is a steel gear. The gear (with zero draft) is fastened to the steel plate with bolts from the back. A sprue is made from the same material as the gear (carbon steel), and a hole is drilled in the face of the gear for insertion of the sprue. In this casting, the sprue also acts as a riser.

Pin Hole Problem

Ejector pins are designed for removal of the shell from the pattern, and holes for the ejector pins are drilled in strategic places to aid in the separation process. Finally, ejector pins are cut and welded to a separate plate to be placed under the pattern at the right time to allow the ejector pins to protrude through the face of the pattern. These ejector pin holes pose a problem, however, because their presence when the mold is made would produce raised portions in the mold cavity.

Two possible alternatives are:

☐ Suspend the ejector pin plate under the pattern plate so the ends of the ejector pins are flush with the face of the pattern.

☐ Use a separate plate under the pattern with individual "fillers" or "plugs" placed in the ejector pin holes to eliminate the holes during mold fabrication. The first of these possibilities resulted in excessive ejector plate warpage and uneven heat distribution on the pattern plate caused by the insulating air space between the two plates; thus, this alternative was rejected. The second solution proved effective and simpler to construct and maintain.

When the mold is made, thickness of the shell wall is controlled by two variables: pattern temperature and sand curing time. Raising the temperature or increasing the curing time will increase shell thickness.

Procedure to Form Shell

☐ Assemble the pattern, dump box, sprue, and ejector pin plugs and heat to 400°F. Heat can be obtained from a forge, bench furnace, or enameling kiln. Temperature of the pattern can be determined with a melt stick.

☐ Coat the assembly with a silicone mold release agent.

☐ Drop the shell sand into the dump box frame, allowing the sand to cover the pattern completely.

☐ Remove the sand-covered pattern from heat after 15 seconds. Allow the sand to remain in the dumping box for an additional 2 minutes before dumping out the uncured sand.

☐ Remove the sprue, dump box, and ejector pin plugs from the pattern and plate. Place the pattern plate on top of the gear and remove the mold from the pattern.

☐ Place the dump box on a flat metal surface to produce the drag portion of the mold. Use the shell making procedures described earlier to form the flat back drag (except that ejector pins are not needed). Release the mold from the plate with the blade of a screwdriver, and clamp the cope and drag parts of the shell mold together to produce the completed mold cavity. (Industry uses special clamps or fastening devices, but the two mold halves can be held firmly together in a flask using green sand tightly packed around the outside of the shell.)

☐ After skimming the metal to remove slag, pour the molten aluminum directly into the sprue of the shell mold.

☐ After the casting has cooled sufficiently, break open the mold and remove the gear from the sand.

The end product is a cast gear with a fairly smooth surface finish; relatively little machining is necessary to complete the piece. Although this example is a simplification of the shell molding process, it will acquaint students with a casting process not usually employed in the industrial-arts shop.

HOW TO MIX WATER- AND OIL-BASED SAND

Are you using oil- or water-based sand in your foundry? If you use both, you are part of a minority. Using both types of sand in the foundry can be a problem, but the solution can be simple and inexpensive.

Because foundry concepts are basically the same for both the oil and water process, many programs use exclusively oil-based sand. Although industry uses both water- and oil-based sands, the majority of industry foundry work is done with water-based sand. Oil-based sand is used for special casting problems, although it is held to a minimum because of higher costs.

A small area of the production laboratory can be set up using a wall grid system that would allow both types of foundry sand to be used concurrently without contamination problems.

Two separate ram-up areas, each containing three

Fig. 6-130. Pouring area is just outside ram-up stations. Up to four flasks can be poured at once.

individual ramming stations, were constructed by forming 26-inch high concrete block wall barriers to contain the two different sands. This height allows workers to move their full flask from the ram-up bench to the wall, then from the wall to the pouring area. The concrete blocks were donated by a construction company, and were laid by a volunteer professional blocklayer. See Figs. 6-130 and 6-131.

The entrances were set as far apart as possible with 10-inch step-up thresholds. Inside each entrance are two wire mesh grates that help prevent tracking sand outside the ram-up areas. Each ram-up area contains its own tools and mullers to provide added protection against sand contamination.

The pouring area was set up just outside the walls by strapping refractory brick with a 3-inch steel band. Up to four flasks, regardless of the type of sand, can be poured at any one time with this system.

Sand waste should be minimal and contamination will be eliminated. Water and oil do mix—with the right foundry design.

BUILD A FOUNDRY SAND MULLER

Sand tempering is one of the most important aspects of foundry work. A sand muller is a significant asset to a successful casting for both green and oil base sands. See Figs. 6-132 and 6-133.

Construction incorporates the use of lathe, milling machine, and welding operations. Purchase bearings first in order to up-date dimensions on drawings. Fits of shafts are determined by bearing size.

The two axles are different lengths to allow the

Fig. 6-131. Block wall separates ram-up areas and prevents sand contamination. Individual station tools line the walls.

wheels to mull the sand on two different paths. Caps on the outside of the wheels are pipe flanges with a plate welded over the end, drilled, and tapped for a grease fitting.

The wheels can be fabricated from cast or sheet aluminum. The weight of the wheel has little effect on the mulling because the twisting action of the rolling wheels blends the sand and clay particles with the water.

Keep rotation of the main shaft to around 40 rpm.

Motor combinations and pulley combinations can be adjusted as required.

Mount the axles on pivot blocks to facilitate wheel height adjustment. Then bolt the blocks to the main shaft, and mount the plows with these mounting bolts.

The plows are designed to scrape the sand from the sides of the drum, off the bottom, and to direct the sand in front of the mulling wheels. The edges of the plows should be hardfaced, and can be made adjustable.

Fig. 6-132. Axles of two different lengths ensure that the wheels mull the sand on two different paths.

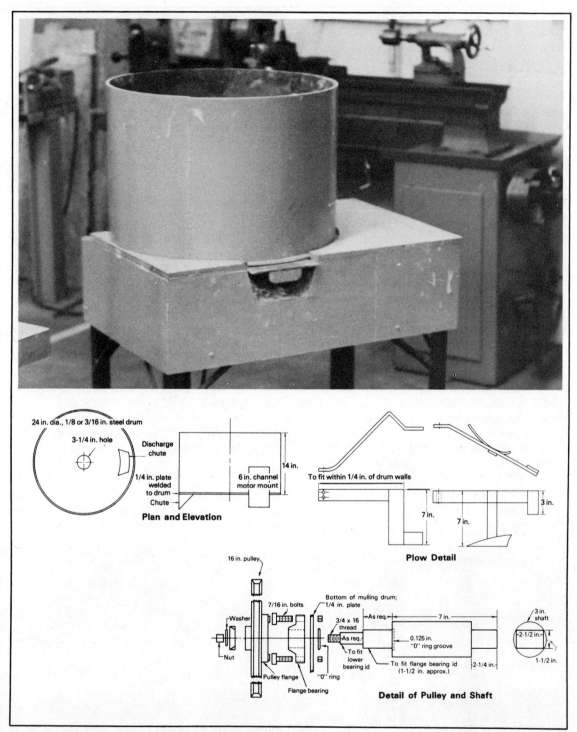

24 in. dia., 1/8 or 3/16 in. steel drum

3-1/4 in. hole

Discharge chute

14 in.

6 in. channel motor mount

1/4 in. plate welded to drum

Chute

Plan and Elevation

To fit within 1/4 in. of drum walls

7 in.

7 in.

3 in.

Plow Detail

16 in. pulley

Washer

Nut

7/16 in. bolts

Bottom of mulling drum; 1/4 in. plate

3/4 x 16 thread

As req.

To fit lower bearing id

As req.

7 in.

0.125 in. "0" ring groove

To fit flange bearing id (1-1/2 in. approx.)

2-1/4 in.

3 in. shaft

2-1/2 in.

1-1/2 in.

Pulley flange

Flange bearing

"0" ring

Detail of Pulley and Shaft

Fig. 6-133. This sand muller is an asset to any foundry program.

One hundred pounds of sand can be mulled in about 4 minutes, and smaller mullers can be built with this basic design.

DOUBLE-END CORING

This double-end coring candlestick project is ideal for materials and process objectives. You design a candlestick, make a split turning on the wood lathe, make core boxes, and ram up the mold to be poured in either aluminum or brass in the foundry.

This activity is a real challenge. It teaches design and problem solving, while resulting in a marketable finished product. It also can be adapted to mass production. See Figs. 6-134, 6-135, and 6-136.

Preparation. The design drawing should include complete dimensions for length and diameter. When it is finished, cut and glue together the stock for the split turning. Be sure to put a piece of paper between the two halves. For added safety, place a screw through the surplus stock in each half of the turning, where the screws will not show. If the screws are put in the turning, they will show up when it is rammed in the sand.

Turn core prints on the lathe before the turning is split. Drill two holes through the core prints to serve as locating points for the turning after it has been split.

Making the Core Boxes. A split core box is needed for each end of the candlestick because each end will be a different diameter and shape. The boxes can be made of wood, metal, or other durable material. The split core box is made of two pieces, aligned with precision dowel pins (Fig. 6-135). Follow these steps to make the core box:

☐ Cut stock to rough dimensions.
☐ Dowel both halves together and square stock to proper dimensions.

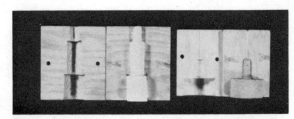

Fig. 6-135. Two stepped core boxes are aligned to make the candlestick. At left, the top piece; at right, the base.

☐ Drill holes, the same size as the core prints, for core boxes. It might be necessary to step down the core size as it goes into the casting, because of changes in the diameter of the candlestick. The stepped down core would also give a quick chill to the molten metal. This would help control shrinkage of the casting—especially in the heavy sections—because they are the last places to solidify. Make several small holes in the bottom of the core box so that CO_2 gas can penetrate all of the core sand.

In the average shop, the CO_2 and air-set processes are the most economical for making cores. Many shops don't have core ovens or shell-coring facilities. For the CO_2 process, materials needed are washed silica sand (99.9 percent pure), sodium silicate, and CO_2 gas. If air set is to be used, the materials needed are washed silica sand (99.9 percent pure), sodium silicate, and a catalyst.

Once cores are made, the pattern can be rammed. To adapt the pattern to higher-production work, the split pattern can be mounted on a matchplate, as in Fig. 6-136.

CASTING JEWELRY

Exquisite jewelry can be cast by several different methods. The two most popular methods are sand casting and centrifugal casting. Commercially, centrifugal cast-

Fig. 6-134. The finished candlesticks.

Fig. 6-136. The split pattern can be mounted on this matchplate for high-volume production.

Fig. 6-137. The equipment needed and the four principal steps in casting jewelry with sand.

ing has many advantages. It makes possible mass production, and even intricate jewelry with undercuts can be easily reproduced. It is a simple matter to produce a wax pattern from a rubber mold using a centrifugal machine or wax injector, if quantity reproduction is desired. Rings are usually made by sand casting. The process' chief limitation is that a pattern used for sand casting cannot have an undercut that will cause the sand to break away when the pattern is removed.

The original pattern for a ring is commonly made of beeswax or a wax similar to that used by dentists. Very often a lead ring will be cast from the wax pattern to serve as a permanent pattern for sand casting rings of gold or sterling silver. The casting method to be followed, however, is the same whether a wax or lead pattern is used. Ring casting only will be described. The same technique can be used in casting a flat piece. See Figs. 6-137 through 6-141.

Preparing the Flask for Sand Casting

Sand is packed into a rectangular or cylindrical container called a flask. The flask is composed of two equal parts fitted together by means of pins in the lower part (the drag) which fit into lugs on the upper part (the cope). Flasks can be purchased or made easily from 3-foot pipe to which pins and lugs are welded.

The sand used is very fine and is tempered with either water or glycerine. The latter is more convenient because it remains in a condition suitable for casting for a considerable length of time. Water-tempered sand, on the other hand, must be prepared each time a casting is to be made. Moreover, there is less danger of the mold exploding when glycerine-tempered sand is used. This type is recommended.

The drag is placed on a table with the pins facing upward. Over the pins is placed a metal plate equipped with an attached half-round rod having a diameter equal to

177

Fig. 6-138. Two samples of sand-cast jewelry.

the ring size. The convex side of the half-round rod must face upward. The cope is positioned over the drag pins.

Sand is sifted through a riddle into the cope until the pattern is covered by 1 inch of sifted sand. Unsifted sand is then added until several inches cover the pattern. Next, the sand is firmly packed around the half-round rod with the fingers and finally with a rammer. Unsifted sand is added (until it extends several inches above the cope) and packed with a rammer. After the cope is tightly packed, surplus sand is removed with a strike bar. Any flat piece

of metal serves well as a strike bar.

The flask is turned over and the drag is taken off and the steel plate with the attached half-round bar removed. The pattern is placed on an arbor having a diameter the same as the ring size. The pattern should fit snugly over the arbor. When a lead pattern is used, its shank is usually cut so that the pattern can be pressed tightly to the arbor. The arbor is installed over the depression in the cope sand, with the pattern shank down and the setting up, and pressed down until it fills the depression. As this is done,

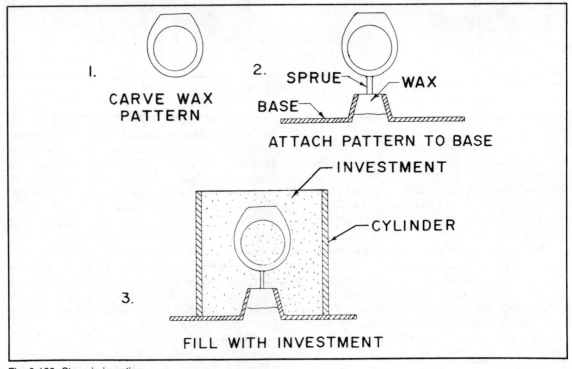

Fig. 6-139. Steps in investing.

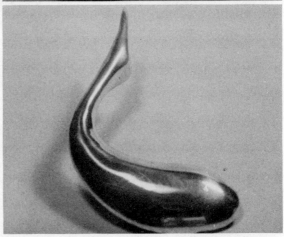

Fig. 6-140. From top to bottom, an investment casting machine; a "tree" of centrifugally cast items after casting, but before finishing; and three samples of centrifugally cast and finished jewelry.

the shank of the ring pattern makes an impression in the sand.

Parting compound (talcum powder works very well) should now be dusted on the pattern and sand. The parting compound should be contained in a cloth bag that is coarse enough so that shaking the bag deposits a thin,

even layer of compound. With parting compound covering the mating surface, it is possible to separate the drag and cope of the flask without disturbing the sand in either part.

The drag is placed on the cope in proper position. Sand is then sifted into the drag until the layer is ap-

Fig. 6-141. A wax pattern attached to a crucible form plate.

proximately 1 inch thick. Another inch of unsifted sand is added, and the sand is packed tightly with the fingers against the pattern. A rammer is used to pack the sand even more tightly in the drag. More unsifted sand is added until the sand stands several inches above the top of the drag. Finally, the sand is rammed, and a strike bar is used to remove surplus sand.

The drag is disengaged from the cope by lifting carefully and tapping the side of the flask lightly with a hammer to loosen the sand from the pattern and arbor. After the drag has been set to one side with the impression up, the pattern and arbor are carefully removed. There should be a smooth, exact impression of the ring in the sand at this stage.

To fill the space left by the arbor, a core is used. The core is constructed by packing sand into a metal pipe having an inside diameter that is exactly the same as the diameter of the ring arbor. The packed sand core is removed from the pipe with a rod having a diameter slightly less than the inside diameter of the pipe. The core is caught in the palm of the hand and, after loose sand is blown from the drag, placed in the drag impression left by the arbor.

A sprue opening must be cut into the cope. A satisfactory method for making this opening is to press a ⅛-inch diameter rod completely through the sand from the shank impression to the top of the cope. The tang of a needle file serves very well for making the sprue opening. After the sprue opening is made, a conical or funnel-shaped opening in the sand on the top of the flask is cut with a knife. This opening facilitates the pouring of the molten metal into the flask.

The cope is turned over, and a few fine lines are scratched with a scriber from the ring impression to the edge of the flask. The lines allow air to escape from the ring impression when the molten metal is poured.

Loose sand is blown from the cope, and the cope is placed in position over the drag. Cope and drag must fit tightly together. At this point, the flask is assembled, and the casting is ready to be poured.

Melting and Pouring the Casting

Melting metal and casting the ring are relatively easily done. Metal is placed in a hand crucible, and a small amount of borax is added to prevent oxidation of the metal during the melting process. The amount of metal necessary for the casting can be roughly estimated by weighing the lead pattern and adding a little extra to fill the sprue and a portion of the funnel-shaped gate.

The metal is melted with a torch using bottled gas, or natural gas, and compressed air. The flame is directed into the crucible on the small pieces of metal. When the metal becomes molten and takes on the appearance of a puddle of mercury, it is poured into the gate opening in the cope. The metal should be poured rapidly and the torch kept on the metal until the actual pouring takes place. After the metal has been allowed to harden, the ring casting is removed from the flask and placed in water to cool, but this must not be done until it has lost its cherry red color. When cool, the ring is scrubbed to remove particles of sand and placed in a pickle bath to dissolve oxides. After removal from the pickle, it is rinsed in water and dried. The sprue is cut off with the end nippers or a jeweler's saw. As a final step, the ring is filed, buffed, and polished. If the ring is to be set with stones, it is done at this time.

Introduction to Centrifugal Casting

Centrifugal casting is identical to the lost wax process *if* the original piece is first constructed of wax and used as a pattern for casting. It is possible to reproduce almost any piece of jewelry, no matter how intricate, by the centrifugal casting method. The piece to be duplicated is used as a pattern in constructing a rubber mold which allows rapid and inexpensive production of wax patterns. The patterns are invested to form a mold for the metal.

The craftsman, who wants to produce an original piece, must first make a pattern of wax. The pattern should be formed on the end of a short, straight tube, or rod, 3/32 of an inch or ⅛ of an inch in diameter. The rod serves as the sprue when the investment flask is constructed.

Investing the Pattern

The pattern must be solidly adhered to the sprue base if it is to be invested satisfactorily. After a crucible form of proper size is selected, the center depression is filled with dental wax. The crucible form is placed on a smooth surface, with its metal dome facing up. The sprue is inserted through the opening in the dome and fastened to the wax base. Around the sprue, about ¼ of an inch below the lowest point of the pattern, a small ring of wax is added to form a reservoir. The reservoir serves to furnish metal to the casting while it cools.

When the pattern has been attached to the base, it is washed with a detergent. The washing operation assists in getting water-based investment to adhere to the wax surface. A fine camel's hair brush is used to paint all surfaces of the pattern with a coat of investment having the consistency of thick cream. Care must be taken to brush all air bubbles from the surface because a bubble, regardless of size, will leave a space for metal during the casting.

As soon as the painted investment has begun to set, a steel cylinder is placed over the crucible form plate. Sufficient investment to completely fill the cylinder is mixed and poured over the painted wax pattern. To prevent the formation of air bubbles near the pattern, the mold should be vibrated slightly. Vibration causes bubbles to rise to the surface.

Investment is mixed with water. If it is measured according to volume, a satisfactory proportion is 1 part of water to 2 parts of investment. The water is placed in a container and the investment added gradually while the mixture is stirred. Care must be taken not to form air bubbles, and the mixture must be free of lumps.

When the investment has set, the crucible form base is removed, leaving a funnel base leading directly into the sprue. The metal sprue pin is also removed. The opposite end of the flask is made smooth by cutting away surplus investment so that the investment is even with the end of the steel cylinder. The investment must be allowed to dry for an hour or longer, depending on its size, before burnout is begun.

Eliminating the Wax

The flask is heated to a moderately high temperature to eliminate the wax. This is done by placing the flask in a furnace and gradually increasing the heat from room temperature to approximately 1300°F. At that temperature, the investment glows red when it is viewed through the sprue hole. The change of temperature should occur over a three- or four-hour period. A good procedure to follow is to allow one hour to bring the investment temperature from room temperature to 500°F, another hour to raise the temperature to 600°F and a final hour to reach 1300°F.

The flask is allowed to cool in the furnace until it reaches a temperature of 700°F or 800°F. It should remain in the furnace until the metal is ready to pour. If the flask cools too much, cracks, which will be detrimental to the casting, may form in the investment.

If a furnace is not available for burning out the wax, satisfactory results can be obtained by gradually heating the flask in a soldering furnace or with a torch. The flask is heated until the investment appears bright red in color as it is viewed through the sprue hole.

Casting with a Centrifugal Machine

The centrifugal machine used by dentists will be found to be very satisfactory. The machine must be balanced to obtain the most satisfactory casting and to prevent damage to the machine. It is balanced after the pattern is invested and before the wax is burned out. This is accomplished by placing the invested flask and crucible in position for casting with the weighted arm directly opposite. The weight is adjusted until the arm is balanced over the upright shaft. The weights are tightened in position, and the retaining nut that holds the horizontal arm to the vertical shaft must also be tightened.

After the wax has been burned out, the machine is wound by grasping the weight arm and turning it to tighten the spring. Two or three turns should be sufficient for small castings. For larger pieces four or five turns will be required. The machine manufacturer's suggestions regarding the number of turns necessary for casting pieces of various sizes should be followed.

The crucible is placed in position and loaded with enough small pieces of metal to do the casting. A small quantity of borax is added to the metal to prevent oxidation during heating.

The flask is carefully removed from the furnace with large tongs and installed in the machine. Heat is immediately applied to the metal in the crucible, and as soon as the metal becomes molten, the weighted end of the casting machine is grasped firmly and pulled to release the stop pin. The torch is withdrawn simultaneously and the arm released. Centrifugal force drives the molten metal into the cavity and produces a dense casting that shows exceedingly fine detail.

The machine should be allowed to run down. The flask is removed, placed on a metal surface, allowed to cool in the air for a minimum of 5 minutes, and dropped into a pan of water. When cool, the investment and casting are removed from the steel cylinder. The casting is placed in a pickle bath to remove oxides, then rinsed and dried. The sprue is cut away with nippers or a jeweler's saw, and the cast piece is ready for polishing.

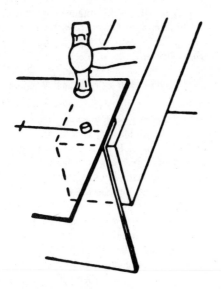

Chapter 7
Beginning Projects

A WORTHWHILE LEARNING EXPERIENCE IN MET-alworking can come from the first project described in this chapter; it is a multi-faceted project. It involves, first, a wide variety of operations despite its low cost and ease of construction. Other assets include its interest and usefulness. Almost anyone can proudly display an air rifle, bow, or gun on an attractive rack that he has "custom made" for himself. If you prefer, the basic design can be adapted to become a tie rack, coat or hat rack, or even a rack for kitchen utensils. Only a few simple modifications are necessary to adapt the hangers to a particular situation.

The learning experiences include cutting stock to length, scholl work, peening, forging, grinding, filing, drilling, riveting, welding, and finishing. The total cost of this wide range of experiences in metalworking is about 50¢.

The back piece (28 inches long) and hangers (each 8 inches long) are made from ⅛-×-1-inch band iron. Both ends of the back piece are shaped, but only one end of each hanger is shaped. Some of the end shapes that can be used are shown in Fig. 7-1. To shape the end, the metal is heated and the thickness at the end is tapered and flared. The desired shape is then rough cut with a hot chisel and finished by grinding. All burrs should be removed by filing when the shaping has been completed.

The rivet holes should be drilled before any bending or forming operations are done. While this sequence is not essential, it is much easier and helps to illustrate the importance of a procedural plan. The ⅛-inch holes are located and drilled on both the back and hanger pieces. The exact distance between hangers is not crucial and can be determined by the shape of the object or objects to be displayed. For most guns, however, a distance of 14 inches to 18 inches between the hangers has been found to work satisfactorily.

To display a gun in a level position, it is sometimes necessary to make one hanger slightly higher than the other. Using a "profile" of the gun, you can determine this (as well as the desired spacing of the hangers). For a profile, simply trace the outline of the gun on wrapping paper.

Bend the hangers to form as shown. Note that the projecting end of each hanger is bent out slightly. This is done to eliminate scratching the finish of the gun stock. Assemble the hanger pieces to the back using ⅛-×-⅜-inch soft iron rivets.

The scrolls are made from two pieces, each 21

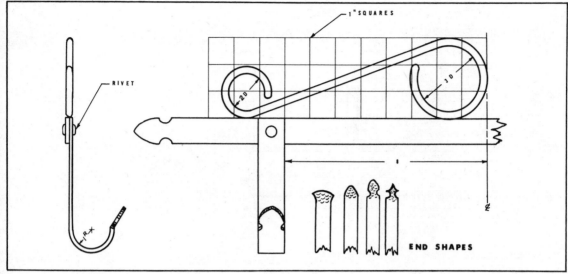

Fig. 7-1. End shapes.

inches long, of ¼-inch round stock. It is best to smooth and round the ends of each piece before they are formed. The rounding and smoothing of ends gives the project a more decorative appearance. A true scroll (an expanding curve) can be used or a pleasing form can be made by bending each end into circles of different diameters. The rack shown in Fig. 7-2 used the two circles. The major diameter used was 3 inches and the minor diameter was 2 inches. The finished scrolls are assembled to the back piece by brazing or welding.

Several substitutions can be made for the ¼-inch round stock. Such substitutions include ¼-inch square, 10-gauge wire (or larger), or similar materials.

Drill two ⅛-inch holes for mounting the rack to the wall. If the rack is mounted directly to the wall, the distance between centers of the studs should be known before the holes are drilled. By using a 28-inch back piece, the rack can be mounted directly on walls having studs on any center from 16 inches to 26 inches.

Smooth any remaining burrs or rough spots on the project and remove the mill scale and oxides. The project can then be finished as you prefer. Flat black enamel is the traditional wrought-iron finish and is quite attractive on this type of project. Hangers can also be lined with leather or felt strips to further guard against marring whatever item is arrayed on the finished rack.

WROUGHT-IRON LEGS

Two jigs are required for making wrought-iron table legs. One is a bending jig for forming the legs while the other is a positioning jig to hold the legs and the right-angle plates for fastening the legs to the table while they are brazed or welded.

Materials for Bending Jig

One sheet-steel plate, ⅛ × 8½ × 26.

One angle iron for reinforcement under edges of plate, ⅛ × 1 × 1 × 69.

One black-iron pipe, ¾ × 1.

Two studs, ½ × 1½.

Two #13 nuts, ½.

Two machine bolts, ⅜ × 1.

Two wing nuts, ⅜.

One angle iron, ⅛ × 1 × 1 × 5.

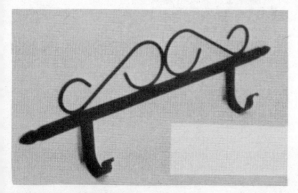

Fig. 7-2. A wrought-iron rack.

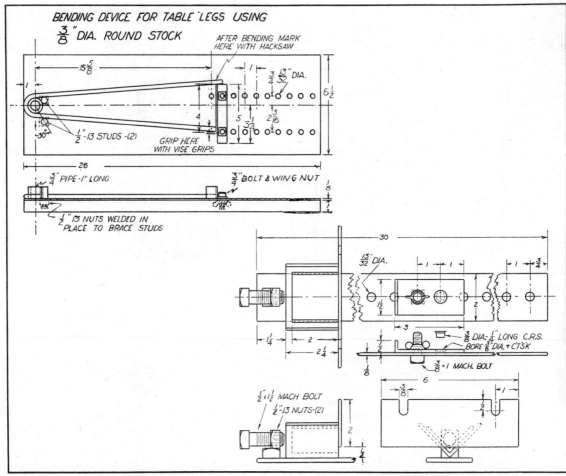

Fig. 7-3. Wrought-iron legs.

Figure 7-3 gives most of the details for fabricating the jig. When the pipe is welded to the plate, care must be taken so there is a minimum of build-up or else the ⅜-inch rod used for the legs will not form snugly around the pipe. The 13/32-inch stud holes should be drilled after the stop and pipe are in place. These are tapped, the studs inserted, and nuts welded in place on the under side.

When forming the ⅜-inch legs, stock should be cut off about 2 inches longer than twice the desired length. The stock is heated to a bright red in the center and one end is placed in the stop and clamped in place with vise grips. The other end is then pulled around the pipe and studs to the opposite side of the stop. Some tapping may be necessary to form the radius if the stock is too cool. The leg is then marked with a hacksaw and allowed to cool before cutting.

Materials for Positioning Jig

One machine bolt, ½ × 1½.
Two #13 square nuts, ½.
One band iron, ⅛ × 2 × 30.
One angle iron, ⅛ × 2 × 2 × 2¼.
One angle iron, ⅛ × 1½ × 1½ × 2.
One band iron, ⅛ × 2 × 6.
One band iron, ⅛ × 1½ × 3½.
One machine bolt, ⅜ × 1.
One wing nut, ⅜.
One C.R.S., ¼ × ⅜.

Figures 7-3 through 7-6 show a piece of 30-inch band iron used for the body of the jig. More weight and rigidity would be added if 3-inch channel iron was substituted. The smaller piece of angle iron is brazed inside the larger

Fig. 7-4. Rubbing down the finish on the end tables. The wrought-iron legs were forged.

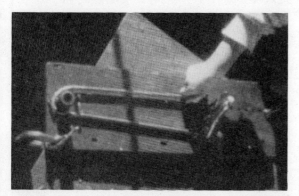

Fig. 7-5. Bending jig of sheet steel for forming iron legs.

Fig. 7-6. Positioning jig used when welding on end plates.

piece as shown in Fig. 7-3. The outside corner should be filed so it nests properly. The small piece of C.R.S. is used as an alignment pin for the stop.

The right-angle plates for attaching the legs to the table are made from a piece of ⅛-×-1-×-8-inch band iron that is cut through the center at a 45-degree angle and then welded together, forming a 90-degree flat plate. The outside corners of these plates should be rounded slightly so they will fit into the angle of the positioning device. Holes are drilled in these plates for the screws for attaching to the bottom of the table. The plates are brazed or welded to the ends of the legs in the positioning device. The legs and plates are given a coat of flat black paint.

The finished products are neat, attractive, and accurate.

BAR TWISTER INCREASES
YOUR OPTIONS IN ORNAMENTAL IRON

The ability to twist steel flats and square stock easily greatly increases the range and quality of ornamental iron projects you can make in the metalshop. It's an excellent means of linking several machine tool and welding operations into one group project. The bar twister is capable of twisting ⅝-inch square cold rolled steel without difficulty. It can be mounted on a welded angle-iron frame or made as a table top model. See Figs. 7-7, 7-8, and 7-9.

A variety of machine-tool operations are involved. Most of the lathe work is straight turning with some boring and thread cutting. The spindle, jackshaft, gear blanks, crank handle, and rails are turned on the lathe. The vertical milling machine is used for boring and end milling. The most difficult operation involves cutting gears using a dividing head and horizontal milling machine. Vertical and horizontal bandsaws are used to saw rough stock, contour, and slit-saw the tailstock. The shaper can be used in place of the vertical mill to finish out the outside contour of the tailstock. All flat stock (see Table 7-1) is ground on the surface grinder. A drill press is used to drill and power tap all holes.

Fabricate the headstock from two ⅝-inch hrs plates with ¼-inch hrs side plates. Drill and bore the headstock plates one on top of another to ensure proper alignment. The spindle is 12 pitch, 44 teeth. A 22-tooth gear is on the crank handle shaft, which runs to a 44-tooth gear on the jackshaft and a 22-tooth gear meshing with the spindle gear. The total reduction is 4 to 1.

Machine the chuck on the headstock from a piece of 5-inch-diameter-×-2-inch steel. A 2-×-2-¾-inch square is milled in the chuck to hold the split die assembly. The headstock and tailstock dies are interchangeable. The dies must be hardened and ground to assure durability. Most iron projects can be produced with the following dies: ¼-inch square, ⅜-inch square, 7/16-inch square, ½-inch square, ⅝-inch square, and an adjustable die to handle up to 1½-×-¼-inch flats.

185

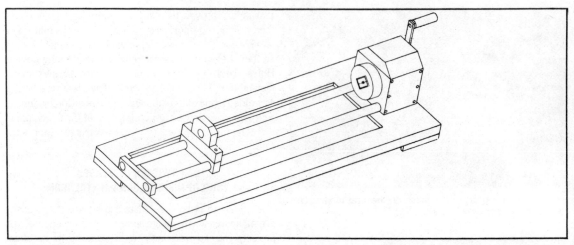

Fig. 7-7. Diagram of bar twister.

Machine the tailstock from a 9-×-7½-inch piece of hrs. Bore two 1½-inch diameter holes 6 inches on center horizontally. The tailstock slides on two 1½-inch diameter crs bars which enable you to twist any length bar, or portion of a bar, up to 5 feet.

A SET OF CANDLESTICKS

Looking for a high-interest machine shop project that can be made either individually or in mass production? Constructing these candlesticks, designed for large-diameter candles, meets those requirements. See Figs. 7-10. Use either 2017T4 aluminum or ASTM B-16 SAE 72 brass, and proceed as follows.

Cut the base from ¾-×-3-inch stock, and finish square on the vertical mill. For greatest accuracy, machine the ½-inch hole and the counterbore on the milling machine as well. Machine the 25-degree angle on the lathe. Hold the base on a threaded mandrel. Fit a hex nut into the counterbore and tighten the base against a shoulder on the mandrel. This facilitates matching and polishing.

The top should be completely machined on the lathe. Do not machine finish the .376 diameter that fits into the stem top until the stem has been drilled to receive it. Machine the diameter for press fit.

Forming tools can be ground for most radii on the stem. But the radii could also be formed freehand. If you want precision matching of the stems, of if you are mass producing them, a contour turning lathe is recommended. Machine finish the .502 diameter that press fits into the base after the base has been drilled and reamed. This gives you leeway for correcting the diameter if the hole diameter is machined too large.

ALUMINUM YARD LAMP

This yard light consists of six assembled aluminum castings and a single gas mantle. The lamp can be used with a double mantle or it can be electrified.

Fig. 7-8. Capable of twisting up to a 5-foot length of bar of ⅝-inch square crs, the bar twister is a valuable tool for making ornamental iron projects in the shop.

186

Fig. 7-9. Cutting gears on the horizontal mill is the most difficult of the required machine tool operations.

Figures 7-12 and 7-13 give complete details for making the patterns. They should be laid out using a 5/32-inch shrink rule. If you make aluminum patterns from the wood masters, allow for double shrinkage.

The base (part A) is designed to fit a 3-inch od pipe. This pattern can be molded as a flat back by parting down ⅛-inch to the 2 11/32 inch diameter. We counterbored a molding board 5/16 of an inch deep by 2⅜ inches in diameter and set the boss in this recess. This allows simple molding and good casting detail without any flash.

Part B, the body, is the most difficult to mold and a step-by-step procedure is given below.

Part C, the top, is molded as a loose pattern in a 9-×-12-×-12-inch cope. You can center the pattern on a molding board that has a recess of 5/16 × ¾ × ½ inches deep to compensate for the hinge boss extension. This is a double-roll molding experience because the green sand in the drag, which is 2 × 12 × 12 inches, cores out the inside of the top. Feed this mold direct to the center of the top (see Fig. 7-14).

Part D, a spacer, and Part E, a cap, can be molded as flat back in the same flask. This allows you to calculate a feeding system. You can use a 1:3:3 ratio. The one (1) would be the area of the sprue. You can use a ½-inch diameter sprue and round the area off to .2. The runner would carry .2 by 3, or .6. You would cut .6 deep by 1 inch wide. Using one ingate to each mold cavity, divide .6 by 2, and each ingate would be cut .5 by .6. Consult AFS book on gating and feeding non-ferrous metals. The eagle, (Part F) can be molded as a loose pattern and you can develop some skill in parting down to the nonuniform parting line.

You can feed the casting into the 15/32-inch diameter boss. This makes for easy cleanup and provides good directional solidification. A follow block made out of low shrink plaster could also be introduced as a new learning experience and provides exposure to another molding technique.

Finishing can be accomplished by etching and painting. Your local gas company will cooperate on the mantles.

Part B, the center section, is molded in a 9-×-12-×-12-inch cope section. You can place four 22-gauge sheet metal separators in the four glass areas (Note View D: typ 4 corners). This keeps the molding sand from filling the center section. This will be filled by sand from the 2-×-12-×-12-inch drag section.

☐ Place a ¾-×-14-×-14-inch molding board on the molding bench stringers.

☐ Place the cope, top up, on the molding board.

☐ Center the pattern bottom up, and with the sheet-metal inserts in place, in the center of the molding board (see Fig. 7-14).

Table 7-1. Materials List.

Part	Description
legs and top	25′ x 2 x 2 x 1/4 angle
frame braces	15′ x 2 x 1/4 hrs
floor mounts	8 x 2 x 1/4 hrs
way support plate	2′ x 4 x 1/4 hrs plate
headstock support plate	2′ x 10 x 1/4 hrs plate
way support	9 x 2 x 1 crs
ways	10′ x 1-1/2 dia crs
tailstock	10 x 7-1/2 x 2 hrs plate
headstock	10 x 7-1/2 x 5/8 hrs plate (2)
crank	1′ x 1 x 1/2 hrs
handle	6 x 1 dia brass
handle	7 x 1 dia hrs
handle	3 x 1-1/4 dia hrs
gears	2 x 2 dia crs (2)
gear	1-1/2 x 4-1/4 dia hrs
spindle	5 x 6 dia crs
chuck	4 x 6 dia hrs
headstock cover	8 x 10-1/2 x 26g aluminum
bearings	Nice 1635 DC (2)
Allen bolts	1/4-20 x 1 (6)
set screws	1/4-20 x 3/4 (9)
Allen bolts	10-24 x 3/4 (12)
bolts	3/8-16 x 4 (2)
bolts	5/16-18 x 1 (2)
bushings	3 x 1 dia brass
bushings	2 x 1-1/2 dia brass
bushings	2 x 2-1/4 dia aluminum

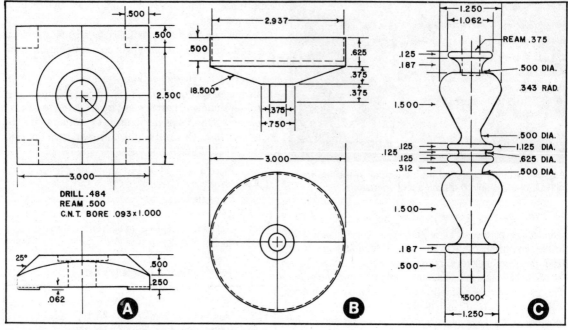

Fig. 7-10. The base (A), the top (B), and the stern (C).

☐ Apply parting compound to the molding board and pattern.

☐ Riddle sand over the pattern and molding board to a 3-inch height.

☐ Hold the pattern with one hand and, using a hand rammer, ram the sand.

☐ Riddle additional sand and ram until mold is rammed slightly above the cope top.

☐ Using a strike off bar, strike off the surplus sand and place a bottom board in position on the cope top.

☐ Roll the cope and remove the molding board and inserts.

☐ Place the drag on the cope and apply parting compound to the pattern.

☐ Riddle sand and ram until the sand is above the drag bottom.

☐ Strike off the surplus and place a bottom board on the struck off area.

☐ Have someone help you roll the mold.

☐ Remove the board and draw two diagonals from opposite corners. Where they cross, mark an X on the sand.

☐ Using a 9/16-inch diameter sprue cutter, start at the X and cut to a depth of 3½ inches.

☐ Form a pour basin at the sprue top (see Fig. 7-14).

☐ Vibrate the cope and draw it from the drag. The pattern usually remains on the rammed sand in the drag.

☐ Vibrate the pattern and draw carefully.

☐ Cut lapping gates in the cope section ½ × ⅝ inches (see Fig. 7-15).

☐ Blow off all loose sand with a bellows and place the cope on the drag.

☐ Move to pouring area.

☐ Pour this casting at 1350° and use alloy 319 or 356.

PATTERNS IN PERFORATED STEEL

One of the most versatile materials available to metalworkers is perforated steel. It can be purchased in a variety of designs, and will lend itself easily to cutting, welding, riveting, soldering, bending, forming, and enameling. Used in conjunction with wrought iron, and highlighted by polished brass or copper, it adds a distinctive touch to many projects.

The projects described in this section represent only a few of the countless ideas that can be developed through the use of this material.

Candle Holder

The pleasing contrast between polished brass and flat

188

black metal highlights this attractive candle holder. The body is made of perforated steel, and the design shown in Fig. 7-16 represents only one of the many design varieties available. Another interesting feature is the larger drip cup for the center candle. Materials needed include:

1 pc. #22 ga perforated steel, 9″ × 9″
2 pc. ¼″ d wrought iron, 10″ long
4 pc. rubber or plastic feet, ¼″ id
3 pc. ⅞″ d brass tubing, 1″ long
2 pc. #20 ga brass, 1¾″ d
1 pc. #20 ga brass, 2½″ d
Solder, lacquer, and flat black enamel.

Procedure. Cut perforated metal to proper size (9 × 9 inches) with tin snips or squaring shear. The design will dictate the exact size of the perforated steel for the body of the candle holder. Measure 1 11/16 inches back from each corner and cut corners at 45-degree angles. Here, again, the exact measurement will depend on the arrangement of the perforations.

Bend ¼-×-10-inch round iron to lengths with the hacksaw and file both ends smooth. Measure the center of the legs and bend to 90-degree angles in a vise or jig. Clean the legs and sheet metal both physically and chemically, and solder legs to sheet metal with the propane torch. Check positions of legs as shown in Fig. 7-16.

Cut the three brass disks to the proper sizes, file the edges smooth, and raise the disks slightly to form a shallow cup shape. Next, cut three 1-inch lengths of ⅞-inch diameter brass tubing. File both ends of each cylinder square to sides with a single-cut file. Tin one end

Fig. 7-11. A completed set of candlesticks.

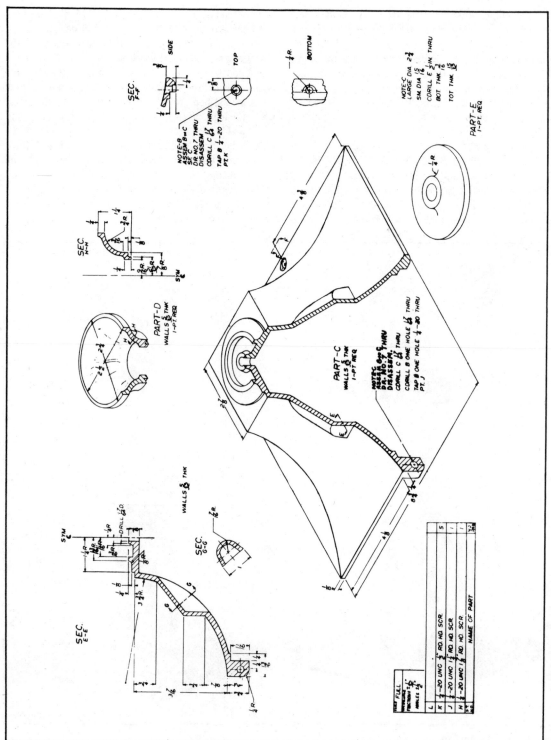

Fig. 7-12. Details for making patterns.

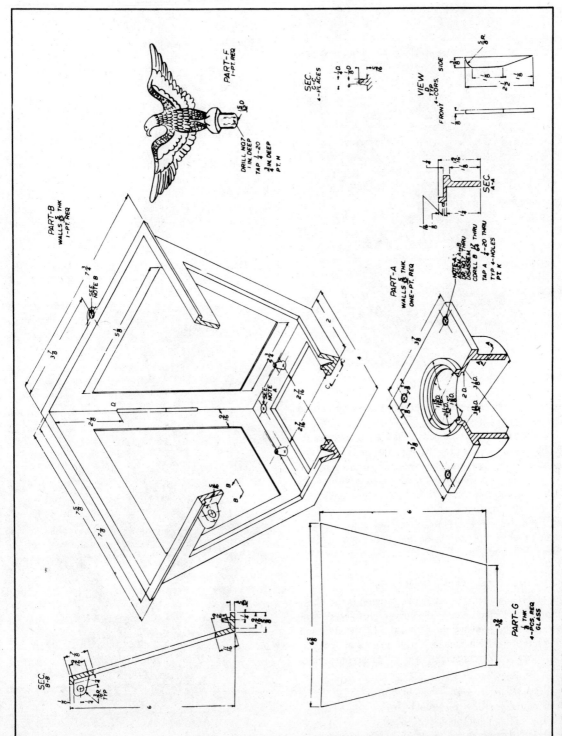

Fig. 7-13. Details for making patterns.

Fig. 7-14. Feeding the mold.

1 pc. 20 ga brass, ¾″ × 8″
3 pc. ⅛″ d × ⅜″ rh rivets
1 pc. ⅛″ threaded pipe, ⅝″ long
2 pc. ⅛″ locknuts

Lacquer, flat black enamel, key or push-through type socket, plug, 6′ of #18 lamp cord.

Procedure. Measure the ⅛-×-1-inch band iron to 12 inches in length, mark with scriber, and cut with hacksaw. File both ends square, using double-cut and single-cut files.

Enlarge the drawing to full size, using 1-inch square graph paper. Grip the ⅛-×-1-×-12-inch piece in a vise and bend the ends with a hammer until they match the enlarged drawing of the back. Centerpunch the metal where indicated on the drawing for the hanger hole, and the two rivet holes at A and B. Drill a 3/16-inch hanger hole at the top of the back, and drill two ⅛-inch rivet holes at A and B. Countersink rivet holes with a 3/16-inch drill.

Measure the ⅛-×-¾-inch band iron to 8 inches in

of each cylinder and sweat solder it to the center of each disk, using the propane torch.

Solder the completed candle cups to the perforated steel as shown on the drawing, again using the propane torch. If another method of fastening is preferred, use rivets for this step. Then buff the candle cups with rouge, wash with soap and water, allow to dry thoroughly, and apply a coat of clear lacquer.

Paint the legs and perforated steel with flat black enamel. Press rubber or plastic feet on the legs, and the project is finished. See Fig. 7-17.

Pin-Up Lamp

One of the interesting features of this lamp is the brass foil reflector located behind the curved perforated steel front. As can be seen in Figs. 7-18 and 7-19, the steel and brass serve as the lampshade. A pair of lamps of this type will serve as background lighting for a living room or den. Materials needed include:

1 pc. ⅛″ × 1″ × 12″ wrought iron
1 pc. ⅛″ × ¾″ × 8″ wrought iron
1 pc. 22 ga perforated steel, 5″ × 8″
1 pc. 36 ga brass foil, 5″ × 7″

Fig. 7-15. The completed lamp.

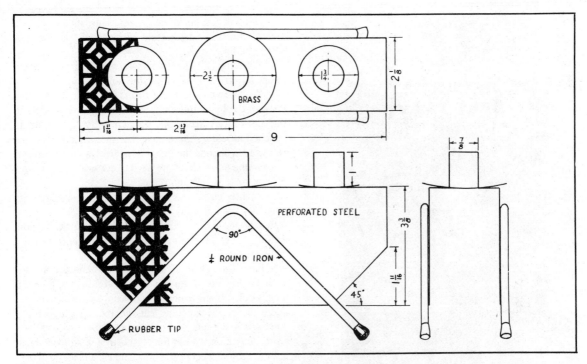

Fig. 7-16. Candle holder.

Fig. 7-17. The finished candle holder.

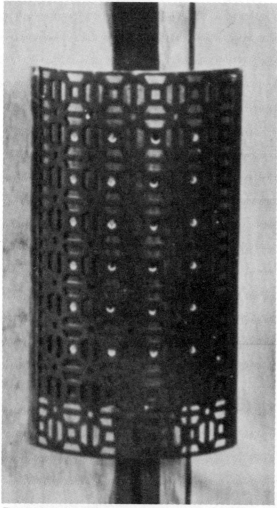

Fig. 7-18. Pin-up lamp.

two sides of the perforated steel. This should leave a 1-inch strip along the bottom of the steel that does not cover the foil.

Place the two sheets of metal over a piece of maple to act as a backing block for the next operation.

With a ⅛-inch drift punch and hammer, punch holes through the brass foil only, where there are cut-outs in the perforated steel sheet. Generally, one hole is punched for each square inch. The brass sheet acts as a reflector to bounce the light off the wall, and the perforations in the brass sheet are used to allow a small amount of light to pass through them.

Slightly curve the perforated steel sheet along its length on the slip rolls. The top view in Fig. 7-17 illustrates the curve. Next, rivet the steel sheet to the support arm at point C. This point is 1 inch above the bottom of the sheet as shown in the side view.

Paint the assembly with flat black enamel and set aside to dry. Polish the brass sheet on both sides with steel wool, rubbing in one direction only, then lacquer and allow to dry. Meanwhile, cut the two 20-gauge brass pieces to ¾ × 8 inches. Fold the brass pieces along their entire length on the bar folder set to ⅜ of an inch. Then buff, wash, and lacquer the brass pieces and allow to dry.

When all pieces are dry, assemble the reflector by placing the polished brass foil behind the perforated steel sheet. The two long strips of brass are then pressed over the two edges and tapped lightly with a mallet to keep the foil in place.

As a last step, install the threaded pipe with the two locknuts, wire and assemble the socket and plug.

PERFORATED METAL PLANTER

Smart table and mantle accessories can be made simply and inexpensively by using perforated steel and aluminum.

This versatile material will give you a chance to design, to be creative, and then see the project through to completion.

Although the design shown in Figs. 7-20 and 7-21 are of the gift-item variety, this material is equally suitable for larger projects such as home decorations, etc.

An outstanding feature of working with this material is that a minimum of metal-working equipment is needed. Perforated metal is easy to cut with tinsnips, it solders well, and bends sharply. It can also be fabricated by spot-welding or riveting, depending on the equipment available.

The dimensions given in Fig. 7-20 are only approximations. This is because perforated steel is available in

length, mark with scriber, and cut with hacksaw. File both ends square, using double-cut and single-cut files.

Bend the metal to the proper shape (see Fig. 7-17) using a bending jig and a vise. Locate and centerpunch position for ⅛-inch threaded pipe that holds the socket.

Drill ⅛-inch holes for rivets at A, B, and C. Drill 13/32-inch hole for ⅛-inch threaded pipe. Rivet support to back, using two ⅛-inch-diameter-⅜-inch rh rivets.

With tin snips or squaring shear, cut the 22-gauge perforated steel to 5 × 8 inches. Actual size is determined by the type of pattern of metal you are using. Cut the 36-gauge brass foil to 5 × 7 inches in the same manner. Next, place the perforated steel over the brass foil in such a position that the foil is even with the top and five distinct designs. This necessitates changing dimensions slightly according to the pattern to avoid a raw edge. This is also true of perforated aluminum.

To make a typical project, the following operations will be done. Use squaring shears, a file or emery cloth, the box and pan brake or a vise and bar for rolled edges, a metal bender, a spot welder or soldering iron, and the paint sprayer.

Perforated steel is manufactured by the Cross Engineering Company and perforated aluminum by Reynolds Aluminum Company. Both products are distributed by industrial-education supply houses.

LOG HOLDER

Steel and fabric, combined in a single project, often give interesting and pleasing results. In this project, steel is used to form a frame, and fabric is used as a sling. It serves well as a log holder or, on a smaller scale, as a magazine holder. More experimentation could aid in developing other design variations.

Materials needed are shown in Fig. 7-22. In approaching the project as a log holder, the frame requires two pieces of ½-×-30-inch, cold-rolled rod and four

pieces of ¼-×-17½-inch cold-rolled rod. The sling requires approximately one-half yard of 36-inch fabric and some matching thread. Canvas, sailcloth, or duck are good fabric choices and can usually be obtained in a wide range of colors. Leather, another choice for the sling, produces an exceptionally pleasing result. Colored burlap is an interesting choice if the sling is to be used as a magazine holder. Other materials needed will depend on the method selected for attaching the fabric to the bottom rails. Two methods are illustrated in B of Fig. 7-22. One method uses gripper snaps and the alternate method uses grommets set into the fabric and a leather thong to lash the fabric to the rail. Directions and tools for attaching these items are shown on the packages and can be purchased at any fabric or novelty store.

Cut two frame ends ½ × 30 inches and four rails ¼ × 17½ inches from cold-rolled rod. All matching items should be ground to the correct lengths and burrs should be removed. In addition, a slight spherical radius should be ground or filed on the frame ends.

Bend the frame ends and check carefully against each other for alignment. On each frame end, lay out and center punch the location for the rail holes; drill eight holes in the frame-end pieces ¼ of an inch in diameter and

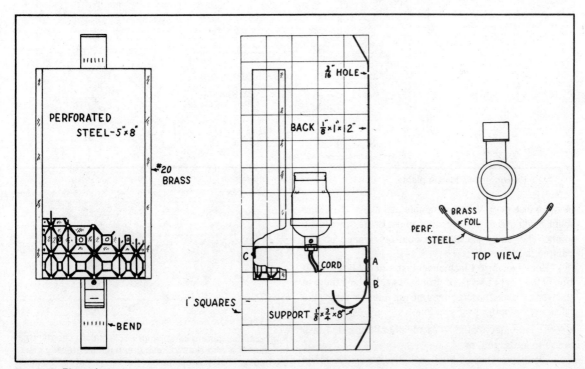

Fig. 7-19. Pin-up lamp.

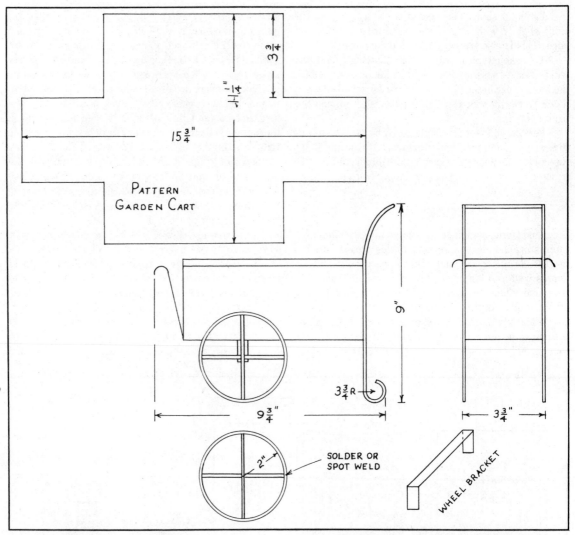

$3\frac{3}{4}$

$1\frac{1}{4}"$

$15\frac{3}{4}"$

PATTERN
GARDEN CART

9"

$3\frac{3}{4}$ R

$9\frac{3}{4}"$

2"

SOLDER OR
SPOT WELD

$3\frac{3}{4}"$

WHEEL BRACKET

Fig. 7-20. Design details for the planter.

⅜ of an inch deep. Next, assemble and check the alignment and fit of the rails and frame ends. Braze or weld the joints. The joints and metal should be cleaned up and painted flat black.

Hem the fabric 1 inch on all four sides. Locate position of the gripper snaps or grommets and attach them to the fabric. Drape the sling over the top rails and attach the fabric to the bottom rails as follows:

☐ grommet method—use leather thong and lash fabric to lower rail, or

☐ gripper-snap method—fold the fabric around the lower rail and secure the snaps.

Fig.7-21.This garden-cart planter would make a charming gift for someone who likes to have green things growing inside the house. This is an example of the things that can be made with perforated metal.

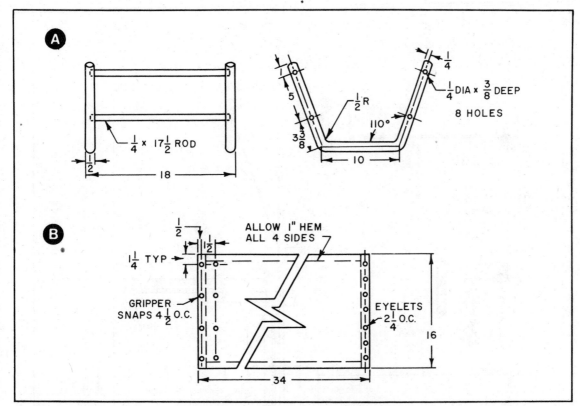

Fig. 7-22. Frame (A) and fabric and fastener details (B).

PORTABLE LECTERN

A free hand with frame design will result in many unusual shapes and styles. It should always be kept in mind, however, that the finished product is intended to be functional and attractive.

This lectern meets many of the criterions for a mass-production project: it has commercial value, it requires a minimum amount of tooling, jigs, and fixtures, and the fixtures needed can easily be developed. It offers an opportunity to develop basic manipulative skills, and it lends itself well to an operational breakdown to demonstrate the application of industrial processes and techniques.

Figure 7-23 illustrates assembly positioning, with the top inverted. It should prove quite satisfactory because it is completely portable and folds up into a compact package. It was made from No. 8-gauge half-hard aluminum flat sheet. Several additional models have also been made from much lighter-gauge material. The lectern is assembled by using pop rivets, but spot welding or

brazing would be just as effective. Any enamel or lacquer can be used as a finish.

Capable of reaping public-relations dividends, this project can be very economically produced, and ready markets can be found with local groups.

ALUMINUM/WOOD STILTS

The stilts shown here have a cast aluminum foot-piece. Figures 7-24 and 7-25 should furnish anyone experienced in patternmaking and foundry practice with ample information to work up patterns.

Label 1 in Fig. 7-24 shows a split (two-part) pattern of the footpiece made of clear white pine. The web is made of ⅛-inch plywood.

Label 2 in Fig. 7-24 shows a rough casting of the aluminum foot-piece, showing (A) the body of the footpiece, (B) sprue, (C) risers, and (D) vents. It is necessary that venting of the mold be adequate to eliminate air pockets.

Label 3 shows the finished cast aluminum foot-piece mounted on a dummy leg. This unit is hand finished with

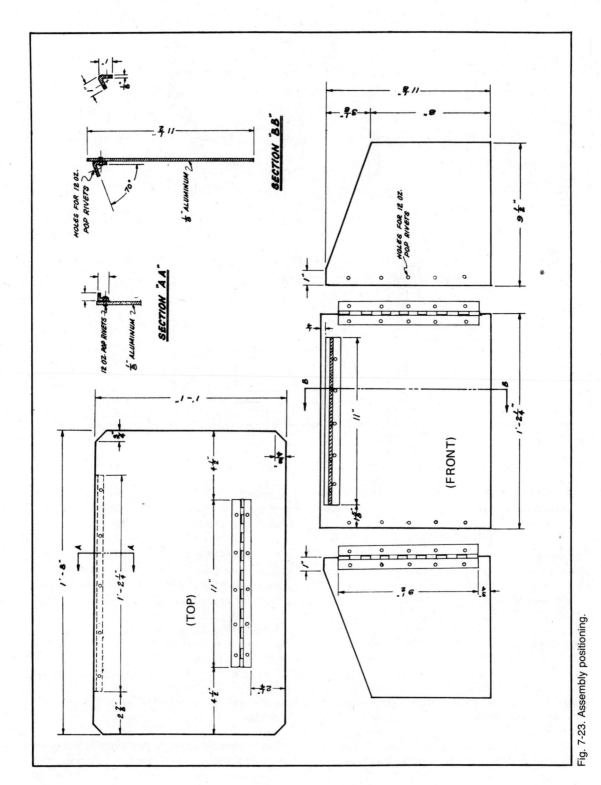

Fig. 7-23. Assembly positioning.

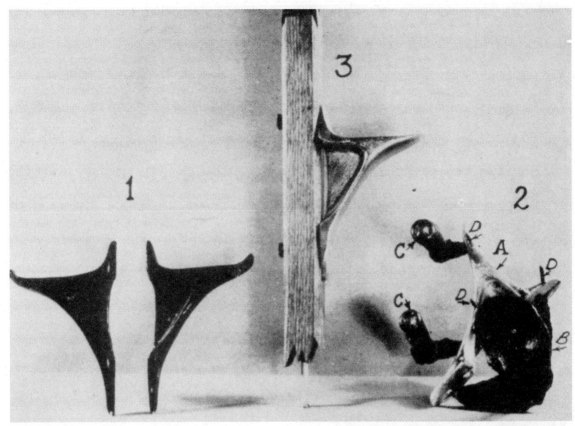

Fig. 7-24. Stilt details.

files and abrasives. If your shop is equipped with a milling machine or a metal shaper, the part of the foot-piece that fits against the stilt leg can be machine finished. Drill two 17/64-inch holes in the foot-piece on 4¾-inch centers. Countersink these holes for ¼-×-2¼-inch flat-head bolts. Brass bolts are recommended for ease in removal to adjust for greater heighth. Use lock washers under nuts to assure safe assembly.

For the stilt leg use 2-×-2-inch-6-foot (approximately) straight-grained wood stock. Chamfer the edges, full length, and round off the ends slightly. Sandpaper smooth. Beginning approximately 8 inches from the bottom end of the leg, drill five 9/32-inch holes, 4¾-inch centers. Two coats of shellac are recommended to protect the wood from exposure to the elements. See Figs. 7-25 and 7-26.

ALUMINUM NUTCRACKER

The nutcracker shown in Figs. 7-27 and 7-28 is an ideal

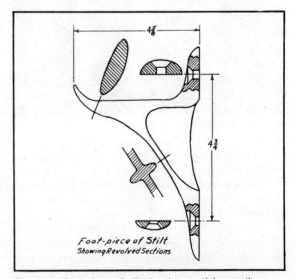

Foot-piece of Stilt
Showing Revolved Sections

Fig. 7-25. Foot-piece of stilt showing revolving sections.

Fig. 7-26. The finish stilts in use.

project for the machine shop, especially for the vocational machine shop.

It has several virtues. First, of course, it is a useful article. Then, too, it can be set up either as an individual project or as a production project.

In making the nutcracker, it is advisable to purchase 1-×-2-inch aluminum and machine the body block from these. The tensile strength of the article made in this way is greater than a casting, and the project is not so easily broken when in use.

The gear and rack are made on a horizontal mill using a dividing head and index plate. This furnishes an excellent opportunity to teach gear cutting, indexing, and the related math so necessary in machine-shop training.

The lathe work, threading and tapping, filing, and polishing are not too difficult for the average metalworker. The results, naturally, will depend on the individual.

A MAGIC PITCHER

Almost everyone seems to be fascinated by magicians and magic. One of the most interesting and popular tricks used by magicians is the "pitcher that never empties." The device employs a very simple law of physics stating the water seeks its own level. The "gimmick" in this trick is that the pitcher is actually two containers in one. A cylinder is soldered inside the outer shell in such a way as to provide an air space between the two containers. This air space is actually used as a reservoir to hold water back every time the pitcher is "emptied."

The pitcher must be filled prior to use. As noted in Figs. 7-29 and 7-30, the liner has two very small holes punched in it, one located near the bottom to let the water in the air space—the other hole located near the top to allow air to escape to prevent back pressures. Filling the pitcher takes some time to allow the water in the cylinder to seep into the cavity. Water should be added until the cylinder will accept no more.

The magic pitcher is very easy to use. After it is full of water, you need only to pour the water out in the conventional manner. The water in the cylindrical part will be emptied and when the pitcher is righted the hole in the bottom of the cylinder will allow water from the air space to seep into the cylinder until the two levels are equal. This process can be repeated about a dozen times before the water is completely exhausted.

Planning and Construction

The pitcher poses a design problem and a shop problem. Construction follows usual sheet-metal procedures with patterns being transferred to metal, parts being cut, shaped, or formed, and assembled by hand soldering. It is suggested that the body be made first and the bottom added to it. The wired spout should then be added to the body. The cylindrical liner is inserted and soldered in place with the handle fixed in place as the last step.

Additional Notes

□ You might want to omit the cylindrical liner if a plain pitcher is desired.

□ Brass or copper can be substituted in place of tinplate.

□ Other methods of development can be used in place of radial to get a greater variety of designs.

Whether the pitcher is used as a decoration, a magical trick, or a combination of the two, there will be many hours of enjoyment for anyone who designs and makes a magic pitcher of his own.

FREE-FORM METAL DISHES

Free-form designs, widely accepted in the furniture and home-furnishings industry, lend themselves to such items as metal fruit dishes, ashtrays, and table center-pieces. The raising technique, used in forming container shapes from metal by "stretching" metal, is not an exacting process and is suited to free-form designs of dishes made from metal.

Some of the metals that can be used for making free-form dishes, and their inherent assets as well as shortcomings, are:

Aluminum. It is inexpensive, but it scratches very easily. Furthermore it is difficult to anneal once it is hardened from being worked.

Pewter. Although this metal is easily worked it is also easily bent out of shape because it is quite soft. It is relatively expensive.

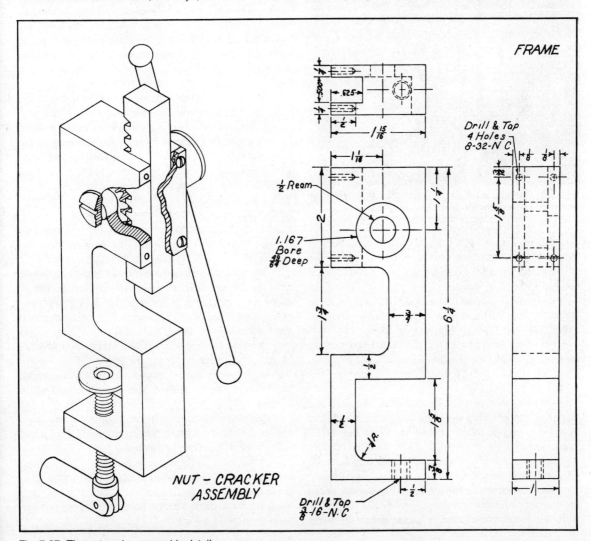

Fig. 7-27. The nutcracker assembly details.

Fig. 7-28. This nutcracker can be used either as an individual project or as a production project in the shop.

Silver. This is a lovely metal to work with, but it is too expensive for the beginner.

Brass. This alloy would be nice to work with, but it tends to be hard to work.

Copper. This is the metal used in making the items shown in Fig. 7-31. Some procedural suggestions for making free-form dishes from copper follow.

Sketch on heavy paper the shape that you want to form. Keep in mind the purpose of the dish. For example, if you plan to make a dish to hold flowers, it must be deep enough to hold waer.

Cut out the paper pattern you have sketched and trace it on copper. It is a good idea to use blue layout fluid to make an easy-to-follow scribed line (A of Fig. 7-31). Remember that the eventual depth of the finished item will take up some of the width. Allow for this factor in your free-hand sketch.

The finished article will not be the exact shape as the flat piece of metal that you start out with. The copper, or whatever metal you choose to work, should be fairly thick; 16 gauge or heavier. The 10-gauge stock, which, although a little more expensive than 16 gauge, produces a pleasingly heavy finished piece.

After outlining the shape on the metal sheeting, cut it out with a metal-cutting band saw (B of Fig. 7-31), cold chisel, sheet-metal snips, or whatever tools you have handy. File the edges smooth and free from irregularities.

A short section of a log, 1 foot in diameter by 2 feet in length, makes an excellent forming block. Gouge out a shallow depression, 2 inches to 3 inches in diameter and 1 inch deep, in the top of the block.

Hold the metal blank at an angle (C of Fig. 7-31) and begin working it near the edge, using light hammer blows. The spot where the metal is being hammered should be over the depression in the forming block. Do not hammer too hard in any one place on the metal. The metal is formed by many light blows distributed evenly all around the blank. Turn the metal after each blow—really, tap.

We used art-metal-forming hammers, but ordinary ball peen hammers will also do the job.

Copper can be raised considerably before it hardens, but when it resists hammer blows, it should be annealed. This is simple. Heat the metal evenly until the first glow of red appears. Then quench it in acid to clean the black oxide from the surface. Beware of acid splatter.

The acid solution is comprised of 1 part of sulfuric acid to 11 parts of water. Scouring powder can also be used to clean the metal. If you do use the acid solution, though, scrub the metal thoroughly in water and dry completely.

The forming process goes on and on and on and on until the sides of the dish are raised to whatever size or shape you prefer. Perfect symmetry is not exactly preferable because this effect can be achieved more easily and more accurately by stamping.

Once the forming is completed, the finishing process begins. You can file and round the edges and then polish them on a buffing wheel charged with tripoli compound. Or the edge can be peened with a small, round-nosed hammer.

Additional surface treatment might be enameling a design on the surface, following standard enameling techniques. It can then be lacquered.

Novel color patterns can be achieved—prior to the lacquering—by baking the item in a kitchen oven. It is recommended that you experiment with the last step using scraps of copper before doing it to a dish that has been painstakingly formed.

TROWEL PROJECT GIVES VARIETY

Garden trowels as a project are readily acceptable to most metalworkers. The project offers sufficient variety of tool processes and use of materials to be adaptable to any shop situation. In this case, aluminum was used throughout, but sheet steel for the body, ⅜-inch square mild steel for a handle shank, and a turned wood handle could be substituted with equally good results. The following description will deal only with the fabrication of an aluminum trowel.

The body is made of .091-inch thick 24 ST aluminum alloy (see Fig. 7-32). After the body is laid out, it can be

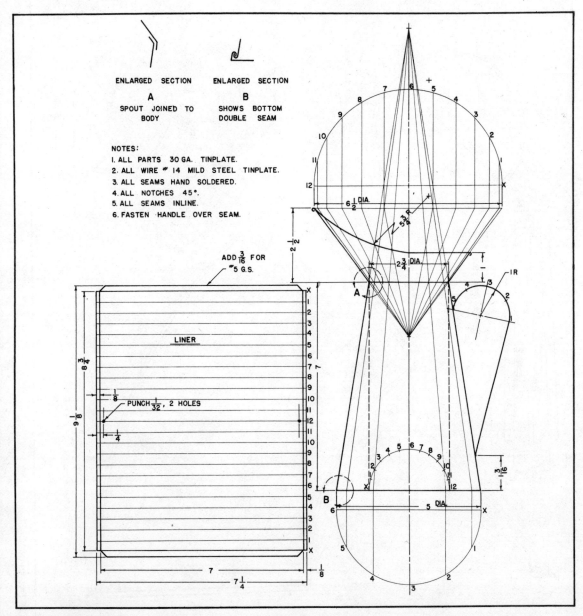

Fig. 7-29. Design details.

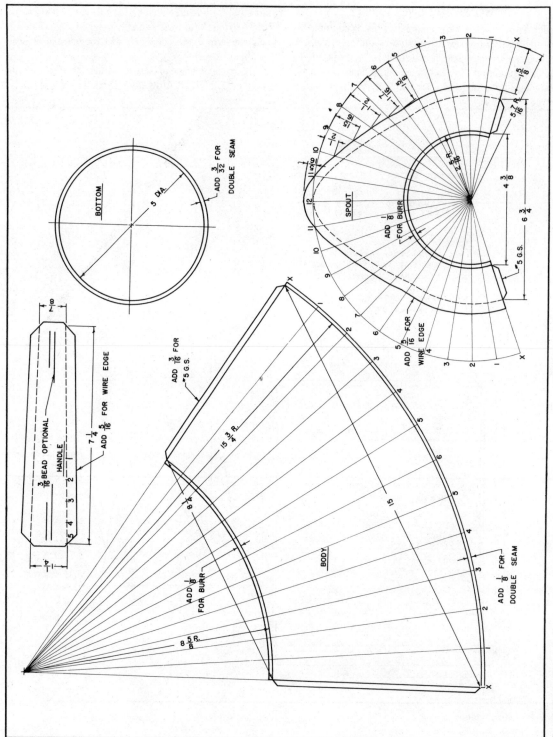

Fig. 7-30. Design details.

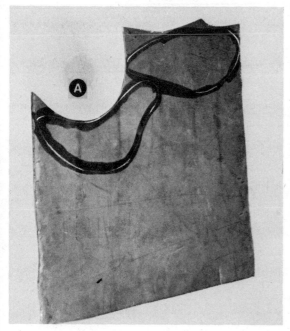

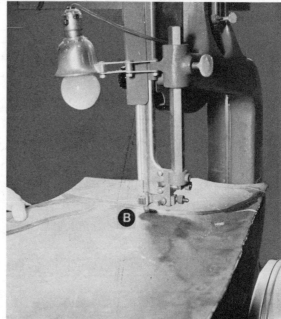

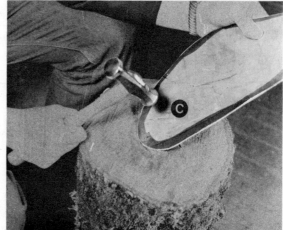

Fig. 7-31. Sketch a pattern (A), cut the shape (B), and work the edge (C).

roughed out by hand sawing, shearing, or by use of a metal-cutting band saw. Finishing to layout lines is accomplished with files and the edge is finally burnished. Forming rolls are excellent for curving the body, but in their absence a sheet-metal stake and mallet would be found suitable.

Rivet holes should be laid out after the body is formed because they can become distorted in the forming process. The holes should be countersunk from the inside of the trowel to receive the ⅛-inch countersunk rivets. The degree of finish desired on the body as well as the handle will determine whether or not you choose to use

abrasive cloths and buffing equipment. Most metalworkers will prefer to put a very high finish on the trowel if aluminum is used.

A little foundry practice is employed in making the handle. A two-piece pattern was used to make a green sand mold and casting. If metal-working machines are available in the shop, the handle can be finished on the lathe and shaper. In the absence of a metal-turning lathe, the handle can be finished by mounting on a wood-turning lathe. The latter method will require some special consideration to prevent damage to tailstock center if a spinning center is not available and will also require a

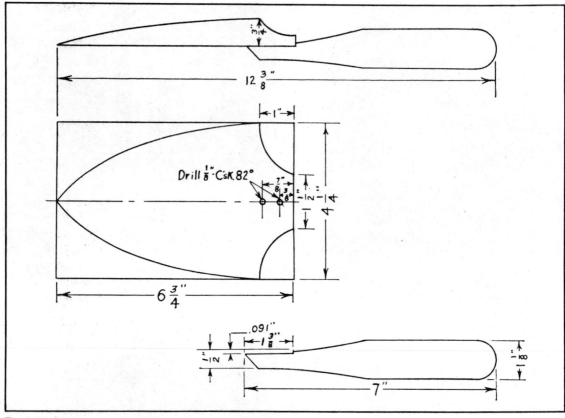

Fig. 7-32. Garden trowel details.

slotted faceplate to receive a lathe dog. A scraping tool made of a heavy file will suffice for the preliminary finishing which would have to be followed up by finishing with a file and abrasive cloth. The offset to receive the body can be produced by filing.

Holes for rivets in the handle are countersunk to give a flush surface to the handle. Use countersunk rivets, peen them into the countersunk holes in the handle, and finish off with a file.

BUILDING KNIGHTS FROM
NUTS AND BISHOPS FROM BOLTS

Designing, planning, and constructing this chess set affords you the opportunity to weld and braze metals of different properties and thicknesses. This can be a stimulating and challenging experience for the welders.

Various metal finishes can be applied to the chess set. If time is taken to design and plan a chess set carefully, it can be constructed for a small fraction of what a commercial model would cost. See Figs. 7-33 and 7-34.

Cut copper and brass squares very accurately so that they will fit together properly.

Finish squares with emery cloth and cement on plywood with a heavy-grip cement. Alternate the brass and copper squares in eight rows of eight squares each.

Fig. 7-33. The finished chess set.

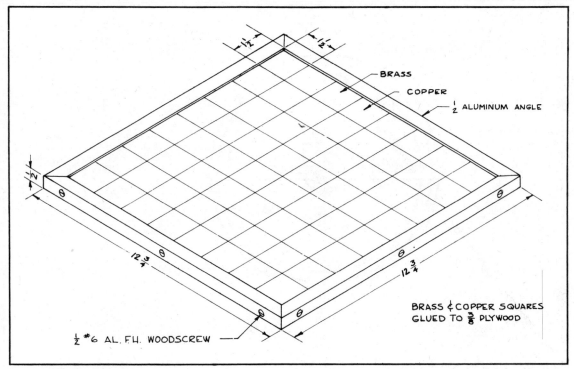

Fig. 7-34. The chessboard.

Mitre, drill, and countersink the aluminum angles. File parts as needed and mount with three screws to each side.

Make sure project is clean and dry. Spray with clear lacquer.

The following is a parts list for the chessboard.

1 ⅜″ × 12¾″ × 12¾″ plywood
4 1/16″ × ½″ × 12¾″ aluminum angles
32 1½″ × 1½″ 20-ga. copper
32 1½″ × 1½″ 20-ga. brass
12 ½″ #6 aluminum fh wood screws

A GYROSCOPIC TOP

This project has educational value in many subject fields—not only is machining of metal, welding or brazing, and metal forming involved, but mathematics and physical science as well.

You will learn a variety of operations in making this project, including straight turning, knurling, drilling, taper turning, turning work held on a mandrel, forming rings, brazing or welding, and threading. Many items of related information such as unified thread system, tap drill sizes, classes of fits, brazing techniques can be examined.

To construct the frame, cut the stock to length and chamfer the ends so that the joint will hold after brazing. Form the rings on a slip-roll forming machine. The holes in the frame for the screws and the bumper ring are drilled and tapped while clamped to an angle plate. A fixture can be made for this operation.

The spindle is used as the mandrel for holding the flywheel for machining. All diameters on the wheel and spindle must be concentric or the top will be out of balance.

The machine screws must have center holes drilled in the end to provide seats for the spindle. Paint the frame before assembly to complete this attractive educational toy. See Figs. 7-35 and 7-36.

BUCKLE UP

Scraps of brass and copper can be made into belt buckles. A design can relate to an event, place, person, or thing. Examples are the Liberty Bell, tomahawks, cannons, profiles of colonial leaders, arrowheads, and keystones. (See Fig. 7-37).

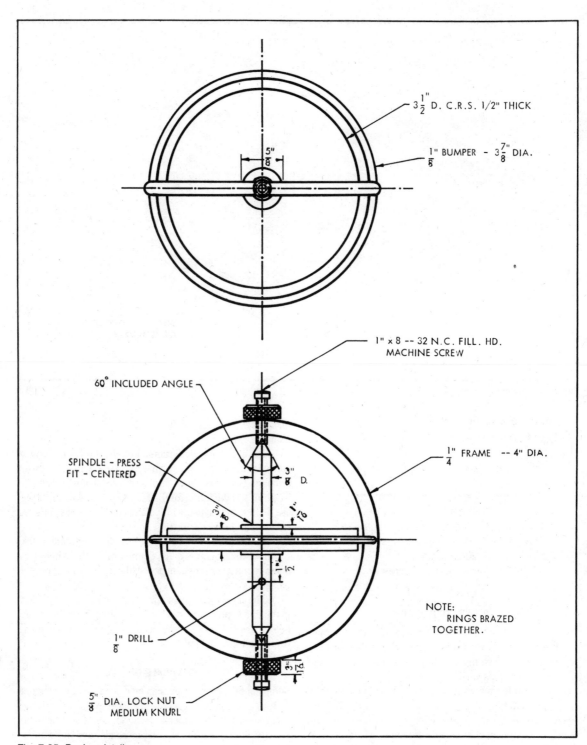

$3\frac{1}{2}$" D. C.R.S. 1/2" THICK

$\frac{5}{8}$"

1" BUMPER - $3\frac{7}{8}$" DIA.

1" × 8 -- 32 N.C. FILL. HD.
MACHINE SCREW

60° INCLUDED ANGLE

$\frac{3}{8}$" D.

SPINDLE - PRESS
FIT - CENTERED

$\frac{3}{16}$"

$\frac{1}{16}$"

$\frac{1}{4}$" FRAME -- 4" DIA.

$\frac{1}{2}$"

1" DRILL
$\frac{1}{8}$"

NOTE:
    RINGS BRAZED
    TOGETHER.

$\frac{5}{8}$" DIA. LOCK NUT
MEDIUM KNURL

$\frac{3}{16}$"

Fig. 7-35. Design details.

208

Fig. 7-36. A completed gyroscopic top.

After a design is created, a piece of 12- to 20-gauge brass is selected, cut, and shaped for the buckle body. A brass welding rod or sheet brass is shaped for the belt loop holder and keeper. These are silver soldered to the back side of the buckle body. An overlay of 18- to 24-gauge copper is cut with a jeweler's saw, filed, and soft soldered to the buckle body. The buckle is cleaned with fine abrasive, then buffed to a high luster. Any necessary engraving is added; then the buckle is sprayed with water-clear acrylic enamel to prevent oxidation.

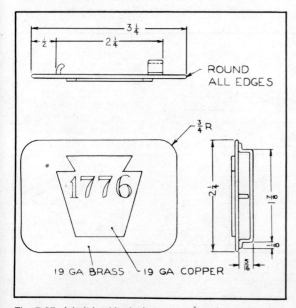

Fig. 7-37. A belt-buckle design.

PERSONALIZED BUCKLES IN THREE METALS

Personalized belt buckles is an art metals project that can be used as a fund raiser. Readily fabricated with a minimum of materials and equipment, the project gives you experiences with a variety of metals, fastening methods, and finishing techniques.

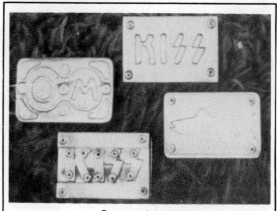

Construction calls for problem solving

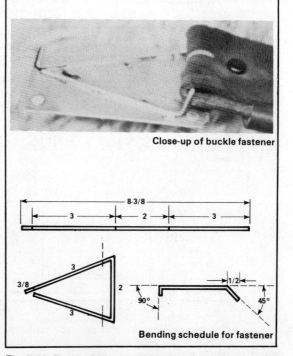

Close-up of buckle fastener

Bending schedule for fastener

Fig. 7-38. Buckle designs and details.

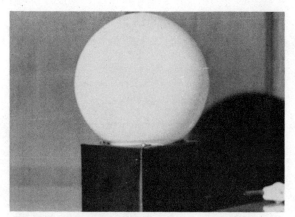

Fig. 7-39. This opal globe lamp is a good beginning project.

BUILD A GLOBE LAMP

This opal globe lamp can be assembled with standard metalworking tools. The lamp requires development, layout, cutting, bending, fastening, abrasives, and finishing. During construction, you will use: disc gauge, rule, scriber, prick punch, bar folder, hand drill, box and pan brake, stake, setting hammer, rawhide mallet, aviation snips, hand punch, straight snips, squaring shears, spot welder, riveting hammer, rivet set, and file.

☐ Cut 28 gauge sheet metal to size and remove sharp edges and burrs.

☐ Tape pattern to metal and transfer lines.

☐ Fold metal in this sequence: (a) hem (b) top (c) end flap (d) crease each corner slightly (e) complete each corner bend on stake.

☐ Spot weld flap.

☐ Drill 9/64 in. holes for rivet at each corner. Set rivets with preset head up.

☐ Construct bracket, punch and bend, and spot weld.

☐ Punch hole for electrical cord.

☐ Clean with steel wool, solder seam if desired, and paint. Rub paint off rivet heads for highlight effect.

☐ Fasten electrical socket to bracket with Class A sheet metal screw.

☐ Complete electrical wiring; attach globe. The globe should have a base of about 3⅛-inch diameter. Smaller bases usually fit; larger bases often fit after trimming with aviation snips. See Figs. 7-39 and 7-40.

First design a buckle and prepare a plan sheet to include sequential construction steps, tools and materials needed, and a full-size sketch. The buckle is made of 2-×-3-inch pieces of sheet copper, brass, and aluminum and nonferrous wire, if needed. With the use of all three metals, you must solve a variety of fastening problems. Through soldering or solid or blind riveting the main pieces are generally sandwiched together to add thickness, weight, and rigidity to the piece. Design elements can be cut out, engraved, or added on. Peening, engraving, buffing, etc., add to the texture of the buckle. The buckle back is made of ⅛-inch diameter steel wire, soldered to the work (see Fig. 7-38), and after cleaning and buffing, several coats of lacquer are applied.

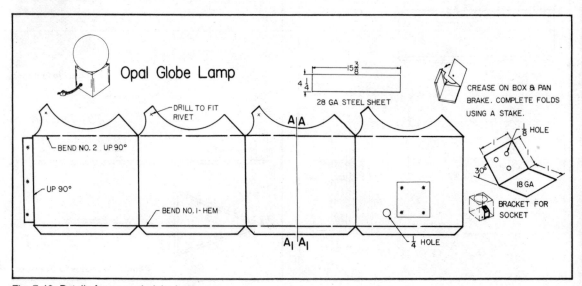

Fig. 7-40. Details for an opal globe lamp.

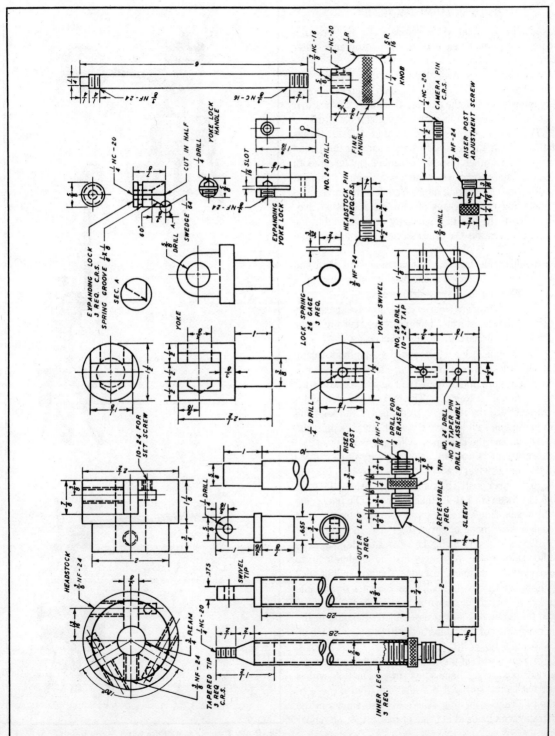

Fig. 7-41. Aluminum tripod details.

BUILD AN ALUMINUM TRIPOD

This aluminum tripod will serve as a sturdy, versatile, and lightweight tool welcomed by the photographer, star gazer, or projectionist.

Because it is unusually light in weight, it is a convenient traveler, especially where a high degree of portability is desired. With the exception of minor hardware, it is made of aluminum tubing and aluminum bar stock.

The leg tips are reversible. One end of the leg tip has a tapered point that is used when mounting the tripod outdoors. The other end has a rubber tip for smooth surfaces. The tripod can be angled or swiveled in almost any direction. By making minor changes, it can be used for mounting various types of cameras and small telescopes. With the use of a specially designed table-top attachment, it can also be used as a base for holding a slide projector.

Building this tripod will challenge your skill and ingenuity. It can be made in any machine shop that has a lathe, a shaper, a mill, and a drill press.

The project offers a variety of learning experiences in turning, milling, slotting, tapping, thread cutting, angle drilling, reaming, laying out, and measuring.

The aluminum bar stock and the aluminum tubing should be selected from hard stock. The degree of hardness should approximate 2024-T4. The wall thickness for the legs should be 18 gauge. The parts made from cold-rolled steel are the three tapered tips for the legs and their expanding split locks, the three headstock pins, the camera pin, and the riser-post adjustment screw.

A press fit is used to fasten the three tapered leg tips, the three swivel tips, and the sleeve connecting the yoke to the riser post. The camera pin is held in the yoke swivel by means of a 10-24 thumb screw. The flat spring for the expanding yoke lock can be made from either 26-gauge sheet metal or springsteel. The inner legs are threaded on one end to fit the reversible leg tip. The handle can be made from steel instead of aluminum to avoid mating aluminum threads. The expanding lock should be wedged with a ball peen hammer or suitable dapping die punch as shown in section A of Fig. 7-41. When the expanding lock is assembled, it should fit the inside diameter of the tubing and still be able to slide up and down freely.

Proper tension of the riser post is obtained through the riser post adjustment screw in conjunction with a short but heavy spring and a disc cut from a piece of leather or rubber matting. The steel ball shown in the illustration can be used in place of the leather or rubber disc.

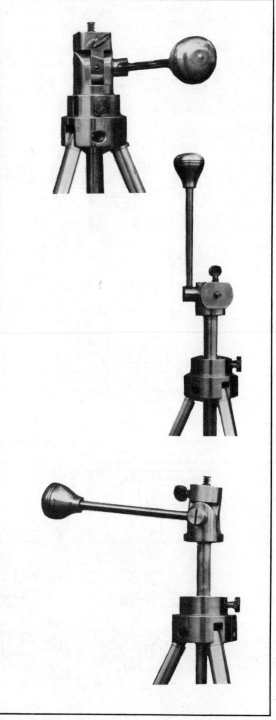

Fig. 7-42. Three views of the head of the tripod.

Assembling the tripod is not difficult if all the parts have been carefully made. The expanding yoke lock must fit the yoke with a "push fit" to attain maximum locking action. The swivel leg tips should fit the slots in the headstock with a snug fit. Finally, the three headstock pins for fastening the legs to the headstock should be tightened lightly against the swivel leg tips and locked in place with a No. 8-32 set screw to insure maximum rigidity of the tripod. See Figs. 7-42, 7-43 and 7-44.

MATCH-PLATE PATTERNS

When quantity production of small castings is required, a match-plate pattern can offer several advantages. In addition to establishing the parting plane and eliminating parting down as required on many loose patterns, match-plate patterns allow gating systems to be attached or cast in the plate as well as the riser if needed, this saves time and money. Match-plates provide more than one mold cavity and also establish machine locating points and core prints. Thin section patterns that would normally warp can be attached or cast into a plate to provide pattern stability.

Match-plate patterns can be made of ¾-inch fir plywood with the pattern or patterns attached, or they can be made by attaching the patterns to a ⅜-inch aluminum plate, which may have an air-operated vibrator attached to it to facilitate drawing of the plate.

While match-plate patterns can be pressure cast in precision plaster molds or sand molds, a greater amount of polishing and clean-up is required when sand casting plates. When cast in plaster, the metal is held in a lined steel tube with a cap and air connector. An air hose is attached to the connector, and 5 pounds of air pressure is applied. The paper breaks, and the aluminum is forced into the precision plaster mold. The tube is offset to the side of the plate and the ingate is cut off after shake-out. Aluminum match-plates can produce up to 50,000 cast-

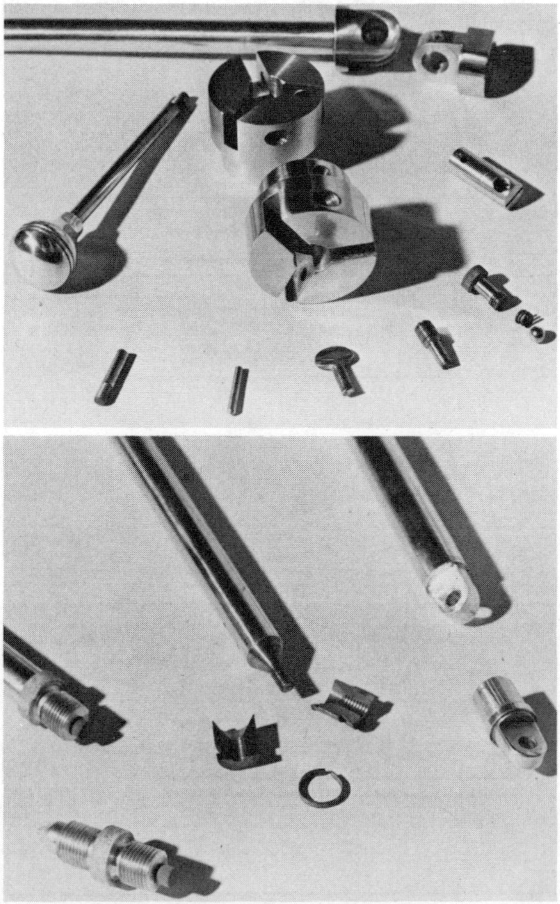

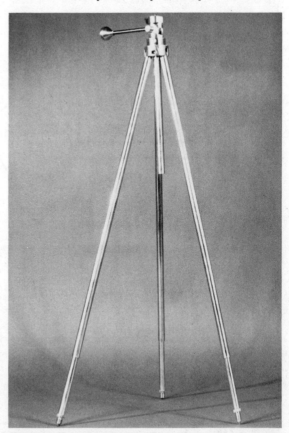

Fig. 7-43. Parts for the tripod's head and feet.

Fig. 7-44. The completed tripod.

ings with greater dimensional accuracy than wood or plastic.

Here is the procedure for making a match-plate.

☐ Ram up the desired pattern mold as you regularly would to produce a casting.

☐ Carefully remove the pattern from the mold and set the mold aside where it will not be damaged.

☐ In the center of the gypsum board, lay out the outside dimension of the intended match-plate. The gypsum board will serve as a spacer between the cope and drag of the mold (see A of Fig. 7-45).

☐ From a hole punched or drilled in the spacer, cut out the shape of the intended match-plate.

☐ Cut holes in the gypsum board spacer to receive the pins of a large flask. When cutting the holes, make sure the hole for the match-plate is centered around the pattern.

☐ After making sure the mold is clean and free of loose sand, sandwich the gypsum board spacer between the copy and the drag.

☐ Weight the mold to prevent blowout and follow normal safety procedures in pouring aluminum (see C of Fig. 7-45).

☐ When the aluminum solidifies, remove the match-plate from the mold; then, clean and inspect it for casting defects, and cut off the sprue. Drill holes to fit the flask in which the match-plate will be used (see D of Fig. 7-45).

☐ Ears can be attached as shown in Figs. 7-46 through 7-49.

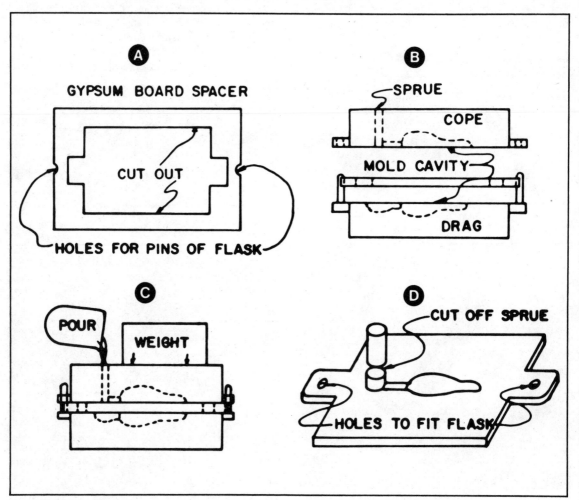

Fig. 7-45. Match-plate design.

214

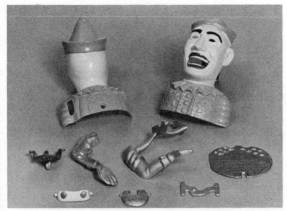

Fig. 7-46. Match-plate patterns can provide more than one mold cavity. This nine-piece Humpty Dumpty mechanical bank is reproduced from two cast aluminum match-plates.

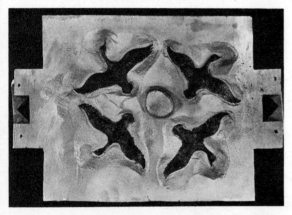

Fig. 7-47. Cope and drag sides of a sand cast aluminum plate with spacing of four patterns having nonuniform parting.

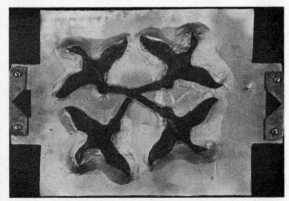

Fig. 7-48. Note feeding system as cast. Patterns and feeding system have been darkened to accent the parting down.

Fig. 7-49. Patterns can be attached to a ⅜-inch aluminum plate (left) or to ¾-inch fir plywood. Aluminum plate can have an air-operated vibrator attached to facilitate drawing of the plate.

A steel frame ⅜ × 1 inch can be fabricated to the needed flask size and used in place of the gypsum board. The steel gives a quick chill and improves directional solidification.

A SHAD DART PROJECT

The shad dart lure is deadly on any species of game fish. It also makes a great shop project. In fabricating the lure, you will learn such machine and metalshop operations as casting, grinding, drilling, milling, and tapping.

The advantage of the shad dart over other types of lures is its versatility. It can be retrieved steadily, jerked, or worked slowly behind a float. The smaller size darts catch trout and panfish, but also lure larger species who feed on small, schooling bait fish. Larger-size lures sink deeper and can be seen better.

The lure is made by casting a metal with a low melting point into a tapered, cylindrical body, formed around a jig hook. The front of the lure is the larger end of the taper, with a flat surface slanted at about a 60-degree angle, causing the lure to wiggle when retrieved steadily and rise in the water when sharply pulled.

Equipment and Materials. To make the lure, you will need a heat source capable of converting metal, such as lead, to a molten state, a ladle for holding and pouring the metal, jig hooks, and a shad dart mold. Lead can be found in used tire balance weights from gas stations, plumbing supplies, or old sinkers. Jig hooks come in sizes from eight (smallest) to one (largest) and in different shank lengths. The long shank model is best for shad darts because the body of the lure takes up so much of the hook.

The mold is best made of zinc or aluminum, but other materials such as plaster, wood, and plastic are adequate. A commercially available cast aluminum mold can be purchased, but the resulting product is rough and needs considerable trimming and filing—a poor option when you can make a precision mold that will produce a lure ready to tie and paint. Making several molds in mass production or individually is a good advanced machine shop project.

The most difficult procedure in making the mold is to accurately grind the drill bit to the correct taper for forming the dart. Otherwise, mold construction requires straightforward machine operations. See Fig. 7-49 and 7-50.

Casting. When heating the lead, be sure you have adequate ventilation. Some lead contains impurities that give off harmful fumes. Place hooks in position in the mold, and heat the mold a little before pouring. Wear safety glasses and do not add new lead to the molten lead. This could cause moisture to drop into the molten metal making it spatter.

The darts will solidify quickly so you can remove them at once. If you are using a precision mold, snap off the sprues with the cutter. If you are using a standard mold, remove the darts first, cut off the sprues with wire snips, then trim and file.

Dressing and Painting. Before painting, tie on hair or a feathered tail, using size A nylon thread. Popular materials for dressing are calf tail, which can be purchased dyed, or marabou plumes, which have a lifelike, wiggling action in the water. But almost any natural or synthetic material that is long enough will suffice. Some fisherman swear by cat and dog hair, claiming good results, low cost, and an unlimited supply.

To prepare hair for tying, cut it as long as possible, and even it up by pulling out the extremely long or short hairs. A vise will help to hold the hook while you tie. Lay the hair parallel to the hook shank, and wrap several turns of thread around both shank and hair. Tie off the thread with a couple of half hitches, and cut off the excess hair. Continue wrapping the thread over the hair until all the butt ends are tied down and smooth, leaving the slender, tapered ends to trail behind the hook.

Use an undercoat of white paint to bring out the brightness in the final colors. Lacquer is a good choice because it dries fast. Cover the thread wraps to keep thread and hair from coming apart. Some popular designs are red, white, and yellow, or red with black dots dabbed

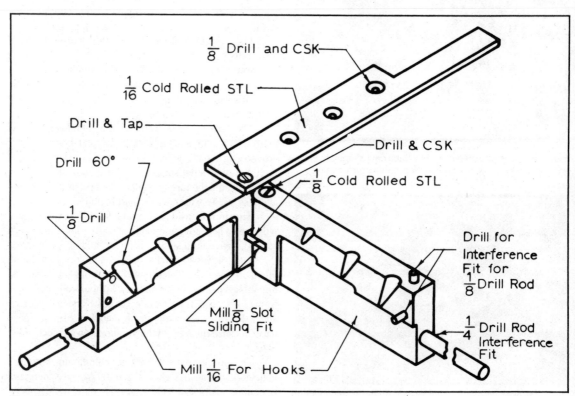

Fig. 7-50. A shad dart mold.

Fig. 7-51. Start to finish sequence.

on with a nail. But don't let standard patterns keep you from experimenting. Take pride in your lures and personalize your designs.

A MULTIMACHINE PROJECT

This key chain project has much to recommend it. It is simple in design, low in cost (including the "good luck" penny), is a multimachine, multioperation learning experience and is a realistic simulation of industrial process.

Before going into production, analyze the steps involved, work out the problems, and develop a written procedure sheet. You will need a hydraulic press and stamp. See Figs. 7-51 through 7-55.

☐ Shear 2-inch squares from 3/32-inch aluminum.

☐ Mark one corner of each square with a layout dye for piece location in next two steps.

☐ Rough an 11/16-inch hole in center of stock in a vertical milling machine setup.

☐ In same setup as above, finish hole .750 d with end mill.

☐ Countersink both faces lightly in a drill press, and load parts on arbor. Random loading makes cutting smoother.

☐ Turn to 1.750 ± .005 on an engine lathe.

☐ Set up milling machine (horizontal) with gear cutter or slitting saw and an indexing or a dividing head, and mill desired design.

☐ Strip arbor and tumble pieces to remove burrs and sharp edges.

☐ Make setup in drill press and drill 5/32-inch hole for chain.

☐ Deburr hole in drill press or by hand.

Fig. 7-52. Turning the stack.

Fig. 7-53. Milling the design.

Fig. 7-54. Stamping the piece.

Fig. 7-55. Punch with work in fixture.

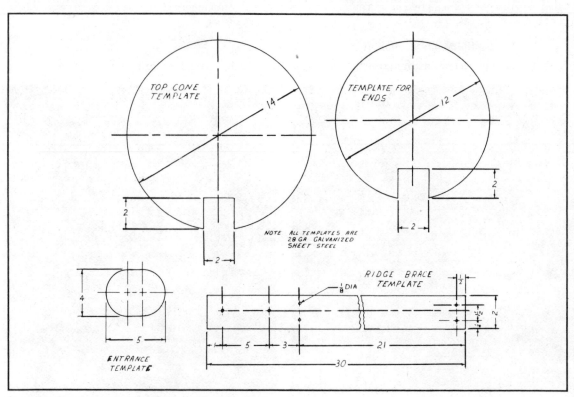

Fig. 7-56. Template patterns, with suggested dimensions.

☐ Set up a holding fixture in hydraulic press. Insert aluminum disk and penny.

☐ Press lettering into piece. Action will hold penny in place.

☐ Polish or leave satin finish from tumbling.

☐ Paint letters, assemble chain, and inspect.

BUILD A WOOD DUCK HOUSE

With this simple wood duck house project you can learn mass production processes while recycling materials. Sheet-metal templates, a vertical band saw, electric hand drill, tinsnips, hand seamers, pop rivet gun, and hammers are all the equipment needed. Nevertheless, a slip roll, bar folder, and drill press are helpful bench and power tools. See Figs. 7-56, 7-57, and Table 7-2.

You can use discarded offset printing plates from a local newspaper for the bodies of the houses. Wood for the top, bottom, and back brace can be made from scraps from old pallets, crating, or sawmill drops. The top is covered by a conical-shaped piece of sheet steel. This prevents predators from sitting on the house, reaching into the entrance, and stealing the eggs. The only new materials usually purchased are the cloth for the ladder so the day-old ducklings can climb out of the house, pop rivets to secure the cloth to the body, and roofing nails to nail the body to the ends and back brace.

The houses need not be made to exact dimensions, but should be about 2 feet high and 12 inches in diameter. The entry hole should be an oval 4 × 3 inches located a minimum of 18 inches from the bottom of the house. Rivet a piece of ¼-inch square hardware cloth, 2 inches wide, on the inside of the body from the lower edge of the hole

Table 7-2. Materials List.

Part	Qty.	Description
Ridge board	1	2 x 1 x 30 pine
Bottom	1	12″ d x 1 pine
Top	1	14″ d x 1 pine
Top cone	1	15″ d x 28 ga. galvanized sheet metal
Body	1	22 x 36 x 1.010 scrap aluminum
Ladder	1	1/4″ sq. x 2 x 18 hardware cloth
Nails	18	7/8″ galvanized roofing
Pop rivets	4	1/8″ d x 1/4″ aluminum

to the bottom of the house. Drill small holes in the bottom to drain out rain water. Painting isn't necessary, but if it is preferred use a light-colored paint which will not absorb heat. A dark paint will make the nest too hot. Place 3 inches to 4 inches of sawdust in the bottom of the house for bedding.

The houses are most useful when mounted on trees 10 feet to 40 feet above the ground, or on a post adjacent to ponds that have a stationary water level. The best location is near streams and ponds where the hen will take her day-old brood. Houses should be installed by March 1, as the hens start looking for a nesting site in late March.

HERE'S THE HITCH!

This trailer project is easy to build and it is functional. Moreover, it is designed to conserve metal by minimizing scrap.

The material for the bottom and sides is formed from 18-gauge galvanized iron on a hand brake in lengths of 10 feet. The metal for the bottom is 36 inches wide; a split sheet is used for the sides, which are 18 inches wide before they are formed.

The purchased wheels are a lightweight, wheelbarrow variety. You can make two short axles of 1-square-inch stock turned down to ¾-inch round on the ends to fit the wheels, but a piece of ¾-inch round rod welded to the angle would work just as well.

As finishing touches, you can add "fenders" and built-in stake brackets for a wooden stake bed. This can be painted in a contrasting color. See Figs. 7-59 and 7-60.

Fig. 7-57. Final phase of the project is mounting the house in readiness for a hen wood duck.

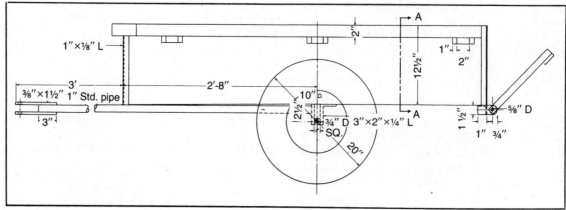

Fig. 7-58. Hitch design details.

CHAIN BREAKER IN ENGLISH OR METRIC

Anyone who does trail riding and has had a chain break in the field will know that, without the proper tools for the job, it is nearly impossible to make the necessary repairs. Having a chain breaker readily available in the tool kit can be a big help because the breaker does not do what its name implies—break the chain—but rather simply re- moves the pin from the links so chain repairs can be made. Thus, making a drive-chain breaker is sure to provide plenty of motivation in the machine shop among bicycle-motorcycle fans. It is a practical problem-solving device you can really use.

Cost-Price Factor. A chain breaker—roughly a cubic inch in size—usually retails for about $4, while the

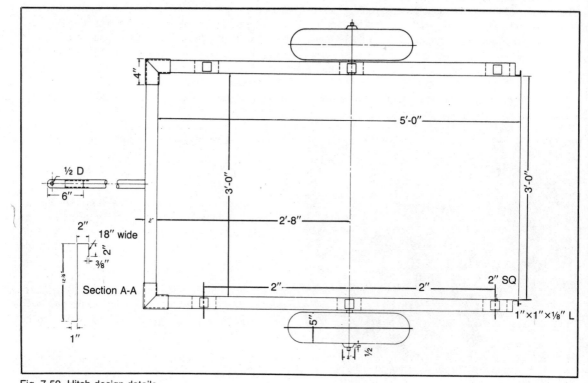

Fig. 7-59. Hitch design details.

220

Fig. 7-60. The completed hitch.

one you can make in the machine shop will cost about 30 cents.

Such a cost-price advantage is very often difficult to achieve for project ideas. The craftsman can rarely compete with the prices of mass-production manufacturers. This is a project you can make and sell at a handsome profit and still be underselling the retail price.

Furthermore, you can use the breaker at home to make repairs—not just on bicycles and motorcycles, but on lawn mowers, for example. Although the particular chain breaker described here (see Figs. 7-61, 7-62, 7-63 and Table 7-3) will not handle the larger agricultural or industrial type chain, a larger version could be designed and produced specifically to meet that purpose.

Rapid Learning. The project is designed to introduce the beginning machine shop student to basic machines and processes and also to provide you with an initial appreciation for absolute accurate measurement. The breaker introduces you quickly to machining, how to do simple operations on each machine, and how the symbols and instructions indicated on a drawing relate to the operations to be performed.

This does not mean, however, that the shop must be heavily equipped in order for the chain breaker project to be used. The breaker can utilize as many operations and machines as the shop can accommodate. The machine shop could include power sawing, milling, drilling, shaping, and surface grinding. But, at the same time, if facilities are more limited than this, as in a general shop,

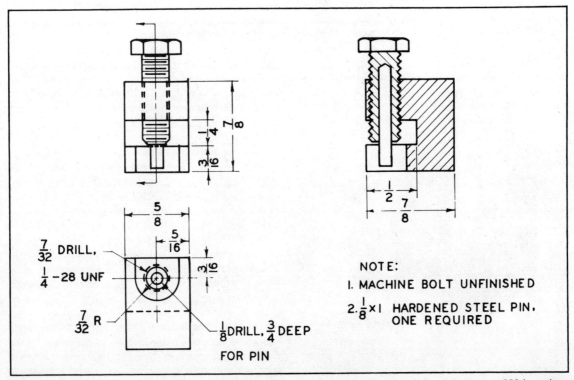

Fig. 7-61. The English-measured version of the chain breaker expresses all fractional dimensions as ±.020 in. unless otherwise specified.

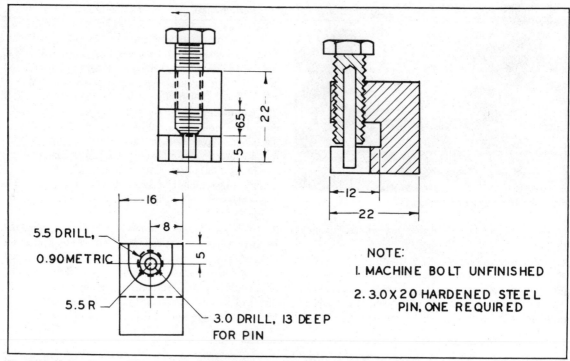

NOTE:
1. MACHINE BOLT UNFINISHED
2. 3.0 X 20 HARDENED STEEL PIN, ONE REQUIRED

5.5 DRILL,
0.90 METRIC

5.5 R

3.0 DRILL, 13 DEEP FOR PIN

Fig. 7-62. Metric chain breaker shows fractional dimensions as ±.10 mm unless otherwise specified.

for example, the entire project could be made by using just the drill press and some simple hand tools.

One of the best features of the chain breaker as a project is that it offers a wide range of learning experiences at a low cost without using large amounts of stock.

Fig. 7-63. The completed chain breaker.

The breaker does not require any expensive or exotic materials for manufacture, and it is small enough to fit into limited storage space. Furthermore, if you make an error in the course of building the drive-chain breaker, you can begin again without wasting any more material than a cutoff.

Going Metric. The drawings, along with the step-by-step directions, for the chain breaker are shown here in both English (Fig. 7-61) and metric (Fig. 7-62), in order to add further relevance to the project as a learning experience for those who are working in a shop environment where metrics are playing an increasingly important role. The two drawings here, it should be noted, do not represent an English version accompanied by an English version converted directly into metric; rather, they show a distinct and separate English version and metric version, each making use of standard sizes within its own system.

Shops that have already been outfitted with metric equipment can make immediate use of the project in the metric form offered here. Shops still working completely within the English system can use the English-dimensioned plans and instructions.

A brief word of explanation is in order concerning

Table 7-3. Drive-Chain Breaker Directions.

English	Metric
1. Cut material for the chain breaker body from 1 by 1 in. crs.	1. Cut material for the chain breaker body from 1 by 1 in. crs (used because metric-sized steel is still unavailable except by special order).
2. Square the chain breaker body to within 1/16 in. of dimensions given, using horizontal mill.	2. Square the chain breaker body to within 2 mm of dimensions given, using horizontal mill.
3. Surface grind each of the surfaces to .020 in.	3. Surface grind each of the surfaces to .10 mm.
4. Mill 1/4 in. slot, 1/2 in. deep using vertical mill.	4. Mill 6.5 mm slot, 12 mm deep using vertical mill.
5. Locate the center and drill a 7/32 in. hole.	5. Locate the center and drill a 5.5 mm hole.
6. Tap hole with 1/4-28 UNF tap.	6. Tap hole with .90 mm tap.
7. Locate the center and mill the base of the body with 7/16 end mill.	7. Locate the center and mill the base of the body with 11 mm end mill.
8. Finish the body with files and abrasives, coming as close to indicated dimensions as possible.	8. Finish the body with files and abrasives, coming as close to indicated dimensions as possible.
9. For the bolt and pin, locate the bolt center and drill with 1/8 in. drill, 3/4 in. deep.	9. For the bolt and pin, locate the bolt center and drill with 3.0 mm drill, 13 mm deep.
10. Epoxy 1/8 by 1 in. hardened steel pin into 1/8 in. hole.	10. Epoxy 3.0 by 20 mm hardened steel pin into 3.0 mm hole.

General Directions for Both English and Metric

11. Case harden the breaker body.
12. Assemble the drive chain breaker and place identification on it using stamped initials if this is desired.

the general directions listed in Table 7-3. The reason for hardening the body of the breaker and using a hardened pin is to increase the life of the finished project. Do not harden a bolt or buy a hardened bolt. While it is true that a soft bolt will be the first part to fail if the tool is used with too much force, it is also true that this bolt is readily replaced; the breaker body itself, on the other hand, takes a good deal more time to produce.

CONSTRUCTING A METALSHOP PROJECT THE METRIC WAY

Start out on the right foot (meter?) with this metricated parts bin (Fig. 7-64). Construction of the bin requires light-gauge, cold-rolled steel that can easily be spot welded or riveted. You can spray paint the finished bins either to use in the home or retain in the shop for storage of small parts.

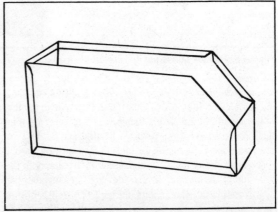

Fig. 7-64. Building this parts bin requires welding and riveting techniques, metricated equipment, and metric measurements.

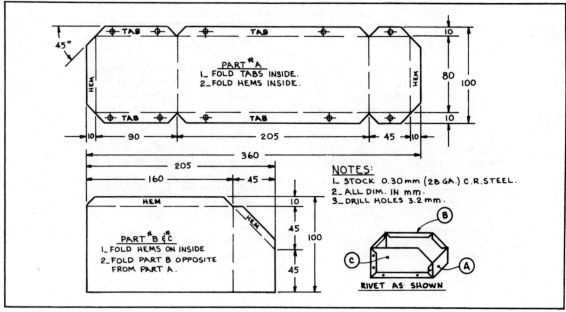

Fig. 7-65. Bin design details.

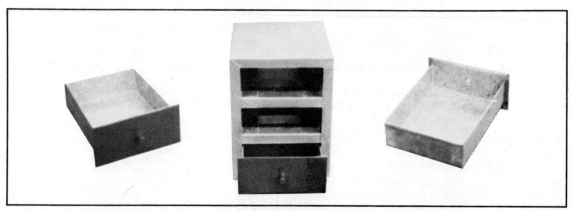

Fig. 7-66. This version is useful for storing small parts.

You will need to "metricate" your existing squaring shear and bar folder. Most squaring shears read in inches, but you can set the stops using a metric ruler or glue dual-dimensioned scales over the English scales. You can metricate a bar folder by cutting 25 mm off of a metric machinist's scale. This can be fastened with epoxy to the left side of the pointer to provide dual measurements.

Note that all dimensions in Fig. 7-65 are in millimeters rather than centimeters. Because the millimeter is the preferred unit of linear measurement, be careful to use shop rules with millimeter scales.

Fig. 7-67. A three-drawer tool box.

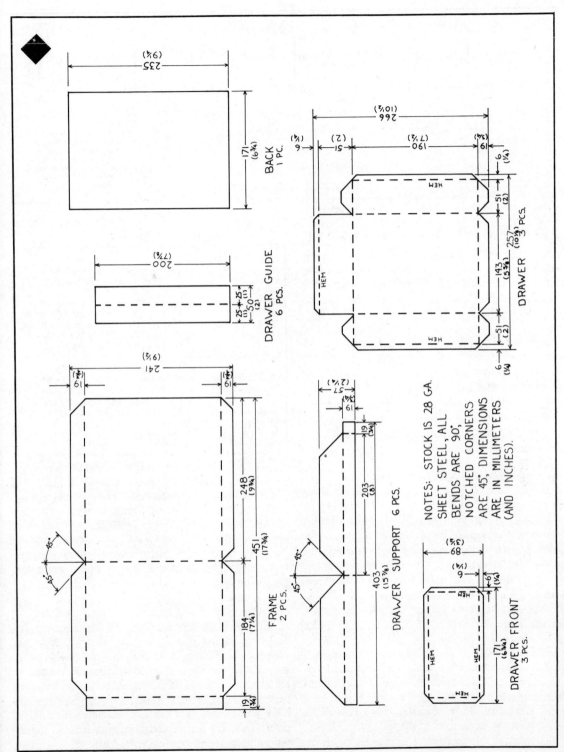

235
(9¼)

171
(6¾)

BACK
1 PC.

200
(7⅞)

25 25
(1) (1)
50
(2)

DRAWER GUIDE
6 PCS.

266
(10½)

6 51 190 6
(¼) (2) (7½) (¼)

HEM

HEM

HEM

51
(2)

257
(10⅛)

3 PCS.

143
(5⅝)

51
(2)

6
(¼)

DRAWER
3 PCS.

241
(9½)

19 19
(¾) (¾)

45°

45°

248
(9¾)

451
(17¾)

184
(7¼)

19
(¾)

FRAME
2 PCS.

57
(2¼)

19
(¾)

45°

45°

203
(8)

403
(15⅞)

DRAWER SUPPORT
6 PCS.

NOTES: STOCK IS 28 GA.
SHEET STEEL, ALL
BENDS ARE 90°,
NOTCHED CORNERS
ARE 45°, DIMENSIONS
ARE IN MILLIMETERS
(AND INCHES).

68
(3⅝)

6
(¼)

HEM

HEM

HEM

6
(¼)

HEM

171
(6¾)

DRAWER FRONT
3 PCS.

Fig. 7-68. Drawing for bench top parts cabinet.

225

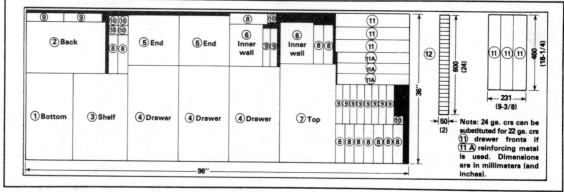

Fig. 7-69. Sheet metal placement (3-drawer tool box).

GO METRIC IN METALS WITH A PARTS/TOOL CABINET

Challenge yourself to develop accuracy in layout, cutting, bending, riveting, braking, spot welding, and assembly procedures while working from either metric or English dimensions. Choose from two designs for a parts or tool cabinet, both of which can be either individually or mass-produced.

A Bench Top Parts Cabinet. The version illustrated in Fig. 7-66, a bench top cabinet, is particularly useful for organizing and storing small parts. The construction procedure is as follows:

☐ Cut 28-gauge sheet steel to the required sizes.
☐ Lay out notches, corners, and bends.
☐ Cut notches and corners where specified.
☐ Hem where necessary.
☐ Brake all 90-degree bends.
☐ Spot weld frame pieces.
☐ Spot weld or pop rivet the drawer support halves to make three completed units.
☐ Position and spot weld or rivet the drawer guides to the completed drawer supports to allow a minimum amount of lateral movement when the drawer is inserted into the finished product.
☐ Insert, align, and fasten each of the three completed supports with guides into the frame to allow for the three equal sized drawer openings. Be sure support guide units are level.
☐ Fasten the drawers.
☐ Position and attach the fronts to the drawers.
☐ Design and attach a drawer pull to each drawer.
☐ If you prefer, spot weld sheet metal divider strips into each drawer.
☐ Fasten the back to the cabinet frame.
☐ Paint the cabinet.
☐ Paint the drawer fronts a contrasting color.

Table 7-4. Tool Box Materials List.

Part No. and Name	Qty.	Description (in millimeters [and inches])		
1—Bottom	1	315 x 530	24 ga. crs	[12-1/4 x 21]
2—Back	1	321 x 500	" " "	[12-5/8 x 20]
3—Shelf	1	351 x 530	" " "	[13-7/8 x 21]
4—Drawers	3	317 x 570	" " "	[12-3/4 x 23-1/8]
5—Ends	2	323 x 315	" " "	[12-1/4 x 12-3/4]
6—Inner walls	2	210 x 263	" " "	[8-1/4 x 10-3/8]
7—Top	1	360 x 610	" " "	[13-7/8 x 24]
8—Outside runners	12	62 x 235	" " "	[2-1/2 x 9-1/2]
9—Inside runners	12	47 x 235	" " "	[1-7/8 x 9-1/2]
10—Drawer pulls	6	60 x 65	" " "	[2-3/8 x 2-1/2]
11—Drawer fronts	3	77 x 450	22 ga. crs	[3-1/8 x 18-1/4]
12—Drawer stops	24	25 x 50	18 ga. crs	[1 x 2]
13—Hinge		16—Handles		
14—Catch		17—Drawer lock		
15—Corners		18—Pop rivets		

A Three-Drawer Tool Box. A slightly more complicated and versatile container, is shown in Fig. 7-67. The plan calls for keeping costs down by making the entire box from one sheet of 24-gauge crs with an alternative thickness of 22-gauge crs for the drawer fronts, and one piece of 18-gauge crs for the stops. See Figs. 7-68, 7-69, and Table 7-4. In addition to the tools and equipment found in the average metalshop, the project requires the use of three offset tools that can be fabricated in several minutes.

After constructing the box, you have the option of adding drawer dividers to fit their tools and equipment, designing and building mechanisms that will lock the drawers when the top lid is closed, or building stops to keep the lid from opening too far and damaging the hinge. Patterns can be made for casting aluminum handles. For personal identification, you can make name tags and pop rivet them to the top of the box. Finishing with wrinkle paint requires no primer, and if you apply it at the proper temperature, it will create a crafted look.

226

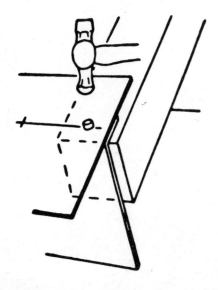

Chapter 8

Advanced Projects

N O ONE ENJOYS WORKING A SHOP WHERE THE AIR is filled with particles that cause sneezing and watering eyes. It bothers visitors and can be hazardous for anyone who spends almost all day in the shop. Most people concerned recognize the problem, but few can afford commercial air cleaners. An alternative is to build an air cleaner using available materials. See Figs. 8-1, 8-2, and Table 8-1.

A fan can be used for moving the air and standard-size furnace filters can be used for cleaning it. Build a box either of sheet metal or plywood. The box size and filter location depends on the individual shop's needs. The fan can be mounted on the bottom (Fig. 8-1) on any side, or on the top. Bottom mounting requires building up the base for clearance. The bottom fan helps heavier materials that have fallen on the floor blown away from machines for easy sweep-up. Also, with bottom mounting, all sides can be used for air cleaning. Nevertheless, be sure to position the unit so that filters can be easily reached for changing.

Where heavy filtration is necessary, save time and money by cutting openings one half the filter size. When the first half becomes loaded, turn the filter around to place the unused half over the opening.

Casters can be mounted on the bottom of the air

cleaner for easy mobility. Save energy by installing a pilot lamp that indicates when the unit is on.

Almost immediately after putting the air cleaner into operation, it begins collecting particles. The filtered materials graphically demonstrate the problem of air pollution.

WORKING WITH SHOP-MADE ROLLS

Cold working can produce a wide variety of metal items. It includes such operations as pulling wire through a die, cold rolling sheet metal, stamping auto body parts, or bending wire to form paper clips. These operations are performed at room temperature. They result in good finish and close dimensional control. Because the metal crystals are permanently deformed by cold working, the metal becomes harder and stronger.

It is important that metalworkers understand the relationships of cold working, strength, hardness, and process annealing. These relationships can be demonstrated easily with tensile samples cut from aluminum bar available from hardware or building supply houses.

To illustrate the effect of cold working, one sample could be reduced 10 percent in thickness. Hardness,

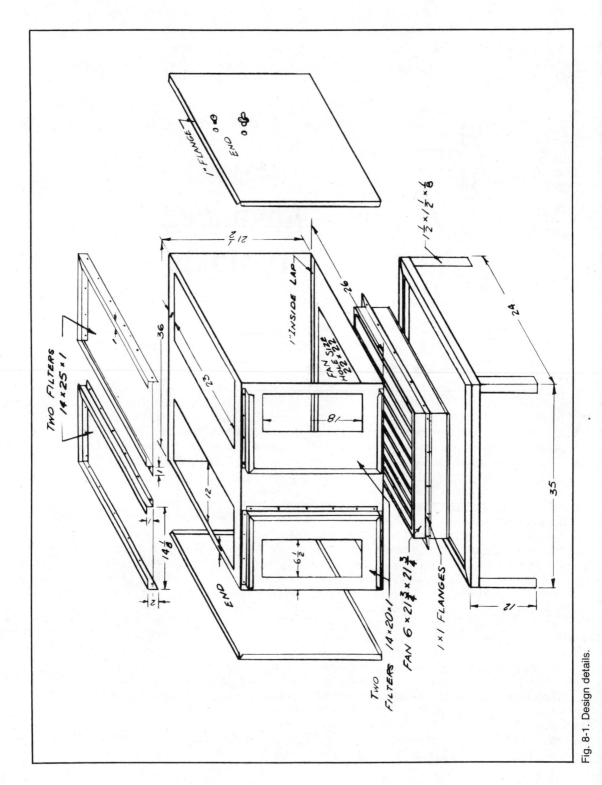

Fig. 8-1. Design details.

Fig. 8-2. This cleaner rids the air of annoying and dangerous particles.

tensile strength, and ductility as measured by percent elongation and reduction in area should be determined for each sample. The broken pieces of a cold worked sample can be placed in a furnace, heated to 343°C. (650°F.) and furnace cooled. Again, determining the hardness will give meaning to the term *process anneal.*

Rolls provide a satisfactory method of cold working a sample. The effect is applied uniformly throughout the sample. A series of samples can be reduced different amounts to study the effect of varying amounts of cold work.

Rolls for the purpose of cold working are available from equipment supply houses. They are power driven and easy to use. They are also expensive.

The frame is assembled by welding. See Fig. 8-3 and Table 8-2. The top roll (I) is raised by the springs (K) between the bearing blocks (N, Q), and lowered by the cap screws (G). The cap screws turn in the nuts (H) welded to the top plate (E) of the frame.

The stand is made from 1-×-1-×-⅛ angle iron. It is 30 inches high. The top is 7 × 8 inches, and the base is 14½ × 24 inches in the direction of rolling. Pads ¼ × 2 × 2½ were attached for the feet.

BUILD A THREE-WHEEL BAND SAW

One sure way of generating enthusiasm in the shop is to complete a project that *does* something. It's a special moment when you turn on the switch and the thing really *works.* Producing a band saw provides advanced training through this project in skills involving lathe, welding, foundry, and assembly techniques. See Figs. 8-5, 8-6, and 8-7. Here's how you can get this high-interest project going.

Only critical dimensions are given—you can easily determine non-critical details. The hubs of the wheels are large enough to accommodate a number of different size bearings. We got ours through government surplus. We

Table 8-1. Materials List.

Qty.	Part	Size	Material
1	Box	36 x 96	24 ga. gal.
2	Ends	23-3/8 x 27-7/8	24 ga. gal.
2	Top filters outside flanges	3 x 26	24 ga. gal.
2	Top filters inside flanges	3 x 26	24 ga. gal.
2	Top filters end flanges	3 x 14-1/8	24 ga. gal.
4	Front filters, top and bottom flanges	3 x 14	24 ga. gal.
2	Front filters inside flanges	2-3/4 x 20-1/8	24 ga. gal.
4	Fan flanges	2 x 23-3/4	24 ga. gal.
1	Base	1-1/2 x 1-1/2 x 1/8 x 118	Angle iron
10 doz.	Pop rivets	1/8 x 3/16	Angle iron
1	Switch		
1	Light		
1	Fan		

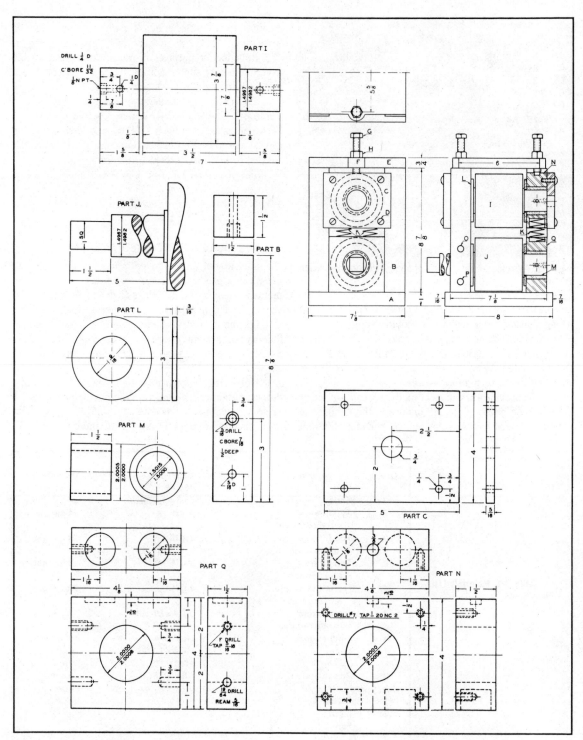

Fig. 8-3. Design details.

Table 8-2. Materials List.

Part No.		Qty.	Description	
A	Base	1	1 x 7-1/8 x 8	AISI 1018
B	Post	4	1-1/2 x 1-1/2 x 8-7/8	AISI 1018
C	End Plate	2	5/16 x 4 x 5	AISI 1018
D	Cap Screws	8	1/4-20 NC x 1" Rnd. Hd.	
E	Top	1	3/4 x 6 x 7-1/8	AISI 1018
F	Lug	2	3/4 x 1/2 x 1	AISI 1018
G	Cap Screws	2	1/2-13 NC x 3" Dog Pt.	
H	Nut, Thick	2	1/2-13 NC	
I	Top Roll	1	3-7/8 x 7	AISI 4150
J	Bottom Roll	1	3-7/8 x 10-1/8	AISI 4150
K	Valve Spring	4	1-1/2 x 1-7/8 long	
L	Thrust Bearing	4	3" dia. x 3/16 thick	Bronze
M	Bearing	4	2" od x 1-1/2 long	Bronze
N	Upper Block	2	1-1/2 x 4 x 4-1/8	AISI 1018
O	Set Screw	4	5/16-18 NC 1-1/2 long	
P	Dowel	4	5/16 dia. x 2	
Q	Lower Block	2	1-1/2 x 4 x 4-1/8	AISI 1018
R	Grease Fitting			

determined plywood sizes and shapes to make best use of a 4 by 8 sheet. All castings were made from scrap aluminum, mostly pistons. You can mount the motor separately or within the cabinet—there is just enough space. Mount the motor so its weight provides the belt tension. Check the wheel alignment after installation, because the frame may have distorted during arc welding.

Be sure to make a jig to fit the frame parts. You can nail wood cleats to a piece of ¾-inch plywood so that the three angle-iron pieces are held exactly as indicated on the drawing (I Frame Assembly). Place protective metal in spots to be tack welded so the wood is not burned too badly.

Make a wheel pattern by gluing wood for the hub and rim on a piece of ¾-inch plywood. This is turned to the sizes indicated. Carefully lay out the spokes and glue them in position. Fillet wax gives the desired radius at several intersection points.

Turn a crown on the surface of each wheel after casting. The draft of the casting provides the initial crown. Turn the largest diameter in the center until it runs true, then with the carriage in automatic feed, turn the cross feed by hand .060 until the tool reaches the edge of the wheel. Reverse the automatic feed, begin again in the center of the wheel, and gradually feed the tool in .060 until it reaches the other edge of the wheel.

The drive wheel is doweled to the shaft flange by 2¼-inch metal dowels, threaded onto the wheel hub. The wheel is then mounted on the shaft and secured with the ⅝ nut, and the entire assembly is mounted between centers and turned to final size. Rubber for wheel coverings was cut from a 4-inch trailer inner tube.

The tension knob is made by sand casting the knob around the ½-inch carriage bolt head. See drawing V of Fig. 8-5. A car valve spring is mounted behind the tension block and over the tension bolt to provide release pressure.

The alignment wheel spacers are cast aluminum (drawing VII of Fig. 8-6). Make the pattern by turning a piece of wood to the inside diameter of the pipe. Next turn six lines, 1 inch apart, on the 7-inch length of stock. (This identifies the places to cut it apart on the casting.) Cut off the two edges of this wood turning and use it as a pattern for casting. This provides spacers for six units.

No plans are given for the lower guide assembly because the lower guide block is identical to the upper one and is mounted on a piece of angle iron ½-inch beneath the lower surface of the table. Do *NOT* mount it

Fig. 8-4. These inexpensive rolls, made largely from scrap materials, are effective in demonstrating a variety of cold-working processes.

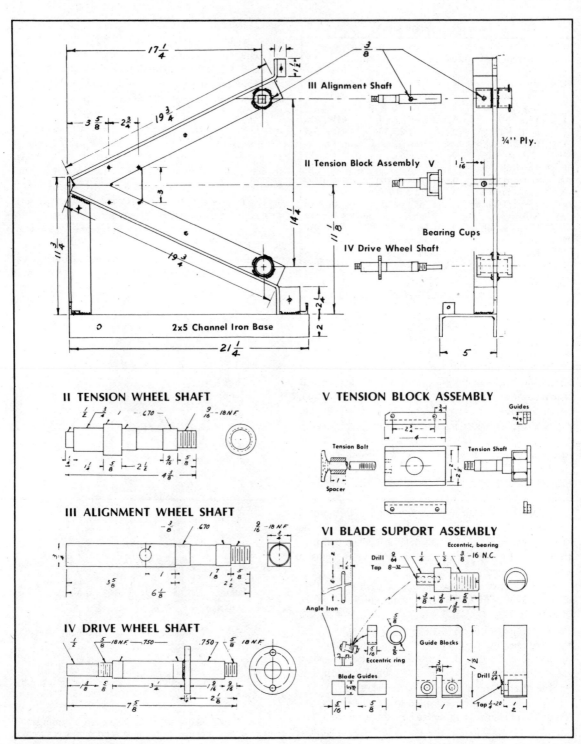

Fig. 8-5. Band saw design details.

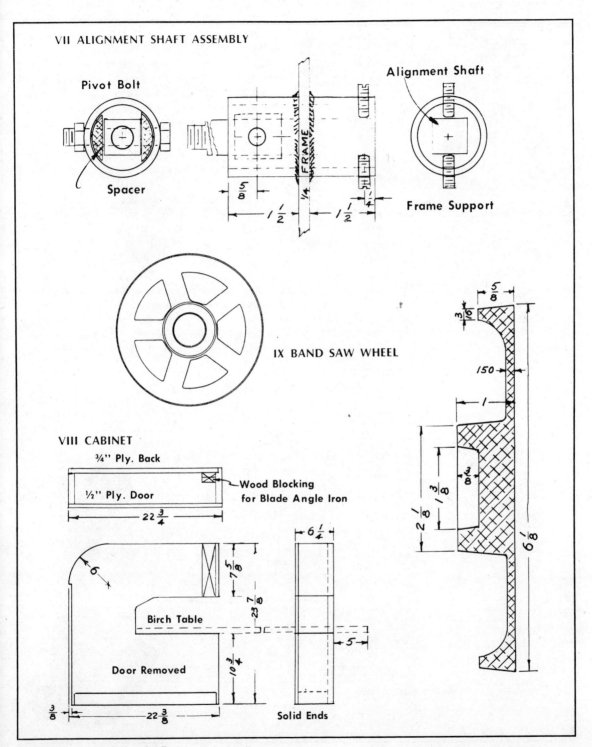

Fig. 8-6. Band saw design details.

Fig. 8-7. Proud workers stand behind their product. Repetitive activities pay off, at least in accuracy.

flush beneath the table because wood chips cannot be removed.

☐ The guide blocks are arc welded to the angle iron.

☐ Braze a piece of 18-gauge crs, ½ by 1, over the 3/16 cut made in the block, then cut the 3/16 slot open.

☐ Braze a boss of 5/16 stock to the top of the block to provide sufficient thickness for the ¼ set screws.

☐ The blade guides of 5/16- ×-5/16 stock should be case hardened to provide good wearing qualities.

☐ The eccentric is mounted in an eccentric ring (drawing VI of Fig. 8-5). This permits some adjustment of the ⅜ hole before it is arc welded in position. Mount at a slight angle so the outer surface of the backup bearing is utilized to support the blade.

The plywood door is held shut by two #10 RH screws. Drive the screws into the wood, remove and cut off the screw heads, thread the shank 8-24, and reinstall in the cabinet.

Lock the wheels to their shafts by cutting the two 9/16 nuts and one ⅝ nut in half. Tighten the halves against each other.

BUILD AN ARBOR PRESS

This arbor press can be used as a general-purpose tool in the house workshop and in most shop laboratories. It is useful in many areas such as ceramics, plastics, electricity, automechanics, and especially metals. With appropriate adapters, the press can be used for assembling miniaturized mechanisms, punching and riveting sheet

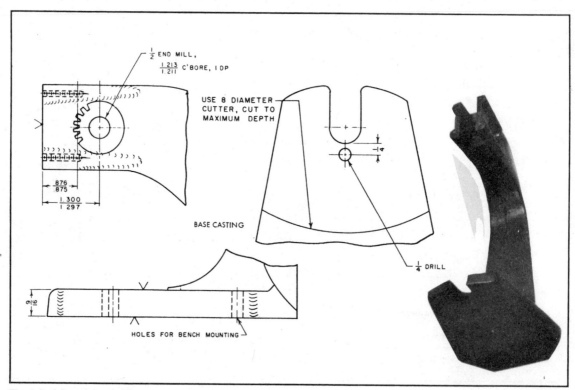

Fig. 8-8. Arbor press details.

metal, pressing designs in leather work, and many other operations.

In addition to elementary operations of straight turning, flat milling, and drilling, the following more advanced operations are necessary for making this arbor press: turning tapers, boring with a boring bar in the engine lathe, boring with the boring head in the vertical milling machine, milling a rack, milling an involute spur gear, grinding flat surfaces, milling with an end-mill cutter, and turning with a mandrel. You will not only learn about many of the basic machine tools, but also about types and kinds of gears, gear sizes, gear nomenclature, gear measurement, precision tools and measurements, types of fits, and fixture design. See Figs. 8-8 through 8-12.

All of the parts, except the cast-iron base casting, can be machined from crs. Various clamping techniques can be employed in the machining of this press. A number of fixtures to hold the casting for some of the operations facilitates the machining of the various surfaces. The

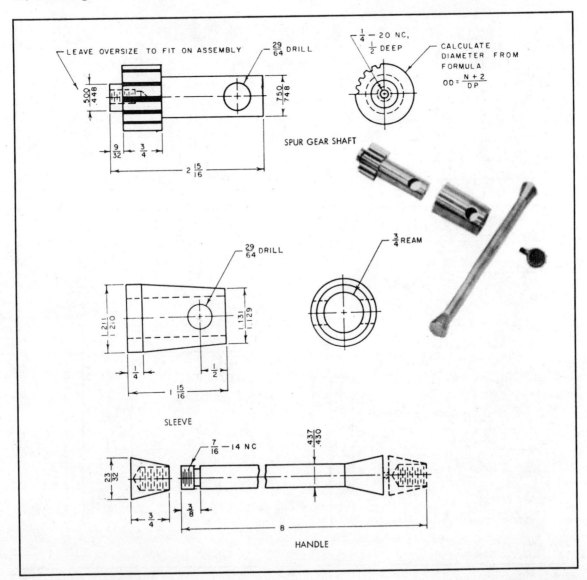

Fig. 8-9. Arbor press details.

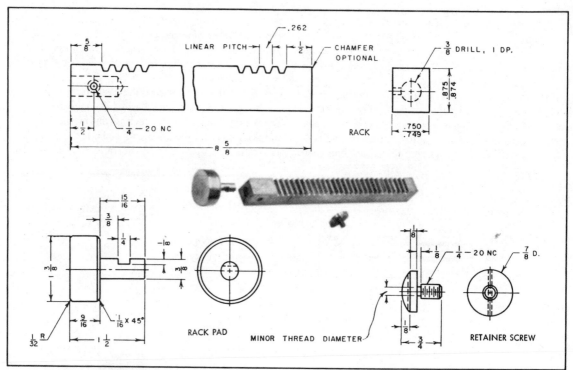

Fig. 8-10. Arbor press details.

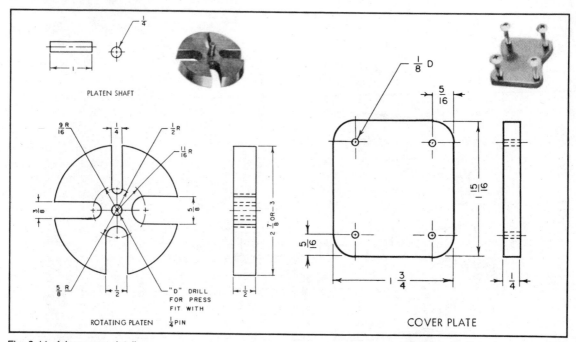

Fig. 8-11. Arbor press details.

236

suggested machines to use in machining the parts, along with a suggested sequence for some of the more complicated steps, follow:

Casting

Using the Shaper, Planer, or Milling Machine. Machine the base and the back of the casting so that these surfaces are 90 degrees to each other. This is essential because these surfaces will be used as locating surfaces in setting up for the other cuts on the casting.

Using the Horizontal Milling Machine. Mill the top surface of the base of the casting by using an 8-inch diameter side-milling cutter. For this cut, the casting is clamped perpendicular to the table with strap or "U" clamps.

Using the Vertical or Horizontal Milling Machine. Machine the front of the head of the casting to provide a locating surface for finding the center of the bored cavity (1.300-inch dimension).

Using the Vertical Milling Machine. Machine the bored hole in the head of the casting by clamping the casting right side up so the handle of the arbor press will be convenient for a right-handed person. It is advantageous to have a specially built fixture to hold the casting for this operation. The base of the casting, however, can be clamped to an angle plate and the head supported with step blocks and fastened with strap or "U" clamps. After locating the 1.300-inch dimension carefully with the cross-feed dial (an edge-finder is helpful), drill a 7/16-inch pilot hole through the casting head.

Enlarge and true the hole with a ½-inch end mill cutter. This will provide the ½-inch bearing on the left side of the head for the spur gear shaft. Bore the $\frac{1.213''}{1.211}$ dimension with a boring head to a depth of 1-inch. If a boring head is not available, a counterboring tool can be made in the shop to perform this operation.

Using the Vertical Milling Machine or Drill Press. Spotface the left side of the head of the casting. This provides a flat surface for the retaining screw. Clamp the casting (bottom side up) in a vertical position. Drill the hole for the rotating platen shaft. Also, drill the holes for mounting the press to a bench.

Handle

Using the Lathe. Turn the $\frac{.437}{.435}$ dimension, the tapers on the knobs, and the recess between centers using the lathe dog. Chuck the part and cut the threads with a die. Reverse the part in the chuck, then drill and tap the 7/16-inch NC thread. Cut the knob off using the parting tool. Screw the knob to the threaded end and face to length. Round the corners.

Rack

Using the Surface Grinder. Grind the part to the specified dimensions.

Using the Horizontal Milling Machine. Clamp the rack in the vise, parallel to the arbor (three or four pieces may be done at once). Using the No. 1-12 diametral pitch cutter, cut the teeth to a linear pitch of .262 of an inch.

Using the Arbor Press. Straighten the stock which has become warped by the rack milling operation.

Rotating Platen

Using the Surface Grinder (Optional). After facing to the approximate size in the lathe, surface grind both sides.

Using the Drill Press. Drill the holes at the bottom of the slots 1/64 of an inch under the finished width of the slots.

Using the Band Saw. Saw the slots to an undersized dimension and tangent to the holes previously drilled.

Using the Vertical Milling Machine. Clamp the platen on a set of parallel bars with strap clamps. Use the appropriate end-mill cutters to mill the slots to the finished dimensions.

Sleeve

Using the Lathe. Chuck the 1¼-inch diameter stock and drill a 11/16-inch hole. Enlarge the hole by boring or drilling with a 47/64-inch drill. Ream to ¾ of an inch diameter. Cut to length by facing both ends. Press the sleeve on a mandrel and mount between centers. Calculate and set the taper on the lathe and turn the sleeve to finished size.

Gear Shaft

Using the Lathe. Center drill the 1¼-inch stock that has been sawed about an inch longer than the finished length. The extra length is needed for clearance when milling the teeth in a later operation. Turn the diameters.

Using the Horizontal Milling Machine. Mill the teeth, using a No. 8-12 diametral pitch cutter.

Using the Lathe. Insert the ¾-inch diameter in the

chuck and face the ½-inch diameter of the gear shaft to length, leaving about 1/64 of an inch of extra length to prevent binding of the retainer screw against the casting.

Using the Drill Press. Assemble the gear shaft with the sleeve and drill the 29/64-inch hole through both pieces.

FABRICATING A DRILL-PRESS VISE

This metalworking project can be constructed in a modestly equipped shop. It involves procedures in foundry work, drill press, threading with a tap and die, and minor lathe work. The finishing of the castings is accomplished on a belt or disc sander, thus eliminating the need for a milling machine. See Figs. 8-13 and 8-14.

The three patterns for the project can be made of wood and modeling clay. Each can be stamped with a number for identification.

It should be noted that in making the mold for the casting, the patterns should be placed in the mold with the flat surface facing down (the opening is in the upper half of the mold when the metal is poured). This is done so that any shrinkage in the casting would not disturb the flat surfaces of the jaws. All drilling and threading of the three castings must be in true alignment and at right angles to the surface.

☐ Make castings #1, #2, and #3.

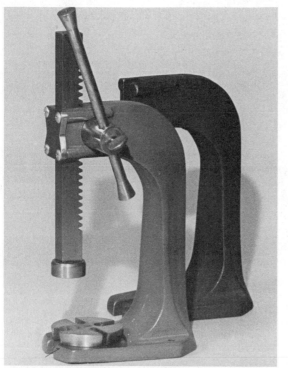

Fig. 8-12. The completed arbor press (foreground) and the base casting.

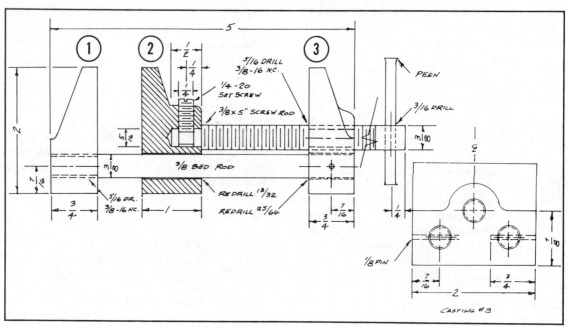

Fig. 8-13. Drill-press vise design details.

238

Fig. 8-14. The finished tool.

☐ In casting #1, drill two 5/16-inch holes at 7/16 of an inch from edges.

☐ From casting #1, drill two 5/16-inch holes in casting #2.

☐ From casting #1, drill two 5/16-inch holes in casting #3.

☐ Redrill two holes in casting #3 to 25/64 of an inch.

☐ Redrill two holes in casting #2 to 13/32 of an inch.

☐ In casting #3, drill one 5/16-inch hole in center at 7/8 of an inch up.

☐ From casting #3, drill one 5/16-inch hole 1/2 inch deep in casting #2.

☐ In casting #1, tap holes 3/8-16.

☐ In casting #3, tap upper hole at 3/8-16.

☐ Obtain 3/8-inch crs RD rod (three 5-inch pieces—two for bed rods, one for screw rod).

☐ With 3/8-16 die, thread 3/4-inch of the two 3/8-inch bed rods.

☐ Turn down diameter of screw rod to fit into 5/16-inch hole in casting #2 for set screw.

☐ With 3/8-16 die thread all but 1/2-inch of 3/8-inch vise screw rod.

☐ Drill 3/16-inch hole 1/4 of an inch in on the blank end of the vise screw rod.

☐ Cut a 2-inch piece of 3/16" RD rod, insert in hole, peen ends, remove burrs.

☐ Assemble project for fit.

☐ In casting #2, drill 3/16-inch hole at 1/4 of an inch in and directly above 5/16-inch hole.

☐ Tap the above 3/16-inch hole in casting #2 with 1/4-20 tap for set screw.

☐ Obtain 1/2-inch set screw 1/4-20.

☐ Reassemble project for fit.

☐ In casting #3, drill 1/8-inch hole 3/4 of an inch deep from each side into bed rods at 7/16 of an inch.

☐ Insert 1/8-inch pins into above holes and cut.

☐ Trim vise on sander for alignment and shape.

This project is an excellent test for workmanship and use of measurements.

PULLEY PULLERS

Producing wheel pullers can solve the problem of designing a mass-produced, inexpensive, simply constructed, and frequently used item. Besides experience with basic machining, the project involves heat-treating, benchwork, layout, assembly, and jig and fixture design.

Making the U brace requires several operations. Drill the stock and grind the radii for both ends before bending. Make a bending jig by machining a piece of tool steel 7/8 of an inch square and 2-inches long. In the center of one end, drill and tap a 1/4-20 NC hole, 3/4 of an inch deep. Heat-treat the jig to harden. Now secure the jig in the vise with the tapped end upward. Slip a 1/4-20 NC bolt through the center hole of the brace and tighten it to the jig. Use a soft hammer to pound the brace into its required shape.

You can construct a special jig with hardened steel bushings to locate holes accurately. In a production situation, this can save a lot of time and material.

The crs threaded rod is turned down at one end to .376 of an inch in diameter and press-fitted with a hardened drill rod cap reamed to .375 of an inch in diameter. Use nuts and bolts to mount the puller arms so that different-sized arms can easily be interchanged.

COMBINATION LOCK

If you are looking for a project for the general metal shop that ranks high in appeal, possesses an unusually great number of learning skills, and is extremely functional, here it is!

This combination lock (Figs. 8-17, 8-18, and 8-19) is designed on the barrel principle to simplify its construction and make it basically a lathe project. There are,

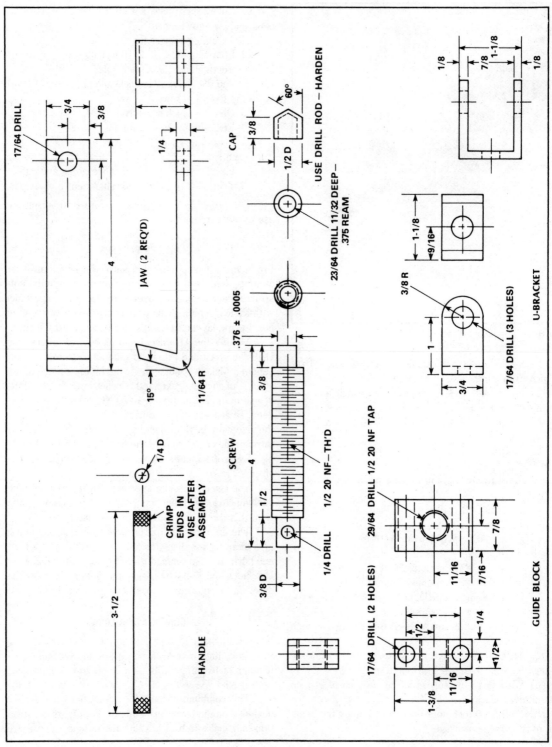

17/64 DRILL

3/4

3/8

1

1/4

JAW (2 REQ'D)

4

15°

11/64 R

CAP

60°

3/8

1/2 D

USE DRILL ROD – HARDEN

23/64 DRILL 11/32 DEEP – .375 REAM

.376 ± .0005

3/8

SCREW

4

1/2 20 NF–TH'D

1/2

3/8 D

1/4 DRILL

HANDLE

1/4 D

CRIMP ENDS IN VISE AFTER ASSEMBLY

3-1/2

1/8

7/8

1-1/8

1/8

U-BRACKET

1-1/8

9/16

3/8 R

1

3/4

17/64 DRILL (3 HOLES)

29/64 DRILL 1/2 20 NF TAP

7/8

11/16

7/16

17/64 DRILL (2 HOLES)

1/2

1

1/4

1/2

11/16

1-3/8

GUIDE BLOCK

Fig. 8-15. Pulley design details.

Fig. 8-16. Examples of pulleys.

however, many bench operations that also provide a wonderful opportunity to concentrate on hand-tool operations. The procedure is relatively simple because there are no close tolerances. An added attraction is the fact that the entire project can be constructed from scrap materials.

The complete lock can be broken down into six separate steps in order to construct the three basic parts: the barrel, the discs, and the staple. Following is a list of tools and materials needed to perform the job:

Machine Tools: Lathe, drill press, grinder.

Hand Tools: 6-inch steel rule, pipe cutter, hacksaw,

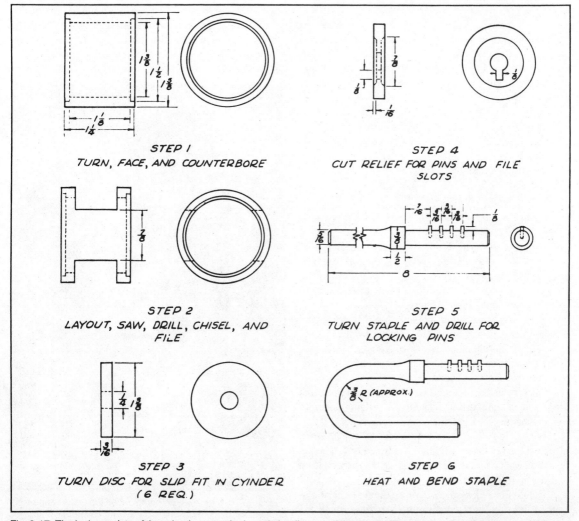

STEP 1
TURN, FACE, AND COUNTERBORE

STEP 2
LAYOUT, SAW, DRILL, CHISEL, AND FILE

STEP 3
TURN DISC FOR SLIP FIT IN CYINDER
(6 REQ.)

STEP 4
CUT RELIEF FOR PINS AND FILE SLOTS

STEP 5
TURN STAPLE AND DRILL FOR LOCKING PINS

STEP 6
HEAT AND BEND STAPLE

Fig. 8-17. The lock consists of three basic parts: the barrel, the discs, and the staple. The construction of these parts is shown here in six steps.

Fig. 8-18. Making an enlarged demonstration model (such as shown below) before the combination lock is built provides a worthwhile learning experience. The model also can be used for display purposes later to interest others in the project. This model has only four numbered discs instead of six, the wooden end discs are larger proportionately than the steel end plates in the lock, and the turn staple has only three pins instead of four.

inside and outside calipers, hammer, center punch, scriber, cold chisel, mill file, file card, drill (No. 40), abrasive cloth, soldering copper, soldering furnace, and oxyacetylene welder.

Materials:
Galvanized iron pipe (1¼″)
Duraluminum plate (3/16″)
Sheet steel (1/16″)
Cold-rolled steel (⅜″ round)
Nail (6d)
Hexagonal nut (5/16″)

From the sketches shown in Fig. 8-17, it will be seen that in Step 1 the barrel should be turned, bored, faced, and counterbored. The first two operations should be skim cuts and performed primarily to remove scale and produce a clean surface. Step 2 is a bench operation and consists of laying out, drilling, sawing, and cutting to remove some stock before filing.

It has been found that the simplest method of performing Step 3 is first to cut the six discs from a plate of scrap aircraft duraluminum by using a 1¼-inch hole saw. Then it is quite simple to mount the discs on an arbor and turn between centers. The two 1/16-inch steel end plates can also be turned in the same manner. In Step 4, the discs are placed in a universal chuck for the relief cuts before the locking-pin slots are filed.

Steps 5 and 6 deal with turning the staple shaft, inserting the pins, and bending the staple hook. The pin holes can be laid out by merely scribing along the side on which it is to be located.

Before the lock is ready to be assembled it is necessary to weld the hexagonal nut on the barrel in such a position that will give the staple support.

The numbers can be stamped on the discs in any

order you prefer. Any arrangement of numbers can be selected. Some prefer to use their house number or telephone number. The final step is to assemble the lock and seal the two end plates in position with solder.

PADLOCK THE METALSHOP!

This padlock combines the basic shop operations and tools with a minimum amount of material. The lock, limited in its security value, is opened by pressing the key against the lock pin and raising the shackle. Removal of the key frees the shackle to open the lock. See Figs. 8-20, 8-21, 8-22, 8-23, and Table 8-3.

Successful operation depends on a good fit of the shackle in the vertical holes. The straight sides of the shackle must be parallel and adjusted for free movement. This should be done before filing the notch. Adjustment can be accomplished with a hammer, a vise, or by heating the piece with a torch.

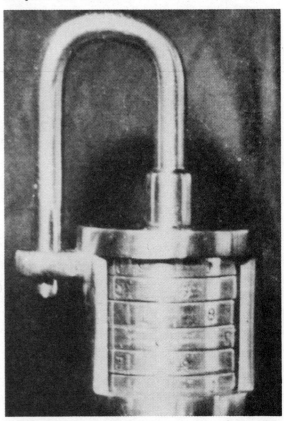

Fig. 8-19. This barrel-type combination lock is an appealing project for both beginning and advanced metalworkers. It offers a great number of learning skills, but is relatively simple to make.

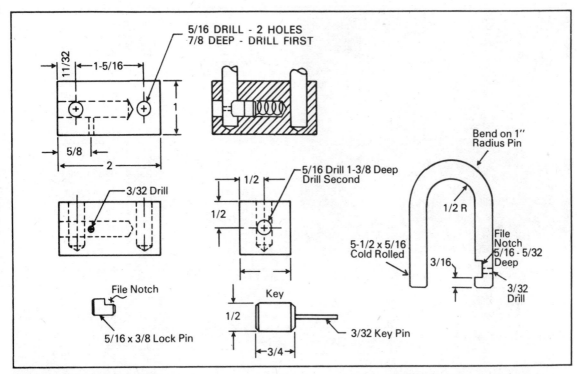

Fig. 8-20. Padlock design details.

Fig. 8-21. The finished lock.

Fig. 8-22. Jig for winding springs.

243

Fig. 8-23. Cross-section of lock.

Table 8-3. Padlock Parts List.

NO.	PART NAME	REQ'D	MATERIAL
A	WHEEL SPOKE	12	1/8 x 6-1/2 ROD
B	WHEEL RIM	2	1/4 x 1 x 42 FLAT CRS
C	HUB	2	1 x 3/4 BAR CRS
D	RING	12	1/4 x 1/4 x 13 CRS
E	AXLE	1	1/4 x 5 HRS
F	BRACE	1	1/4 x 1 x 4 FLAT CRS
G	STEERING ROD	1	1/2 x 4-1/2 HRS
H	HANDLE BAR	1	3/8 x 15-1/4 HRS
I	GRIPS	2	1/16 x 30 ROD
J	CONNECTING ROD	1	3/8 x 15 HRS
K	BACK WHEEL BRACKET	1	1/8 x 1/2 x 9 BAND HRS
L	SEAT ROD	1	3/16 x 1-3/4 ROD
M	SEAT	1	3-1/2 x 2-1/2 x 14 GA. STL
N	SPRING	2	1/16 x 5 ROD
O	BACK WHEEL AXLE	1	1/4 x 1-1/2 HRS
P	BACK WHEEL RIM	1	1/4 x 1/2 x 19-3/8 HRS
Q	BACK WHEEL HUB	1	1 x 1/2 BAR
R	BACK WHEEL SPOKE	4	1/8 x 3 ROD
S	SCROLL	4	1/8 x 7-1/2 ROD
T	PEDAL	2	3/8 x 1 x 1-1/2 FLAT
U	PEDAL ROD	2	1/4 x 4-7/8 HRS

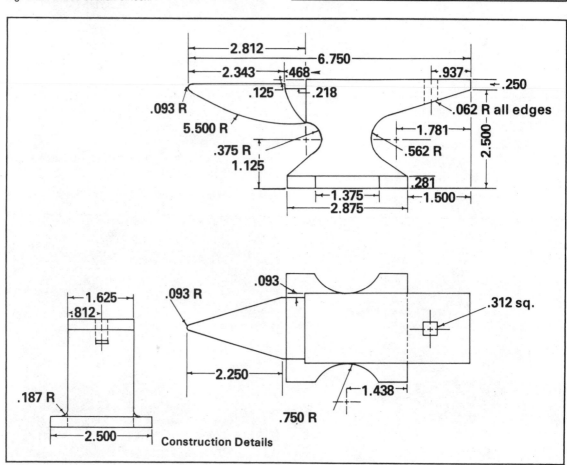

Construction Details

Fig. 8-24. Anvil design details.

Fig. 8-25. This anvil is machined from a solid piece of steel. When finished, it makes an unusual bookend or desk ornament.

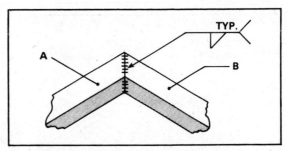

Fig. 8-26. Foundry cart frame details.

The springs are made of 1/16-inch brazing rod or No. 16-gauge piano wire. A crank made of 3/16-inch rod filed down to .175 makes a good device for winding springs.

When drilling the end hole, care must be taken as the drill starts into the vertical hole previously drilled in order to prevent catching. Drill the end hole as deep as possible to allow room for the spring and lock pin.

The 3/32-inch hole drilled in the side makes it possible to hold the lock pin in place with a short piece of 3/32-inch welding rod soldered in the hole.

MACHINE A STEEL ANVIL FROM SCRATCH

Most anvils made in shops seem to be either rough castings that are finished or that are made from part of a railroad rail. This anvil is machined from a solid piece of steel. Such anvils can be used as bookends or desk ornaments.

The anvil is made from 1018 crs. It is brass-plated, painted, or colored. Others, made for use by hobbyists, can be machined from 1042 hrs, hardened and tempered. Only basic machine tools are needed to machine the anvil: lathe, drill press, vertical mill or shaper. If a surface grinder is available, the flat surface can be ground. See Fig. 8-25.

☐ Machine work piece to length from 2½ × 2½ crs.
☐ Lay out centerline for ⅜ r and 9/16 r.
☐ Center punch and layout ¾-diameter and 1⅛-diameter circles.
☐ Drill work piece in drill press or lathe.
☐ Lay out side view and machine on vertical mill and/or shaper.
☐ Lay out top view; machine.
☐ Rough machine horn to contour, then finish to shape by filing.
☐ Finish-polish radii and horn with a slotted rod, using a lathe or drill press. Wrap with abrasive cloth.
☐ Drill hole with a letter "N" drill. File roughly square and broach with a 5/16 square tool bit.

Tolerances and finish are left to the instructor's discretion.

BUILD A MULTI-PURPOSE FOUNDRY CART

The design and construction of this foundry cart arose out

Table 8-4. Parts List.

Qty.	Material	T.	W.	L.	Part Name	Letter
2	Angle iron	1/4	2	36	Bottom frame	A
2	Angle iron	1/4	2	24	Bottom frame	B
2	Steel tubing	1-1/2	1-1/2	35	Grate bottom	C
4	Steel tubing	1-1/2	1-1/2	2	Handle slots	D
4	Steel tubing	1	1	23-1/2	Grate top	E
2	Steel tubing	1	1	2	Handle slots	F
1	Plywood	1/4	23-1/2	35	Bed	G
2	Sq. steel	3/4	3/4	34	Handle	H
1	Sq. steel	3/4	3/4	14-1/2	Handle	J
2	Rubber wheels	3-3/4 dia			Swivel casters	K
2	Rubber wheels	3-3/4 dia			Stationary casters	L

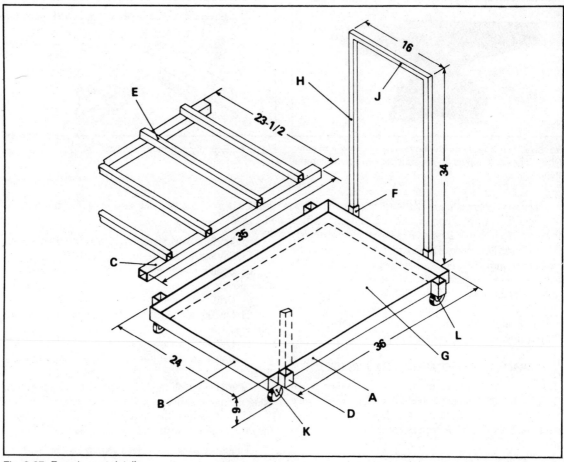

Fig. 8-27. Foundry cart details.

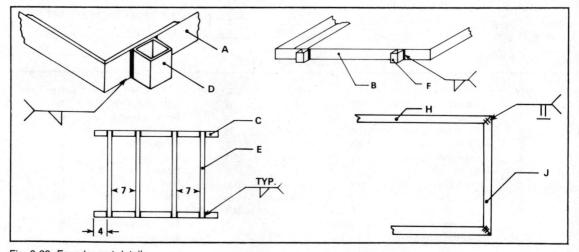

Fig. 8-28. Foundry cart details.

246

Fig. 8-29. The completed foundry cart.

of a need to transport flasks from the sand ramming area to the furnace area of the shop. A cart was needed that would hold at least two and as many as four flasks, pass through a standard size door, and which would catch any molten metal spilled while pouring or that leaked from the flask. Also needed was a cart for transporting lumber from an outside delivery point to an inside storage area. This cart serves these functions and it also can be used for transporting other items. See Table 8-4 and Figs. 8-26 through 8-29.

☐ To construct the frame, cut the 2-inch angle iron pieces at 45-degree angles, and weld them together. Grind the outside corners after welding to remove any sharp or jagged areas.

☐ Weld the casters to the bottom of the frame—two swivel casters at the back, and two fixed ones at the front.

☐ To assemble the grate, cut the pieces of 1-inch and 1½-inch square tubing to length and weld them so that the foundry flasks can rest on the 1-inch tubing. Where flasks measure 13 × 15 inches, you can fasten 1-inch tubing 7 inches apart, ensuring a stable base.

☐ Construct the handle from ¾-inch square solid steel cut at 45-degree angles and welded together. Grind the welds smooth.

☐ To attach the handle to the frame, weld two small pieces of 1-inch square tubing to the frame, and grind the ends of the handle to fit inside the tubing. The handle is then removable so that the casting can be poured without bumping into it and so that it won't interfere with carrying items such as wood.

☐ Insert a piece of ¼-inch plywood into the bottom of the frame, and place the grate over it. Cover the exposed wood with foundry sand to catch spills.

☐ For transporting lumber, weld four additional pieces of 1½-inch steel tubing to the frame. Then insert four pieces of wood into the tubing to stabilize the lumber.

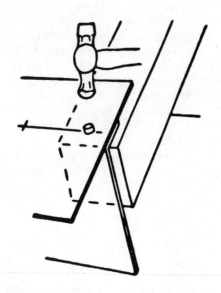

Index

Edited by Steven Bolt